D1188479

Rescuing Our Roots

CONTEMPORARY CUBA

UNIVERSITY PRESS OF FLORIDA

Florida A&M University, Tallahassee
Florida Atlantic University, Boca Raton
Florida Gulf Coast University, Ft. Myers
Florida International University, Miami
Florida State University, Tallahassee
New College of Florida, Sarasota
University of Central Florida, Orlando
University of Florida, Gainesville
University of North Florida, Jacksonville
University of South Florida, Tampa
University of West Florida, Pensacola

RESCUING OUR ROOTS

The African Anglo-Caribbean
Diaspora in Contemporary Cuba

Andrea J. Queeley

JOHN M. KIRK, SERIES EDITOR

UNIVERSITY PRESS OF FLORIDA

Gainesville / Tallahassee / Tampa / Boca Raton

Pensacola / Orlando / Miami / Jacksonville / Ft. Myers / Sarasota

Chapter 4 is based in part on Andrea J. Queeley's "*Somos Negros Finos*: Anglophone Caribbean Cultural Citizenship in Revolutionary Cuba," previously published in *Global Circuits of Blackness: Interrogating the African Diaspora*, edited by Jean Muteba Rahier, Percy C. Hintzen, and Felipe Smith, University of Illinois Press, 2010.

Printed in the United States on acid-free paper

This book may be available in an electronic edition.

20 19 18 17 16 15   6 5 4 3 2 1

Library of Congress Cataloging-in-Publication Data
Queeley, Andrea, author.
Rescuing our roots : the African Anglo-Caribbean diaspora in contemporary Cuba / Andrea Queeley.
pages cm — (Contemporary Cuba)
Includes bibliographical references and index.
ISBN 978-0-8130-6109-2
1. Blacks—Cuba—Social conditions. 2. Blacks—Cuba—History. 3. Cuba—Race relations. 4. Soviet Union—Foreign relations—Cuba. 5. Cuba—Foreign relations—Soviet Union. I. Title. II. Series: Contemporary Cuba.
F1789.N3Q44 2015
305.80097291—dc23   2015017863

The University Press of Florida is the scholarly publishing agency for the State University System of Florida, comprising Florida A&M University, Florida Atlantic University, Florida Gulf Coast University, Florida International University, Florida State University, New College of Florida, University of Central Florida, University of Florida, University of North Florida, University of South Florida, and University of West Florida.

University Press of Florida
15 Northwest 15th Street
Gainesville, FL 32611-2079
http://www.upf.com

This book is dedicated to

Anne Elizabeth Queeley, also known as May Daley,
who left her home to make a life in this place and lived
long enough to leave the memory of her eating mango
at the kitchen table, with me, her youngest grandchild

My mother, who taught me stories

My father, a devout member of the Curious Queeleys

Meredith . . . we were girls together

Contents

Figures

Preface

Same Ship, Different Destinations

Other national and ethnic groupings in Cuba—Spaniards, Arabs, Jews, Chinese—have established solidarity life-lines with their co-nationals and co-ethnics. Black West Indians do not have and desperately need a similar life-line. . . . Help provide food, medicine and clothing for a man, woman or child, who may well be related to your own forebears of the Middle Passage and beyond.

Alberto Jones, "Joining the West Indian Welfare Center"

Alberto Jones is a Cuban humanitarian and activist whose Jamaican parents were among the wave of British West Indian immigrants who arrived in Cuba during the first third of the twentieth century. He made his plea on behalf of the British West Indian Welfare Centre (BWIWC) in Guantánamo in the wake of Hurricane Michelle, which hit Cuba in 2001—when the country was still treading water in the proverbial flood unleashed by the collapse of the Soviet Union. Founded in 1945 by British Caribbean immigrants, "El Centre," as it is called by most, experienced a revival in the early 1990s when the children and grandchildren of these immigrants began a Young People's Department whose mission was "rescatar las raices" (to rescue the roots).

Alberto, who had himself become an immigrant, migrating to the United States and eventually settling in Northern Florida, was involved in this effort, bringing visibility and material resources to the British West Indian Welfare Centre. This was his most recent focus in a long history of local and global social justice work on behalf of people of African descent. "We all came here on the same ship, we just got off at different stops," he explained when I spoke with him after embarking on my own odyssey into the lives of those whose forebears chose Cuba as their port of call. Initially driven by the question of why this group of Cubans sought to rescue their roots in the post-Soviet era,[1] this book is one of the many still-unfolding outcomes of that journey.

Unbeknownst to me, I actually set sail on this voyage into the lives of Anglo-Caribbean Cubans well before reading Jones's plea in that 2001 newsletter. My journey began in 1996 the night I saw *La Cinta*, a calypso group from Ciego de Ávila comprised of descendants of British Caribbean immigrants, perform just outside of Havana. Prior to the show, I approached an older dark-skinned, presumably Cuban man getting a drink at the kiosk that provided *cafecitos* in the morning and *mojitos* at night. I greeted him in Spanish and was taken aback when he responded to me in Jamaican accented English. He was the director of *La Cinta* and proceeded to tell me about the migration of Jamaicans, Barbadians, and people from other British Caribbean islands to Cuba, a journey depicted in Gloria Rolando's film *Los Hijos de Baraguá* (Rolando 1996), which we viewed later that night.[2]

Very soon after our meeting, the director launched into what I now refer to as a narrative of social mobility. He was a man of humble beginnings, yet "gracias a la revolución" (thanks to the revolution), all of his children were professionals. Two of his daughters were nurses and he didn't have to pay "ni un peso" (even a cent) for their education.

As the granddaughter of immigrants whose destiny brought them from Montserrat to the United States rather than Cuba, and a recent college graduate attempting to pay off student loans on a modest salary, I was struck quite close to home by his narrative. From it, I envisioned an alternate reality of which fate had seemingly deprived me. At the time, I had been won over by the apparently sincere affection that Black and mulatto/mestizo Cubans had for their country.[3] Those I came across seemed to experience a sense of belonging that sensitized me to the weight of my own alienation. I began to imagine who and what I would have been if my grandparents had gotten off at a different stop.

Although I had traded in my rose-colored glasses for ones with a more discerning tint in the intervening years between that first trip to Cuba and my graduate research, the implications of Jones's plea intrigued me. It called into question the existence of fault lines in Cuba's social terrain that I had not anticipated. In my hopeful idealism, I had believed that there were, as was so often proclaimed, only Cubans. José Martí, revered founding father of the Cuban nation, had declared it (1893): "Cubans are more than whites, mulattoes, and blacks."[4] The sacred bond between people and nation was forged in the fires of the anticolonial wars. Any violator of this holy sacrament was subject to the wrath of a nation scorned.

So how was it that Jones could speak of solidarity along national and ethnic lines? What sorts of revelations about the politics of racial inclusion lay in those "Black West Indian" communities now in desperate need of a lifeline? How might Afro-Anglo-Caribbean descendants' claims to multiple spaces of belonging come to bear on Black subject formation in Cuba and beyond? And what might this call to ethnic mobilization reveal about the consequences of social and economic restructuring during Cuba's Special Period?

These are among the questions that I pursue in this book in an effort to contribute to popular and scholarly dialogue concerning contemporary racial politics in and beyond the Americas. Cubans of Anglo-Caribbean origin rescued their roots as a strategy to navigate the rough economic and emotional waters of the Special Period, an important facet of which was a resurgence of racial inequality.[5] Thus, although Cubans across the racial and ethnic spectrums continue to grapple with the ongoing insecurity and uncertainty of the reform process and its consequences, Cubans of color are in a particular predicament that has been a catalyst for an increasingly public debate about racism and the emergence of antiracist activism on the island, primarily in Havana.

This debate has included voices from across the African diaspora that are in dialogue with Cuba. I am here referring specifically to the controversial 2009 "Acting on Our Conscience" statement[6] in which African American intellectuals, artists, and activists joined iconic Brazilian antiracist scholar Abdias do Nascimento in condemning racism in Cuba. In addition, a 2012 *New York Times Review* article submitted by Black Cuban intellectual Roberto Zurbano set off a maelstrom of commentary about the state and fate of Cubans of color on the island, in large part due to liberties that the editor took with Zurbano's writing (Zurbano 2013; West-Durán 2013). Although this book, based on research between 2001 and 2009, is not focused on these more recent developments, its insights about the interconnections between Blackness, inequality, migration, and diaspora in the context of seismic shifts in the political and social terrain exist alongside these ongoing debates.

Such insights would not be possible without the willingness of my Cuban collaborators. I am grateful to those who welcomed me into their homes, sharing their stories of triumph, conflict, uncertainty, and survival. I continue to gain personal and intellectual insights from the unfolding of our shared histories of uprooting. It is my hope that shedding light upon their experiences will contribute to our efforts against disregard and distortion.

Acknowledgments

I am grateful for the divine force that has guided and protected me, placing so many good people in my life, for the spirits of my maternal and paternal grandparents, who overcame the adversities that swallowed so many, and for my parents and extended family for their enduring love and support. I am eternally grateful to all those in Cuba who incorporated me into their lives, sharing their time, work, stories, archives, analyses, and homes with me. Their embrace is the force that has sewn Cuba into my spirit. I am also deeply grateful to all of the fierce, dynamic, generous, smart, courageous, and hilarious women in the academy who made me believe that I could one day count myself among them. Special appreciation goes to Leith Mullings and Connie Sutton, two of my mentors who paved the way for so many of us; Dana-Ain Davis, whose dynamic intellect, creativity, organization, and *joie de vivre* never cease to amaze me; Chantalle Verna, for her boundless and unwavering generosity, kindness, and support of the practical, emotional, and intellectual variety; Laura Ogden, without whose advice this quite literally would not have happened; and Devyn Spence Benson, who gave me extensive and insightful feedback on two drafts and then actually agreed *enthusiastically* to read yet another draft of the introduction—on her vacation no less. There is a special place in heaven for you all.

While all interpretations are mine, from the insightful to the mundane to the way off, I owe a tremendous debt of gratitude to the scholars, mentors, activists, and artists whose work has provided foundation and inspiration: Anani Dzidzienyo, Pedro Pérez Sarduy, Gloria Rolando, Alberto Jones, Lara Putnam, Jorge Giovannetti, Aline Helg, Alejandro de la Fuente, Graciela Chailloux Laffita, Roberto Claxton, Don Robotham, Faye Harrison, Ruth Behar, Ed Gordon, Deborah Thomas, Gina Ulysse, Maria Eugenia Espronceda, and Brazilian artist Suzart.

Special thanks are due to Jean Muteba Rahier, Percy Hintzen, and Felipe Smith, the founding fathers of the "Interrogating the African Diaspora" seminar, whose intellectual contributions, vision, and commitment I greatly admire. I am also grateful to all those at so many institutions who have traversed the boundaries between mentor, colleague, student, and friend over the course of this journey: Michelle Hay, Jafari S. Allen, T. J. Desch-Obi, Jana Lipman, Jordan Shannon, Alex Cornelius, Okezi Otovo, Heather Russell, Hilary Jones, Valerie Patterson, Caroline Faria, Jorge Duany, Danielle Clealand, Martin Tsang, Alex Fernandez, and Maya Berry. Your support and camaraderie have been invaluable.

Thanks also to Erika Stevens, Stephanye Hunter, Catherine-Nevil Parker, and Jody Larson at UPF for their patience and hard work in preparing this manuscript for publication.

Final appreciation goes to all those family, friends, and four-legged creatures who have shared their joy, sorrow, time, money, homes, storage space, advice, laughter, music, and much-needed companionship. They have been happier for me than I have been for myself and are too numerous to mention, but I would like to thank in particular: my sister, who is really not what I would call the cheerleading type, for all the pep talks and fashion-filled care packages; Evans, for being my anchor and for swimming in the deep end of the pool; Anike, whose willingness to be vulnerable, take risks and sacrifice for her vision always inspire me to be honest and present in my life; Rachel, for her sense of humor and generosity of spirit, and for bringing my precious niece Ryan into the world; my cousin Laura, for initiating me into what would become my New York experience; James and Chavon for the Prince experience, craft night, and so much more; Khaled, with whom I can always get to the heart of the matter; Jenby for taking the time to ask how and what I'm doing; Yehnana, my running buddy and walking miracle; Ainissa, for her page-countability calls; Ava, the best listener on the planet; Muslima, for having that bottle of Prosecco ready and waiting; and those beautiful creatures who sat with me when no one else was around, taking the edge off of the solitude of writing: Bradley, Greta, Marley, Shelby, Blu, and Orleans.

Introduction

Nested Diasporas, Multiple Mobilities, and the Politics of Black Belonging

Guantánamo, a city of about 100,000 people in southeastern Cuba that is stiflingly hot during the summertime, is relatively unknown to outsiders, unlike the nearby U.S. Naval Base that bears the same name. This city is the location of the revitalized British West Indian Welfare Centre, founded on November 14, 1945, by British West Indian immigrants drawn to Guantánamo by the promise of stable, better paying jobs on the naval base. In August of 2001, during carnival, I found myself in Guantánamo for the first of what would come to be many visits.

At the time of this first stay, "El Centre" was a single-story building with one large room equipped with a desk, a file cabinet of some sort, and the wooden rocking chairs that no Cuban home or social space is considered complete without. Indeed, what identified this space as one dedicated to reaching people and places beyond Cuba's borders were the posters on its walls.

On the wall to the left, a Black Star Line promotional poster featured one of the ill-fated ships purchased with dues paid by millions of Universal Negro Improvement Association members, many of whom were Anglo-Caribbean migrants living in the United States and Latin America. The black masts of the ship were foregrounded by a picture of Marcus Garvey, whose experiences as a migrant laborer in Puerto Limón, Costa Rica, helped motivate him to found the largest Black social movement in history. The Black Star Line was intended to be the route of physical return to Africa as well as to economic independence, self-determination, and racial uplift.

On the wall space facing the entrance of the Centre, the Jamaican flag and the Union Jack sat on either side of a black-and-white photograph of the institution's early leaders. Positioned in front of the Cuban and British flags that sat side by side on the wall behind them, some of these leaders were seated, some standing, and all had dark, stoic faces. Much smaller color photographs of the former Jamaican Prime Minister P. J. Patterson's visit to Cuba and of special events hosted at the Centre in the 1990s completed the layout. With the descendants of early twentieth-century immigrants being increasingly "proud to know [dey] fadah . . . [and] outlooking,"[1] in time, more Anglophone Caribbean flags would come to decorate this space.

As the late afternoon wore into evening at the Centre, increasing numbers of people began to mill about, greeting each other in Jamaican-accented English and conversing in a sort of Anglo-Caribbean-Cuban style Spanglish. Many of them were elders, most middle aged, all traced their origins to an early twentieth-century Caribbean that was integral to the British Empire and had been situated within a world of increasingly intrusive U.S. economic and military power. The Centre, along with churches, fraternal lodges and mutual aid societies, cricket teams, and schools were dynamic cultural spaces for immigrants and their families until the period following the 1959 revolution, which witnessed the dissolution and deterioration of ethnic associations.

Guantánamo's British West Indian Welfare Centre was one of the few associations to remain standing through the revolutionary storm; however, it had lost its former vitality and ceased to be an exclusively Anglo-Caribbean space. This dormant period of the 1970s and 1980s was brought to an end when, in 1992, a group of young professionals decided to come together to form the Young People's Department of the Centre in the wake of the severe economic crisis known as the Special Period, which followed the collapse of the Soviet Union. With the stated goal of "rescuing their roots," they came together to support one another during trying times.

The Young People's Department began with beneficent activities, such as helping the elderly community members (many of whom had themselves immigrated to Cuba in the first third of the twentieth century) meet their basic needs. Soon members were organizing Anglo-Caribbean-related events and celebrations, starting cricket teams and English classes, planning for the reconstruction of the Centre's somewhat rundown building, participating in efforts to reinforce diplomatic ties with the Anglophone Caribbean, and making contact with family members in English-speaking Caribbean countries.

This book comes out of my attempt to understand this community revitalization; the national, regional, and local contexts in which it was embedded; and the significance of this particular story to emergent forms of belonging in contemporary Cuba as well as Black/African/Caribbean diasporic subjectivity. By subjectivity, I mean a sense of self and a way of thinking about others that changes under varying conditions and is informed by social forces and by larger, historically and spatially constituted power relations.

As Michelle Wright (2004) points out in her examination of theories of Black subjectivity, one can adopt a diasporic approach to Black subjectivity, meaning that diaspora is but one way to understand Blackness. This African diasporic counterdiscourse of Black subjectivity or "black self-consciousness," she writes, is evident in the twentieth-century intellectual tradition (2004:3). Indeed, those who have traced the genealogy of the term "diaspora" in reference to Africa date its application to the post–World War II period.[2] During this time when the Holocaust demanded the world's attention to the Jewish experience of enslavement, dispersal, rejection, and attempted annihilation, intellectuals adopted diaspora as a conceptual framework in identifying and thinking through Black subjectivity.

Considerable slippage can be found in the literature between the terms *subjectivity* and *identity*. Identity and subjectivity, concepts developed in modernist and postmodernist and poststructuralist discourse, respectively, have a specific intellectual (and disciplinary) genealogy.[3] I use both terms in this text to refer to one's sense of self and where one belongs. Both are historically and socially constituted, produced through and in relation to power, recognition, and/or exclusions, and can be rendered by a knowing or partially knowing subject. Just as the subjectivities that are produced change over time, space, and place, so do the identities and the identity politics that emerge from them.

However, subjectivities make particular forms of identification possible. For instance, early twentieth-century British West Indian colonial subjectivity that was constituted through military, commercial, and bureaucratic mechanisms made various identities available, one of them being a Black male Protestant migrant laborer. As a young man, this laborer might have had a particularly strong attachment to his Black identity that might have led to further elaboration of this identity by his joining the Garvey Movement. A Garveyite identity emerges out of both a Black subjectivity constituted through terror, discrimination, and solidarity, and a diasporic subjectivity. I am suggesting that in late twentieth-century Cuba, Black and diasporic subjectivities, distinct yet overlapping, allowed for the emergence of an Anglo-Caribbean-Cuban diasporic identity. By the same token, Anglo-Caribbean-Cuban subjectivity makes possible a particular Black identity that challenges the narrative of Black inferiority, the consequences of which became markedly exacerbated during the Special Period. In this project, I am most interested in who my interlocutors understood themselves to be as descendants of Anglo-Caribbean immigrants *and* Black Cubans living through drastic economic and social change, and in the implications of this understanding for the politics of Black subjectivity.

In my interlocutors' narratives about the associations, their families and communities, and current challenges in post–Soviet era Cuba, I was struck by their insistence on demonstrating an alternative way of being Black, one that does not conform to degrading stereotypes of incompetence, intellectual inferiority, deviant sexuality and religiosity, violence, and irrationality, the consequences of which became more dire during the economic reform process. Edward, one of my principal interlocutors and former president of the Young People's Department, illustrated this when he showed me photographs of community events and described how the men from his lodge, most of them descendants of British West Indian immigrants, paraded through the streets of Guantánamo to commemorate Black/mulatto Cuban hero Antonio Maceo. Edward put it this way: "Yes, yes, we participated in the celebration of Maceo. The brothers of the lodge and the Centre we marched, all dressed in our suit and tie, everything in order. It was very important that we were a presence there in the march as Black men who present themselves well to honor Maceo. [Straightens up his posture.] We showed everyone that we are Black and deserve respect."[4]

Edward, whom I affectionately referred to in my field notes as a "race man" because he was particularly passionate and articulate in his analysis of race and the resurgence, struck upon the cord of racial respectability that has long been a strategy used by people of African descent in challenging white supremacist ideology. Middle-class respectability, as a "vision of progress" (Thomas 2004:56), is a signifier of modern subjectivity, that is, an understanding of oneself and others' reading of you as belonging to the world marked "civilized." Its specific variety does, however, differ depending upon the particularities of the context in which it developed, and thus there is an iteration of respectability that is unique to the British Caribbean and therefore most relevant to our story.

In her engagement with emergent nationalism in Jamaica, Deborah Thomas (2004) summarizes respectability as "a value complex emphasizing the cultivation of education, thrift, industry, self-sufficiency via land ownership, moderate Christian living, community uplift, the constitution of family through legal marriage and related gendered expectations, and leadership by the educated middle class" (2004:5). Noting that centering respectability in the construction of national identity necessitates selecting certain practices of the postemancipation Jamaican rural peasantry while excluding those of the urban unemployed, she argues that respectability formed the core of Creole nationalism in twentieth-century Jamaica and is being dislodged by modern Blackness of a different sort, one constructed by urban youth culture, a culture that is heavily influenced by/in conversation with African American popular culture. Similarly, anthropologist Gina Ulysse (2007) argues that Informal Commercial Importers, who travel internationally to procure goods to sell in the Jamaican market and who are dark-skinned working-class women who exude "tuffness" in the Jamaican social imaginary, are pursuing alternative routes to respectability in postcolonial neoliberal Jamaica that put them "out of place" within the gendered socioracial order.

Although I found indications of a similar articulation of Blackness that offered an alternative to respectability among my Anglo-Caribbean-Cuban Rasta interlocutors who came of age during the Special Period, respectability, as Thomas and others have described, continues to be among the strategies of self-making available to Cuban descendants of Anglo-Caribbean immigrants. Building upon the work of scholars who are attuned to the contradictions characteristic of Black subject formation, I argue that this strategy simultaneously challenges and reinscribes the racial hierarchy and Black marginality. Here I am thinking specifically of Michelle Wright's (2004) argument that twentieth-century Black subjectivity as produced in the writings of Du Bois, Senghor, Cesaire, and Fanon while presenting a challenge to the racist discourse produced by Jefferson, Hegel, and Gobineau, does so within a heteropatriarchal nationalist framework. With regard specifically to West Indians, Percy Hintzen's (2010) critique that Black immigrants' deployment of both a "model minority" and "exotic" positionality in the effort to challenge notions of Black inferiority is particularly instructive. According to Hintzen, these approaches "dilute the force of diasporic subjectivity and cultural politics of racial resistance" (2010:58). For Anglo-Caribbean Cubans, the narrative of respectability is affirmative in that it offers a counterideology to *mestizaje* and colorblind nationalism, both of which mute the persistence of racial discrimination and undermine efforts to combat it. However, in various contexts, racial respectability has been defined through and deployed against those people of African descent who neither conform nor aspire to respectable Blackness.

In the case of early twentieth-century Cuba, three African diasporic groups could be identified: Black and mulatto Cubans, British Caribbeans, and Haitians. The connections and ruptures between them were mediated by multiple factors such as class, gender, island of origin, area of settlement, and Cuba's political and economic climate. For those Anglo-Caribbeans in Oriente who were British subjects, which included their Cuban-born children prior to 1940,[5] there were tangible benefits to maintaining distinctions between themselves and Haitians as well as native Cubans. Eligibility for the protection of the British Consulate and speaking English at a time when employers, both American and Cuban, appreciated this skill, were among these advantages.

While this study does not adopt a comparative lens in its examination of the Anglo-Caribbean-Cuban experience, the presence of other Black subjects necessarily interjects itself into my interlocutors' self-understandings and is implicated in diasporic formations. This presence, along with the (re)connection between the Cuban descendants of Anglo-Caribbean immigrants and the contemporary Anglo-Caribbean, illustrates precisely how diaspora emerges out of and is produced through the tension between sameness and difference. And, as Stuart Hall writes, "difference . . . persists—in and alongside continuity" (1990:227). Indeed, his insights in this regard are particularly powerful: "As well as the many points of similarity, there are also critical points of deep and significant difference which constitute 'who we really are'; or rather—since history has intervened—'what we have become.' We cannot speak for very long, with any exactness, about 'one experience, one identity,' without acknowledging its other side—the ruptures and discontinuities which constitute, precisely, the Caribbean's 'uniqueness'" (1990:225). He goes on to write, "The diaspora experience . . . is defined, not by essence or purity, but by the recognition of a necessary heterogeneity and diversity; by a conception of 'identity' which lives with and through, not despite, difference; by *hybridity*. Diaspora identities are those which are constantly producing and reproducing themselves anew, through transformation and difference" (1990:235).

This "difference" is by no means neutral. It is marked by the various racial, cultural, imperial, and national hierarchies born out of conquest, enslavement, and colonialism as well as the regimes of power that have grown under their shadow. Indeed, the distinction between British West Indian immigrants and those who shared their race and class position was an elevating one that my interlocutors, in their narratives of identity, linked to a middle-class, Victorian-inspired imagining of respectability. Immigrants to Cuba were certainly not alone in this as evidenced by a number of scholars who have theorized intraracial and ethnic relations, particularly those in Central America where British West Indians also immigrated in large numbers.[6] Furthermore, in cases focusing on the relationships between Black people who locate themselves in different geographical origins, difference also takes on meaning.[7] This is in part because "peoples defined by the *same* racial category can be rendered Other in *different* ways" (Wright 2004:7). Black subjects are "differently racialized," leading Nassy Brown (1998, 2005) to conclude, based upon her study of three groups of Blacks in Liverpool (Liverpool-born Blacks, Afro-Caribbeans, and ex-colonial West Africans), that "related but distinct colonial histories privilege some blacks in relation to other blacks, a contradiction that defines black Liverpool as an irreducibly postcolonial formation of diaspora . . . [where] diaspora refers as much . . . to antagonisms and power asymmetries as to the links that people make in the hope of overriding these" (2005:6, 127). As we will see, this tension is alive in the narratives of my interlocutors as they *both* reject and assert difference between themselves and other Black people, particularly other Cubans.

My question here is how and why difference is asserted in particular moments. What, for instance, was the impact of radical social change in the guise of the 1959 revolution on diaspora and the differences that it speaks to? Does the current moment, in which Anglo-Caribbean Cubans have rescued an imagined past and made overtures to the people, institutions, and nations that evolved in their absence, constitute the "new form of recognition and consciousness" that diaspora, as "an ideology of mutual recognition," reveals (Hintzen and Rahier 2010:xvii)? And what of the moments of "mutual recognition" between anthropologist and interlocutor? In exploring the disjunctures, or what Hintzen and Rahier refer to as the "fragmented geographies" (2010:xix), that diaspora constitutes, literary critic and historian Brent

Edwards (2003) employs a productive metaphor to elaborate upon Seng-hor's application of décalage. He writes: "Décalage is one of the many French words that resists translation into English . . . it can be translated as "gap," "discrepancy," "time-lag," or "interval." . . . The verb *caler* means "to prop up or wedge" something (as when one leg on a table is uneven). So décalage in its etymological sense refers to the removal of such an added prop or wedge. Décalage indicates the reestablishment of a prior unevenness or diversity; it alludes to the taking away of something that was added in the first place, something artificial, a stone or piece of wood that served to fill some gap or to rectify some imbalance. . . . Décalage is the kernel of precisely that which cannot be transferred or exchanged, the received biases that refuse to pass over when one crosses water" (2003:13–14).

Grounded in this concept, Edwards's analysis of U.S. and Francophone Black internationalists' texts centers translation as a "practice of diaspora" to argue that diaspora is forged through exchanges across diverse subjects. What I hope to explicate in this book are both the contours of the prop used to level the table and the conditions under which that prop is extracted. By pursu-ing this direction of analysis, I am answering Tiffany Patterson and Robin Kelley's (2000) call for scholars to explore diaspora's unmaking as well as its making; "the linkages . . . that tie the diaspora together," they insist, "must be articulated and are not inevitable" (2000:20). I am interested in those "prac-tices of diaspora" engaged in by individuals in this under-studied area of intra-Caribbean migration and Black Cuban identity formation that reveal both diaspora's creation and undoing.

While this investigation requires an understanding of who Anglo-Carib-bean immigrants and their Cuban-born children *were*, it is firmly rooted in the present. It explores Anglo-Caribbean Cubans' experiences of the revolu-tion as well as of the post-Soviet era, which until now have remained unex-plored. These Cubans were certainly not alone in their efforts to make connec-tions with and draw support from their ethnic origins during Cuba's Special Period. As Jones (2001b) alluded to and as I will discuss, other "ethnic groups" revitalized their prerevolutionary institutions and connections abroad. How-ever, Anglo-Caribbean Cuban overtures to diasporic belonging occurred in the context of rising racialized inequality in which Cubans of color became economically marginalized and Blackness increasingly stigmatized.

These Anglo-Caribbean-Cuban practices of self-making shed further light on the kinds of subjectivities, diasporic and otherwise, that emerge in spaces of social transformation carved out by the legacies of both colonialism and Soviet-era socialism. Sharad Chari and Katherine Verdery's (2009) call for us to think "between the posts" of postsocialism[8] and postcolonialism, along with the cases of Cubans who are the children and grandchildren of early twentieth-century Black Caribbean immigrants, provide an answer to what it means to "become something other than socialist or other than colonized" (2009:11) that engages race and Blackness outside the more frequently explored areas of religion, tourism, and popular culture.

In this book, I frame the ways in which those Black Cuban communities sought to rescue their Anglo-Caribbean roots under these conditions as being different strategies of belonging. I evoke diaspora not only as a space of mutual recognition established in the struggle against "the universal politics of misrecognition produced by white supremacy" (Hintzen and Rahier 2010:xi), but also as a space in which frictions around what and who precisely are being recognized are in no way consistent. With belonging comes exclusion. Thus, I am concerned with the tensions between recognition and misrecognition *within* diasporic groups, tensions of the sort that arose (and arise) between British subject and Cuban citizen, the respectable and the rude, the revolutionary and the Rasta, the informant, and the anthropologist.

From British Subjects in Cuba
to Anglo-Caribbean Diasporic Subjectivity

Demographers and historians estimate that between 1898 and 1938 at least 170,000 British West Indians entered Cuba, the majority of them being males from Jamaica[9] (Pérez de la Riva, 1975; Álvarez Estévez, 1988; Wynter 2001; McLeod 2000;[10] Giovannetti 2001; Chailloux and Whitney 2005).[11] According to the 1919 Cuban census, Jamaicans constituted 5.5 percent of the 339,082 foreigners in Cuba (11.7 percent of the total population) while 6.7 percent were categorized as born in the "West Indies, excluding Porto Rico and Jamaica."[12] By 1931, there were 153,846 foreigners of color living in Cuba, which referred to "Jamaicans, Barbadians, Haitians, eastern Caribbean islanders and Africans" (Director General of the Census 1945:736). The entry points in Cuba for Jamaican immigrants were Oriente and Camagüey provinces, which at that time encompassed the entire eastern portion and stretched toward the center of the country.

Among the migrants were unskilled and semiskilled laborers attracted to Cuba by the employment opportunities generated in large part by U.S. economic investment—opportunities that had become increasingly scarce in the British West Indies. They were part of a heterogeneous, mobile labor force that included people from the British, Dutch, and French Antilles as well as Haiti, and that had been circulating through the Caribbean, the Latin American mainland, and the United States since the middle of the nineteenth century. Thus, some arrived in Cuba from the United States, Panama, Costa Rica, and other Central American countries where they had labored on the Panama Canal, Panama Railroad, and plantations that were part of vast agro-industrial complexes owned primarily by U.S.-based businessmen.

The historical research on Caribbean migration to Cuba is a part of a broader exploration into race, immigration, nation-building, and empire in the Caribbean and Latin America from the postemancipation period into the mid-twentieth century.[13] While mine is not a historical study, it certainly draws upon and contributes to these regional and national histories by offering an analysis of the life histories of immigrants and their Cuban-born descendants in Santiago and Guantánamo. Many of them have lived through two watershed moments in twentieth-century Cuban history: the 1959 revolution and the 1989 collapse of the Soviet Union. To date, scholarly examinations of English-speaking Caribbean immigrants to Cuba have not gone beyond 1960. This study is an attempt to push beyond the tatters of the Cold War curtain, turning an ethnographic lens upon these themes of cultural politics and identification processes. It also provides a more nuanced representation of Black Cubans (who must also be recognized as Afro–Latin Americans and Afro-Caribbeans), not only exploring the ways in which they trouble the waters between native and diaspora, but also turning attention away from Havana and toward Oriente.

As I discuss at length in chapter 1, British Caribbean immigrants entered a newly independent Cuba where the highly contested presence of foreign Black laborers contributed to the process of shaping national identity as much as it revealed about that process. Immigrants and their families were subjected to discrimination, exploitation, brutality, and deportation, particularly during the economic crises that followed World War I and the stock market crash of 1929. However, large numbers remained in Cuba even after 1933, the year that every industry and business was legally mandated to employ a workforce that was at least 50 percent Cuban. Estimates of the exact number of immigrants and their Cuban-born children who settled in Cuba vary. Charlton (2005) estimates that 30,000 remained after 1940. Chailloux and Whitney (2005) estimate 33,000 remained after the deportations of the early '30s (2005:62), but in their 2013 publication they state that by 1940 there were approximately 100,000 British Caribbean residents in Cuba both legally and illegally (Whitney and Chailloux Laffita 2013:155). Sánchez Guerra offers that there were around 40,000 "Jamaicans" in Cuba in 1950 (2004:20). Based on data in the 1943 census, I estimate that around 65,000 people of British West Indian origin remained in Cuba.

While the precise number of people of Anglo-Caribbean origin is perhaps impossible to ascertain, we do know that mutual aid societies, churches, schools, fraternal lodges, Universal Negro Improvement Association (UNIA) chapters, and recreational centers sprouted up throughout the island from the beginning of the twentieth century. A strong associational life reveals British Caribbean residents to be dynamic regional, national, and international social actors rather than a one-dimensional, homogenous mass of impoverished, exploited Black laborers whose presence in Cuba was confined within the boundaries of the sugar cane plantations. These institutions acted as mediators between the immigrants and the authorities as well as vehicles through which they created community. Although many immigrants intended to go home someday, in the meantime, their children needed to be educated, their spiritual and social needs met, and their rights and dignity as workers, as Black people, and as human beings had to be protected.

In addition to providing a window into the lives of these Black immigrant communities, the trajectory of these institutions sheds light upon their dynamic relationship to Cuba and Cubanness. After 1940, there were more legally registered British Caribbean organizations than there had ever been, which Whitney and Chailloux Laffita (2013) attribute to Anglo-Caribbean migrants' determination to both "retain cherished traditions and cultural practices and become Cuban" (2013:12). In the decade following the 1959 revolution, private clubs, associations, and organizations that were the institutional extension of difference were, for the most part, dismantled. This included race-based and ethnic associations. The revolution dictated that, in the name of unity upon which national defense depended, there would be no hyphenated Cubans.

The strength of Cuban nationalism is in part what makes the revitalization of Anglo-Caribbean institutions in the 1990s intriguing. In his statements quoted in the Preface, Jones (2001b) is appealing to individuals who are moved to take care of those they believe to be their own. His collapsing of space and time in declaring that all people of African descent who are in the Americas as a result of the transatlantic slave trade are potentially and essentially family is an ethical claim aimed at dismantling difference. Or, better yet, *certain* differences. What is particularly instructive about this appeal is that it (perhaps inadvertently) simultaneously erases and reinscribes difference: the descendants of those who survived the Middle Passage have an inviolable bond, yet "co-nationals" and "co-ethnics" must band together. The ambiguity of these statements leads to that principal set of tensions that I explore in this book, namely, those tensions created through various modalities of belonging that might potentially be at odds—such as race, nationality, diaspora, class, gender, generation, and even economic and political ideologies. These are all mediated by colonial histories, local and global economic conditions, and national, regional, and international politics that are characterized by and generate uneven power relationships. I examine the ways in which this particular segment of Black Cuba interjects into emergent processes of subject-making, thereby expanding upon understandings of the new kinds of subjectivities that the contemporary period is making available to, and perhaps forcing upon, those living this transition.

To be clear, I am in no way asserting that Cubans who can lay claim to English-speaking Caribbean roots and are traversing these tumultuous times constitute a separate group in the tradition of those (allegedly) bounded communities that were once the object of anthropological inquiry. Rather, they exemplify the permeability of group boundaries, the tendency of individuals to occupy multiple, overlapping identities simultaneously, and an engagement in strategic essentialism,[14] all of which illuminate the fraught relationship between race and nation. This relationship and its implications for belonging to the modern state, Hintzen points out, have themselves given rise to diasporic subjectivity (in Hintzen and Rahier 2010:54). Cubans in Santiago and Guantánamo who trace their family to the British Caribbean articulate belonging as Cubans, as Black Cubans, as *orientales*, as descendants of Jamaicans or Barbadians or St. Kittsians and so on, and as members of a larger Black pan-Caribbean and Latin American diaspora.

The claim to a distinct Anglo-Caribbean origin and identity complex does not negate the other modalities of belonging.[15] My presence as ethnographer interested in that particular claim meant that interlocutors were reflecting upon that facet of their identity, a facet that was of course nested within others. Expanding upon Earl Lewis's concept of overlapping and layered diasporas (1995), I use the metaphor of the nest to evoke the space of home, particularly for creatures who take flight and leave the nest for material and social survival. I also visualize this layering as a Russian doll, in which each doll contains another doll within it. This layering has resulted from multiple mobilities, including but not limited to those involving physical displacement from Africa, the British West Indies, and northeastern Cuba to Guantánamo. As whole, dynamic human beings, these Anglo-Caribbean Cubans are simultaneously occupying and speaking to multiple subject positions. Their anglófono roots are but one tendril seeking its source.

As a result, the ethnographic material woven throughout this text might resonate with the experiences of Cubans who share those other subject positions. The task here is not to establish how they differ from other early twentieth-century immigrants to Cuba, or Cubans who experienced professionalization through the revolution, or Black Cubans confronting rising racial inequality as a result of the reforms instituted after the disappearance of Soviet support, or Anglo-Caribbean Cubans in Havana or Cienfuegos as opposed to Santiago and Guantánamo. Rather, this book explores why these Cubans began organizing around this particular facet of their identity, how this identity is imagined, and what these assertions of belonging reveal about diaspora, racial politics, and subjectivity in Cuba at the dawn of the twenty-first century. I argue that this revitalization of Anglo-Caribbean origins was a way of organizing Black people in response to the resurgence of racism in at a time when, unlike in more recent years, organizing *as* Black people in recognition of persistent racial discrimination was still absolutely taboo.

Critical Context: The Special Period—Crisis, Reform, and Rising Inequality

The economic crisis that began in 1989 and forced Cuba into the global market has perhaps initiated as dramatic a shift in Cuban society as the revolution itself. It is in this context that my interlocutors turned toward their Anglo-Caribbean origins. Although there is some debate regarding the exact moment when Cuba's economic crisis began (in addition to whether or when it ended), and whether the collapse of Eastern European and Soviet socialism dealt a lethal blow to an already crippled economy,[16] the gravity of the situation was indisputable.

As with many small economies, Cuba is trade dependent. The Soviet bloc's common market, the Council for Mutual Economic Assistance (CMEA), was Cuba's economic lifeline; it provided access to protected markets and favorable terms of trade. When the Berlin Wall fell in 1989, an average of 84.2 percent of Cuban imports came from Eastern Europe and the Soviet Union. This percentage fell precipitously over the following three years with imports from the Soviet Union dropping by over 30 percent in that first year, and trade with Eastern Europe practically disappearing by 1991 (Zimbalist 1994b:8). Between 1989 and 1993, Cuba's gross domestic product fell by 35 percent, private consumption by 30 percent, and gross investment by 80 percent. Fidel Castro declared the Special Period in Peacetime as the goods and services that Cubans had come to depend on disappeared virtually overnight, the United States tightened its embargo against the island,[17] and the Cuban government implemented drastic reforms in order to prevent further economic deterioration (Brundenius 2002).

These early reforms included the legalization of the U.S. dollar and introduction of a dual economy,[18] the investment in the tourist industry, and legalization of certain categories of self-employment. The changes in economic policy combined with the state's shrinking ability to provide for the minimum of its citizens' basic needs placed Cubans in a desperate position. Not only did Cubans face severe shortages in energy, food, and nearly all essential goods, but also when much-needed goods were available, they were increasingly sold in U.S. dollars while the majority of Cubans were paid in pesos.[19] The already robust black market grew exponentially as Cubans were increasingly caught between the socialist ideology of *conciencia* (consciousness), which values the moral rather than the material, and *la lucha* (the struggle), which refers to the struggle to survive.

While all Cubans certainly felt the shock of the collapse of the Soviet Union and were pressed into these strategies to manage the crisis, the market reforms initiated in order to cope with the crisis placed Cubans of color at a particular disadvantage, regardless of ethnic origins. They were overrepresented in neighborhoods with the poorest housing conditions and thus were unable to convert their homes into guesthouses and restaurants for tourists; they were underrepresented among Cubans receiving remittances from family abroad, since the majority of Cubans living abroad are white; and they were discriminated against in industries where workers were paid in dollars (*pesos convertibles*—convertible pesos, a local currency created in 2004 and tied to the U.S. dollar).[20]

Effectively excluded from the legitimate jobs in the tourist industry due to the policy of *buena presencia* (good appearance),[21] people of more African descent have come to be disproportionately represented in the public aspects of the underground economy. With the growth of the tourism industry in the '90s, Cuba fast became one of the most popular destinations for economizing sex tourists seeking to fulfill their tropical fantasies with women and men of African descent (Davidson 1996; Cabezas 2009). Thus, the most visible workers in the sex industry were those prostitutes, pimps, and hustlers in the street looking for tourists whose racism will be indulged in exchange for foreign currency.[22] *Jineterismo*—which translates literally to "jockeying" but refers to riding the tourists or making a living in the informal tourist economy principally through, but not limited to, sex work—was therefore racialized.

De la Fuente (2001a) argues that such circumstances served to reinforce the Negrophobia and racial prejudice that individual Cubans harbored, but which did not have the same systemic impact prior to the crisis. Indeed, the introduction of the tourist industry provides a prime example of how racial inequality functions in Cuba in the context of the crisis. The more intractable, revolution-resistant elements of the race/class system, such as housing patterns, racial stereotyping, and individual prejudice, are nurtured with the movement toward market relations, taking on a more exaggerated form and leading to more profound consequences, such as increased racial profiling and police harassment.[23]

It is undoubtedly clear that, contrary to Fidel's 1962 declaration that the revolution had solved the problem of racism, discrimination persisted in various spheres in Cuban society after the 1959 revolution, a phenomenon that has been increasingly explored by social science research conducted after the collapse of the Soviet Union.[24] Although some have argued that the revolution worsened conditions for Black and mulatto Cubans, Carlos Moore's (1988) indictment of Castro being one of many, evidence overwhelmingly indicates that the government's redistributive and antidiscrimination policies succeeded in reducing racial disparities in key sectors such as health and education. However, with the implementation of reforms, the racialization of economic inequality in Cuba has been significantly exacerbated. Studies exploring racial attitudes, such as those conducted by de la Fuente and Glasco (1997), Sawyer (2005), and Clealand (2012), indicate that this is in part due to the persistence of social discrimination justified by the belief in Black inferiority.

Thus, the consequences of living in a climate in which Black people are increasingly associated with crime and illicit activity are borne by more than just those who are publicly and visibly engaged in jineterismo. My research suggests that these deeply ingrained ideas about Black inferiority have a pronounced impact outside of the tourist industry, finding fertile ground in the shifting economic conditions. It is in this context that Black Cubans of Anglo-Caribbean descent sought to "rescue their roots."

(Mine)Fieldwork: Race, Nationality, and the Ethnographic Encounter

My own position as a Black American of Anglo-Caribbean descent is indeed present in this analysis as it moved me to grapple with these questions of connection, misrecognition, and the uneven power relations in which diaspora is embedded. In racial/gendered terms I was identified as *negra*, *morena*, or *mulata* (this in an effort to be polite and/or to acknowledge my level of education). My nationality was far less visible. Blacks are Cuban and, if determined to be foreign, we are from another Caribbean island or Africa, our presence in Cuba perhaps attributed to the civilian aid program that offers scholarships for students from other developing countries.[25]

Far from being offended by my exclusion from U.S. nationality, I found myself relieved. It provided me with a cover. It protected me from much of the public attention paid to foreigners by Cubans dependent upon the tourist industry.[26] Moreover, although Cuba might conjure vague ideas about communism or images of tropical cultural vitality for most people in the United States, for Cubans, the United States looms large in the collective consciousness. One need only follow the trail from the Platt Amendment to the Guantánamo Naval Base, to the Embargo, to the Bay of Pigs, to the Missile Crisis, to the Mariel Boatlift, to the Cuban American National Foundation, to the Cuban Democracy Act to get a sense of the close and often adversarial relationship between the two nations.[27] Thus, I was grateful that being Black allowed me to pass, if not for Cuban then for some other less loaded nationality.

At the time of my field research trips (those prior to 2008), Cubans were banned from spaces reserved for tourists even if they had the economic means to patronize the tourist hotels, restaurants, and clubs. This ban was an attempt to separate foreigners from Cubans not working in the official tourism industry.[28] With this practice, along with the racialization of jineterismo, Blackness became a physical marker for not belonging in certain public spaces, namely those frequented by tourists, and signaled criminality. Both the swift and explosive growth of the tourist industry and the resurgence of racial inequality shaped the contours of the social terrain upon which I negotiated my own Blackness and nationality.

Like other Black scholars doing research in Cuba, being at times mistaken for Cuban allowed for a particular point of entry into the social world that revealed this world to be fraught with contradictions (Sawyer 2005; Hay 2009; Roland 2010; Allen 2011). I too was stopped by security at the entrance of spaces frequented by tourists and asked to show my *carnet* (identification card), most likely mistaken for a lone jinetera in *la lucha*. When engaging in participant observation with a group of young Black and mulatto men, most of whom were *rasta modas*,[29] I bore witness to the police harassment to which they were subjected. Indeed, I too became a suspect as on one occasion I recall the police asking me for my *carnet* three times in one hour while I was sitting with them in the park. Were I perceived to be a foreigner, an American no less, how different would such interactions with authorities have been? Would it reduce harassment so as not to reveal systemic discrimination, or invoke more vigilance in order to protect the tourist from the undesirables? Am I a tourist they imagine needs protecting? The answers to these questions are unclear, but what is certain is that at times my non-Cubanness was invisible and I faced the consequences of blending in. Ancestry trumped national origin.

For those aware of my nationality, my identity as not simply a foreigner and a U.S. citizen, but as a Black woman with roots herself in the Anglo-Caribbean signaled a kinship that was at times political, at times cultural. Some common experiences, such as spending an hour every Saturday morning watching *Soul Train*—then two hours afterward practicing all the dance moves—were of course facilitated and, some might argue, generated by the ubiquity and homogenizing force of the U.S. media.[30] Other points of cultural resonance, anything from the politics of hair and interracial relationships to discrimination in the workplace and police harassment to our tough

West Indian immigrant grandmothers, have different roots. I explore this connection in terms of diaspora and am interested in the circumstances under which this belonging to Blackness, and particular articulations of Blackness, is both energized and circumscribed.

Throughout my research, I have grappled with the meanings and consequences of these connections. My own national, racial and ethnic identities served to both connect and create distance. Much like my interlocutors, I had a complicated relationship with revolutionary society, though obviously for quite different reasons. Being a middle-class racial minority born and raised in the United States with commitment to social justice, I swung between hopefulness and disillusionment. Perhaps because my nationality was often obscured by my phenotype, I experienced firsthand some of the contradictions of being Black in a socialist society marked by rising racial inequality. Furthermore, my being a descendant of early twentieth-century Anglo-Caribbean immigrants, one who has personally wrestled with questions of Black cultural heterogeneity, created a certain kinship with my Cuban counterparts. Questions of connection and belonging were a constant companion. Thus the politics of my own subjectivity are implicit in my analysis and I devote attention to this throughout the book.

Of Methods and Madness

Declaring my intention to conduct field research in Cuba back in 2001 consistently elicited hesitant responses from those who were even vaguely familiar with United States–Cuba relations and the politics of a state-controlled society. Was this possible? Was I sure? Was I crazy? As a leading Cuban historian who was kind enough to offer some guidance said, "You can't just drop in on Havana and start asking questions." Prior to the collapse of the Soviet Union, precious few social science researchers conducted ethnographic work in revolutionary Cuba relative to its Caribbean and Latin American neighbors whose societies were subjected to extensive analyses by foreign researchers.[31] Within Cuba, anthropologists Fernando Ortiz and Lydia Cabrera conducted groundbreaking, though not unproblematic, ethnographic research that contributed to transforming the national narrative such that it included the central role played by the Afro-Cuban.[32] While this prerevolutionary research earned Cuba a seat at the discipline's table, after the revolution, intellectual isolation, scarce resources, censorship, and concerns about counterrevolutionary activity placed constraints on the practice of cultural anthropology with its reliance upon in-depth interviewing and participant observation.

Regarding research on race in particular, after 1962 when Fidel declared the problem of racism solved, race became a taboo topic, and while its investigation in the cultural sphere was still permissible, to research and write about it from within the sciences was impossible (Morales Domínguez 2013). Fortunately, there has been an increasing stream of ethnographic research in Cuba since the 1990s. However, obstacles to foreigners conducting research remain, such as funding restrictions, securing a license and the appropriate visas, gaining access to archives that contain information deemed to be politically sensitive, and some Cubans' reluctance to provide the unofficial perspective on revolutionary society.[33] I certainly confronted these in the course of my research, which derailed my intention to follow the disciplinary convention of conducting at least twelve months of uninterrupted fieldwork, but they ultimately provided me with insight into not only the everyday obstructions caused by geopolitics but also into the fact that, as Cubans say, "No es fácil" (It's not easy).

These obstacles became a source of commiseration between my research participants and me. For instance, in 2005, when I paid a visit to Teresa, a spiritist and daughter of Jamaican immigrants, her first words to me were, "How did you escape from that man?"[34] It took me a minute and some additional explaining on her part for me to understand that she was referring to George W. Bush and not a domineering boyfriend she mistakenly believed me to have. Many a conversation began with discussions of "los métodos de Bush"[35] and how I was able to travel to Cuba in the first place. Indeed, each of the five trips of between one and three months in duration for a total of nine months was a sort of triumph over all of the bureaucratic mechanisms that exist to prevent the information exchange and human connection that my presence made possible.

The Sites

While there are sizable communities of Anglo-Caribbean settlement in other areas of the island (most notably in the northern Oriente city of Banes; the northeastern cities of Baraguá, Ciego de Ávila and Camagüey; Manatí in Las Tunas; and Havana), this study focuses on Santiago and Guantánamo for several reasons. Oriente was the point of entry and settlement for most Caribbean immigrants during the first third of the twentieth century. In part for this reason, eastern Cuba is constructed as the most Caribbean part of this Caribbean island and an ideal locale to investigate diasporic formations.

Also, there is a certain bias in research on Cuba created through the focus on Havana to the exclusion of other parts of the island.[36] Knowledge professing to be about Cuba is more accurately about Havana, which, given the regional heterogeneity of the island, is akin to grounding an understanding of the United States on New York City. My selection of Santiago and Guantánamo for this study was in part an effort to intervene upon this.[37]

Furthermore, as Whitney and Chailloux Laffita (2013) point out, there was a disconnect between Havana and Oriente such that the early twentieth-century discourse about Black immigrants that was generated in Havana tells us little about what was happening on the ground in Oriente, where the majority of those immigrants resided. This situation points to the need not only to fill in that gap, but also to generate a regional history that places Cuba squarely within Caribbean history.

Santiago is a city of rolling hills that sits on a large bay and is surrounded by several mountain ranges, including the Sierra Maestra, from which Fidel and his rebel army fought against Batista's army from 1956–1959. At least 130,000 English-speaking Caribbean immigrants disembarked at this bay in the first two and a half decades of the twentieth century to either remain in the city, settling in the neighborhoods of Tivoli, Mariana de la Torre, Carretera del Morro, and Trocha, or travel to the more rural areas in which the *centrales*[38] were located. Formerly distinguished as the capital of Oriente Province and now the capital of Santiago province, Santiago is Cuba's second largest city with a population of 426,841 (as of 2010) and the site of the University of Oriente, which has hosted thousands of students from several Caribbean and African countries.

The city of Guantánamo lies east of Santiago and, with a population of 207,973 (as of 2010), is significantly smaller than Santiago. Capital of the second poorest province in Cuba, it is about a forty-minute drive from the U.S. Naval Base. While English-speaking Caribbean immigrants worked in the surrounding *centrales*, the city's primary significance for this community was as an internal migration destination point during the late 1930s and 1940s when the U.S. military was recruiting laborers for its expansion of the Guantánamo Naval Base. The presence of the naval base had a tremendous impact on the economy and social dynamics of the area as Guantánamo and surrounding towns such as Boquerón and Caimanera developed to meet the needs of U.S. servicemen and civilian workers. British West Indians and their Cuban-born children worked on the railroads, in the brothels and bars, and as laundresses, cooks, and skilled craftsmen, having a significant cultural influence on Guantánamo (Derrick 2001).

The importance of the naval base for the residents of Guantánamo persisted through the early period of the revolution. Guantánamo was one of the stages upon which the drama between the United States and Cuba played itself out in the early 1960s, and workers on the base and residents of the city were often caught in the conflict, as the naval base is on property leased by and under the jurisdiction of the U.S. and the issue of border crossing has been a contentious one. In the contemporary period, families who have members who worked on the base are perceived to be better off in the dollar economy as they have access to a pension in U.S. dollars. Guantánamo attracts few tourists, its dozen or so hotels and *casas particulares*[39] primarily serving those travelers who might be stopping over on their way to Baracoa, a tremendously popular tourist destination. As mentioned earlier, Guantánamo is the home of the British West Indian Welfare Centre (BWIWC), one of the few British West Indian cultural centers on the island that has endured throughout the revolutionary period and the primary institution that the children and grandchildren have sought to revive in the Special Period.

Although I made several trips to Guantánamo, I considered Santiago de Cuba to be my base. During my first two trips to Santiago and my last, I stayed in casas particulares, while on the third, fourth, and fifth I resided primarily in a family home in one of the historically Anglophone Caribbean immigrant neighborhoods. During each trip to Guantánamo, I stayed in private homes, one of which was that of a family of Jamaican origin, and the other belonging to a Black Cuban woman not of Anglophone Caribbean origin.

The insights from this research are derived from a range of sources due to the relationships that I developed with non-Anglo-Caribbean Cubans and Anglo-Caribbean Cubans alike. Indeed, because I formed connections with Anglo-Caribbean Cubans living in the United States, the source of the data is not strictly confined to the island, either. However, all of my semistructured interviews were among Cubans of Anglo-Caribbean descent who had never left the island.

Excluding the six individuals who immigrated to the United States, there were forty participants in this study. I reinterviewed several participants, either because they were community leaders or because I realized that I wanted to extend the depth and breadth of the previous interview. As a result, I conducted a total of fifty-five semiformal interviews.[40] Most of these were recorded; however, on several occasions informants directly or indirectly expressed discomfort at being recorded, sometimes requesting that I turn off the recorder in the middle of an interview as they wanted to share information that they deemed to be sensitive. In these cases, I took notes immediately following the encounter. This speaks to the complications of conducting field research in a state-controlled society where, as one of my interlocutors frequently said, "Here, out of every three people, one is in the security," using three of her fingers to illustrate her point.

Because I located people to interview primarily through referrals, I interviewed those people whose roots in the Anglo-Caribbean were known by other community members. Thus, those people who might have had a parent, grandparent, or great-grandparent who migrated to Cuba, but who perhaps detached themselves from their origins or were unknown to others of Anglo-Caribbean origin, were not part of this study. Therefore, my findings cannot be generalized to all people of Anglo-Caribbean descent in Cuba. Furthermore, while having the former association president as a main referral source was beneficial in terms of identifying potential subjects, it tends to skew the data toward those who were affiliated with and/or participated in the association.

The other segment of the population that was summarily excluded from this study by virtue of the sites where I chose to conduct research was that composed of people who remained in rural areas. Santiago, the municipality, is the second most populous city in Cuba and is the capital of Oriente. Guantánamo is the capital of the province by the same name and, though less populous and with fewer resources than Santiago, it is by no means rural. While historical data indicate that English-speaking Caribbean migrants gravitated toward urban environments, particularly compared to their Haitian counterparts, most were initially agriculturally based (Graham 2013). They lived and worked in and around large plantations owned by U.S. corporations, and this is where many communities were initially established. Due to the range of skills that they possessed as a group and the development of the naval base, both topics that are discussed in later chapters, these people had an opportunity to migrate to and establish themselves in urban areas. This study thus has an urban bias, and accounts of the lives of those elsewhere on the island are not included here.

Language and Terminology

Of the forty participants, fourteen were conversant in English, with seven being or having been English teachers and twenty-two having grown up in English-only households. The interviews were conducted either exclusively or primarily in Spanish, since even those who knew how to speak English seemed to be more comfortable in Spanish. In a few instances, I ascertained this in the course of an interview that began in English when either the interviewee switched to Spanish or when on seeing them struggle to articulate themselves, I realized that my Spanish was more developed than their English and began to speak Spanish myself.

Interviewees tended to say certain phrases and words in English, as well as switching to English under particular circumstances. For instance, those who received their primary education in English recalled such things as the names of teachers as Ms. or Mr. So-and-so, and used English for greetings and pleasantries, prayers, and hymns. In addition, in recounting information about their origins, their family composition, and early experiences in Cuba, they would communicate in English. The names of certain foods associated with the Anglophone Caribbean, such as ackee, breadfruit, bun, soursop, and candy, as well as rituals or religious events such as Nine Night, Christmas, and Harvest, were in English. Also, phrases that they recalled hearing growing up tended to pepper conversations about life in Anglo-Caribbean communities.

What I found to be a more interesting use of English was that people would begin speaking in English when they were discussing things that they did not want others to overhear and understand. My first experience of this code-switching was during my 2001 trip to Santiago, just as I was beginning to become friendly with the Watsons. I was with another Black woman from the United States who had befriended a male dancer who accompanied us on a visit to the Watsons' home. In the course of the conversation, it came up that he had invited us to a *bembe* (African-Cuban religious celebration) in one of the less reputable neighborhoods in the city. We were all seated in the living room, and with him right there sipping *limonada* (lemonade) in his denim overalls *sin camisa* (without a shirt), our hostess switched to English and asked, without changing her facial expression, "Where did you meet this man?"

The more frequent situations in which English was used to make information accessible to fewer ears, actual or imagined, occurred when a speaker was discussing something considered to be taboo. Indeed, the switch to English became a signal that more private information was being shared. An example of this occurred during an informal interview with Mabel, a first generation woman in her seventies who seemed particularly disgusted with the state of economic affairs in the country. We were outside in her yard, and as she was showing me her water tank, plants, and chickens, she abruptly began speaking in English as she recounted a story about a farmer who was jailed for slaughtering his own cow for his family's use.[41] The interaction had a sort of clandestine tone to it, as did many others in which the switch to English occurred as the speaker began overtly or even indirectly criticizing the government. It is not that such criticisms were never articulated in Spanish, but when they were in English, they took on a more serious tone.

Aside from the use of English, three other issues of language need to be noted. The first concerns translation and connotation. For instance, the term *racismo* in Cuba generally refers to institutional discrimination on the basis of race; thus, when a Cuban says that there is no racism, he or she is often saying that the basis upon which the state—and therefore all public society— can deny access has been eliminated. A second issue is the importance that tone and more physical aspects of language have in Cuban Spanish. At one point in my attempt to understand race and how attitudes about it are communicated in a society that is invested in seeing itself as antiracist, I wanted to know what the Cuban word is for "nigger." The word *niche* is an approximation of "nigger"; however, I never witnessed the use of this term. Instead, I found that it was the expression, tone, and context in which a person says *negro* that transforms the word into a racial slur. For instance, when someone refers to a rumba or a *bembe* as "una cosa de negros" (literally, a thing for Blacks), if their tone is dismissive, or there is a subtle shift in their facial expression as if they've just gotten a whiff of rotting meat, or both, then the *negros* is derogatory.[42]

A third issue of language concerns the various terms used to refer to people from the Anglo-Caribbean and their descendants in Cuba, some of which I use in this work. Although people came from all over the Anglophone Caribbean to Cuba, the majority came from Jamaica and thus they are often referred to as *los jamaicanos*. People with family from other islands would be sure to remind me that they were not Jamaican, that this was just the word used to describe all of them.[43] Other terms used in reference to immigrants and those in their communities who might have been born in Cuba but lived in that Anglophone Caribbean world were *los ingleses*, *los antillanos*, and *los anglófonos*.[44] I did not often encounter "West Indian" aside from the "British West Indian Cultural Centre." I most often employ this term in the text when referring to people who were migrants themselves, and when I want to convey a certain adherence to British cultural traditions. I use the emic terms *jamaicanos*, *antillanos*, *ingleses*, and *anglófonos* in direct quotes or in reference to conversations in which those terms were used.

The term *pichones* (young pigeon) refers exclusively to the first generation born in Cuba and can be applied to children of immigrants from any background.[45] Carlos Moore, in his memoir entitled *Pichón* (2008), recalls that this term meant the offspring of black buzzards and was often hurled at the children of Black immigrants with intent to injure. Whitney and Chailloux Laffita explain that over time it has lost its derogatory connotation, but had previously become "a term of derision, a mark of foreignness, indicat[ing] that a person was not only non-Cuban but, more ominously, anti-Cuban" (Whitney and Chailloux Laffita 2013:23). Though I never encountered anyone who had as strong a reaction to the word as Moore describes, I elect not to use it in this book except in a direct quotation. *Descendientes* is a term that people used to refer to anyone who has Anglophone Caribbean ancestry. While these are all rather straight forward, there is some dispute about the connotation of the term *jamaiquino*, which some used interchangeably with or in the same way that others would use jamaicano. When I asked how this term came about or what its significance was, some explained that jamaiquino was a derogatory word that Cubans gave the Anglophone Caribbean immigrants. For some, this term no longer carries a negative connotation. I have elected to use jamaicano to refer to this group while I most often employ Anglo-Caribbean Cubans to refer to their Cuban-born descendants. At times I use the terms English-speaking Caribbean and Anglo-Caribbean interchangeably, although I apply the former more often to the immigrant generation because they were more likely to speak English exclusively.

The overwhelming majority of children and grandchildren of Anglo-Caribbean immigrants in this book are classified as *negro* due to dark skin, kinky hair, and other physical features typically associated with West and

Central African ancestry. Thus, I generally use the term "Black" to refer to them. I use the terms Cubans of color, Black and mulatto or *mestizo* Cubans, and Cubans of African descent interchangeably. Unless otherwise indicated, the descendants of Black immigrants are included in this category. I rarely use the term Afro-Cuban to refer to individuals, but rather to culture and cultural forms.[46]

Documents

With regard to the archival research, I conducted research in the Latin American Collection at the University of Florida, Gainesville; the Elvira Cape Library's special collections in Santiago; the Santiago municipal archive; and the West Indian Cultural Centre in Guantánamo. I consulted lodge documents and the files of past association presidents, including documents concerning the contemporary revitalization that some people were kind enough to share. I mined these sources for any information that would assist me in reconstructing the social and material lives of the immigrants and their families. I reviewed census data, correspondence from the *centrales* on which they worked, by-laws and meeting minutes from the associations that they established, government records concerning control or management of these associations, and personal family records that included passports, birth and death certificates, photographs, letters, articles, fraternity lodge booklets, awards and certificates, and any information chronicling the experience on the U.S. Naval Base.

The Observing Participant

The presence of foreigners is a politically charged issue and subject to regulation, and the process by which I acquired housing as an outsider is itself informative of the social and economic field upon which Cubans, descendants and non-descendants alike, tread. Thus, as a way of highlighting certain key facets of everyday life and introducing the reader to a cross section of those who peopled the social world in which I acted as a participant observer, I will briefly describe the more specific sites into which I ventured.

Mujeres

I arrived in Santiago one afternoon in August with a few important names but, quite predictably, without luggage after having missed a connecting flight in Montego Bay and having been rerouted through Havana. Three names were those of academics who might be interested in my project, one was that of a hotel found on the internet, and one was that of Mujeres del Mar, the *casa particular* where a young woman I met on the plane planned to stay. With a name like "Women of the Sea," accommodations that were a fraction of the price of the two-star hotel at which I stayed for one night ($12 USD a night as opposed to $45), and a location in the center of the city, this casa was where I resolved to stay and sleep in a windowless room with unreliable air conditioning during the hottest month in what I thought was Cuba's hottest city—until I went to Guantánamo.

Occupying the rear section of a two-story edifice that sat across the street from the colonial-style municipal office building, which was painted a sharp white with trim the blue of Cuba's flag's five stripes, Mujeres del Mar had been created out of the second floor apartment of a white Cuban family. The apartment's two bedrooms had been converted into guest rooms for tourists, and Claudia, Flavio, and their teenaged son, Alejandro, lived in a small attic-like space that was above the kitchen and bathroom and accessible by a ladder. All of the rooms faced a narrow hallway/balcony that sat on top of what was essentially the roof of the floor below.

Claudia and Flavio both had jobs in addition to maintaining the business and thus had hired Lidia, a wiry *mestiza* in her early forties who became a close friend and interlocutor, to perform the domestic chores and general hospitality services of the casa particular. Claudia held a mid-level position at a museum and Flavio used a motorcycle (*moto*) he bought with money he made while in Spain to taxi people around the city.[47] They shared the floor with another family—one member of which was a *mestiza jinetera*,[48] the mother of a three-year-old son who had been jailed several times for prostitution. After climbing the marble stairs of a dark, wide stairwell and entering the first wooden door, one had to pass entrances to this family's dwelling areas and bathroom before arriving at a white door anointed with the blue triangle sticker under which was printed *ARRENDAMIENTO* (RENTAL). This signified that the apartment owners were legally permitted to rent rooms.

It was during my first few days at this casa particular that I met two Cubans who would prove to be my link into another social world of Santiago: that of the *rasta modas*.[49] The encounter occurred one evening while I was walking down the street with a Black American woman who was also traveling. We were on our way to Parque Céspedes from an area called The Boulevard where there is a small park surrounded by a dollar store, bank, church, and a few restaurants, one of which was an ice cream parlor that sold small cartons of ice cream for fifty cents. I heard someone behind me ask me a question and when I turned around to hear more clearly, I saw two young Black men with short dreadlocks. They wanted to know if the ice cream was in *moneda nacional*, another name for the Cuban peso. When I responded, they apologized, saying they thought that we were Cuban. We began to talk and continued this conversation at Parque Céspedes, where we would meet off and on throughout my subsequent years of field research. My friendships with Miguel and Samuel and association with their crew of friends, most of whom were *rasta modas* and all of whom were young Black and mulatto men, exposed me to a reportedly marginalized segment of Cuban society.

Casa Santiaguera

Casa Santiaguera was located around a perilous corner from Mujeres del Mar and down two slickly paved sidewalk blocks along one of Santiago's main streets in the direction of the Alameda, the avenue adjacent to the bay. Based on the connections that I made with the Watsons, a Jamaican Cuban family, during my previous trip, I was able to secure a good rate for long-term stay. Marta, the mulata daughter-in-law of the casa particular's proprietor, was the close childhood friend of Melvina, a first-generation Jamaican Cuban who was a former president of the Anglo-Caribbean Association in Santiago and who was to become one of my closest friends and interlocutors. The proprietor was Elena, a mulata in her seventies—though she was infamous for never revealing her true age. She was a retired teacher from a more rural area outside of Santiago and had participated in the revolution's literacy campaign.

Because Casa Santiaguera was the home of a close friend of one of my principal interlocutors, my stay there allowed me to incorporate myself into the extended network of that family. This network is founded on familial, friendship, and/or collegial ties but is maintained through reciprocity, as is demonstrated by the way in which Melvina "shared" me among her network. As a foreigner in need of certain services, I was a resource and it would have been a violation of social norms if Melvina had not done so. I needed something from her, that is, information and contacts, and therefore I was obliged to offer something in exchange; she would have been accused of selfishness had she not spread whatever it was that I gave.

One example of Melvina's sharing me as a resource was arranging my stay at Marta's casa particular, thus guaranteeing a reliable source of dollar income for the house over a period of months in addition to providing the possibility of gifts and assistance that I might offer. Furthermore, staying at a casa particular that was owned by people in my network allowed me to gain insights into how private businesses in the tourist industry function in relationship to the state, or at least the perception of this relationship. Based on her having this "inside track," Melvina told me that her friends had been approached by security to spy on guests from the United States, Jamaica and Colombia. This explained certain irregularities that I experienced. For instance, on one occasion, my hosts requested the *carnet*[50] of one of my Rasta informants who had come to visit me for a couple of hours when the law officially only requires them to record overnight guests. After recording his information and asking him somewhat personal and superficially innocuous questions, they then followed up with a phone call to Melvina in order to confirm the veracity of the details that he provided.[51]

At the same time that I was able to tap into this network of extended households, as a guest in a casa particular rather than a home, I was able to remain somewhat autonomous and develop the connections that I had begun during the previous trip, some of those being with people who were not considered respectable in the eyes of my professional informants. For instance, Lidia, who still worked as a domestic at Mujeres del Mar, and the young *rasta modas* clearly occupied a different status than the professors, doctors, and other educated people of Anglo-Caribbean descent whom I recruited for the study. Spending time in their homes and in *their* social networks, attending social events, planning and participating in celebrations, visiting their workplaces, and accompanying them on errands provided numerous opportunities for observation of and dialogue about daily life in Cuba. Also, during my 2003 stay I developed ties with a group of young people from the English-speaking Caribbean who were studying at the University of Oriente and provided me with a unique perspective on Cuban social relations.

Calle Jamaica

Upon leaving Santiago after my second fieldwork trip, Melvina invited me to stay in her home during my next stay. By that time, the major construction that they had begun when I left would be complete and they would be ready to have a houseguest for an extended period of time. I had been told that foreigners were prohibited from staying in private homes, and thus I had my doubts about how this would work out, but Melvina insisted that she would take care of it and there was nothing that I should do ahead of time. When I arrived in Santiago that May, she and her daughter met me at the airport and we went directly to her house on Calle Jamaica in Tivoli, a neighborhood in Santiago that had a pronounced Anglo-Caribbean immigrant presence and where I spotted an ackee tree, the national fruit of Jamaica, in a clearing two doors down.

Painted a warm rosy pink and made of *placa* (dry wall), the house was built by Melvina's father as a wooden structure in the 1930s but then rebuilt in the late 1940s. In its most recently remodeled version, it had four bedrooms, a large kitchen, a dining room, a living room, and a sitting room; Melvina's brother was also building an addition onto the roof that would house his bedroom, kitchen, sitting room and workshop. The house's sizable backyard, where there were chickens, ducks, and, at one point, a litter of kittens, in addition to tamarind and avocado trees, was an ideal place to seek relief from the heat and have quiet conversation. It was also where we hung freshly washed laundry on the clotheslines to dry.

The day after my arrival, Melvina announced to me that we needed to go to the immigration office so that they would know that I was staying in their house. She was sure to bring her mother's Jamaican passport and her own *carnet*, repeating that she knew what she was allowed to do in this country and that she did everything according to its laws. I was told at the immigration office that I needed to go to the bank and buy forty-dollar stamps that would authorize me to stay on a family visa.[52] I did so, received authorization, and settled into my space as a member of a professional Jamaican Cuban household. In this role, I participated in domestic chores, helped with marketing, learned how to make *pru oriental*,[53] gave and received advice, commented on the *novelas* as well as the weekly movies, cared for Melvina's nonagenarian Jamaican mother, partook in celebrations of all sorts, interacted with neighbors and friends, and asked a lot of questions.

The following year, the plan was the same but the law had changed. In addition, the location of the immigration office had been moved to one of the grand houses in Vista Alegre. As we approached this new and improved setting, I saw a long line of people coming from the back yard and a shorter line of people on the porch, waiting to enter what was perhaps once the foyer or sitting room. Foreigners—as well as Cubans with foreigners—formed the line that came out of the front door while Cubans without foreigners were sent around back. I could not help but note the parallel to the segregation era United States, when workers and Black people had to enter a house through the kitchen in the back. Ironically, I immediately knew which line to go to: it was the one with older white men and women accompanied by younger, more attractive men and women of color.

Melvina and I were told that the only people allowed to stay in houses on a family visa are spouses, parents, children and siblings. All others can stay up to seventy-two hours while waiting for a response about whether they can get special permission, but after that, they have to stay in a hotel or casa particular. Days can be spent and meals eaten in a private home, but I was not officially permitted to stay overnight.

When we broke the news to family and friends, the general consensus was that this was a move on the part of the Cuban government to increase revenue from accommodations for foreigners given that, in November of the previous year, the Bush administration had passed several laws restricting the flow of resources to Cubans by targeting family visits. Restrictions included prohibiting Cuban Americans from traveling to Cuba more than once every three years, limiting the definition of family to spouses, parents, siblings, children, and grandparents, and limiting the maximum time they could spend to fourteen days. This was one of many times that I was caught in the crossfire of United States–Cuba relations. I opted to make arrangements with Elena, the proprietor of Casa Santiaguera, in which I paid her for the room so that Casa Santiaguera was my official residence, but Calle Jamaica was where I spent most of my time.

Guantánamo: Amorcita's and La Prima Hermana

In Guantánamo, I stayed either with Amorcita, a brown-skinned, slight woman in her early fifties who is a family friend of the Watsons, or with Pamela, the first cousin of Patricia, a Jamaican Guantanamera who left Cuba in 1970 and lived in New York, and with whom I had become acquainted.[54]

Amorcita is a single, retired *militante*[55] living on a pension of less than 200 pesos a month. She lived alone after the death of her mother, a loss that left her with a palpable sadness. Though struggling economically, she expressed gratitude for the revolution as it had improved her family's standard of living. Her brother was a professional working in Havana, and she had worked as a municipal level bureaucrat. Beautiful antique furniture crowded her small two-bedroom apartment, an ironic contrast to the empty spaces found in her refrigerator.

Pamela's home was considerably larger and peopled by family members but also marked by grief. She lived with her male partner, daughter, grandson, severely handicapped son, William, and mother, Mabel, the daughter of Jamaican immigrants whose first husband and father of her children was from Jamaica. Mabel's second husband had suffered a heart attack and died in the house seven years earlier. While in this household, I also participated in marketing; attended social activities at the Centre, in the homes of other descendants, and during carnival; and spent hours in conversation with members of this extended social network.

As a participant-observer in these communities in Santiago and Guantánamo and among these individuals I have briefly described here, I took part in activities both mundane and irregular. For instance, in addition to navigating the markets and shops in order to procure daily necessities, I attended events that were periodic, such as birthday celebrations, *rasta moda* house parties, excursions and gatherings of young people from Melvina's daughters' church group, rumbas frequently held in the *barrios marginales*,[56] dances and activities sponsored by an organization of *danzoneros*[57] to which one of my older informants belonged, and various concerts and recitals that featured anything from *rap cubano* to classical music. In terms of annual celebrations, I participated in carnival and the Festival of Fire, also known as the Caribbean festival, which is a celebration and affirmation of the connection between Cuba and other Caribbean countries.

The content of the interviews that I conducted was necessarily impacted by my observations as I took part in the daily life of the cities in which my research participants lived. The major questions were directed toward gathering information about the interviewee's English-speaking Caribbean family, such as time of arrival, island of origin, and occupation; individual, familial, and community responses to and experiences in the revolution; and the impact of the Special Period and Cuba's transition. Through the course of the research, different subtopics emerged that ranged from attitudes about race and the experience of Blackness in Cuban society across time to the generational gap to religion to the role of women in Anglo-Caribbean communities. I not only adjusted the line of questioning depending upon the individual informant's particular background, interests, and openness, but also made additions and deletions with the emergence of particular themes.

Journey through the Book

This book relies upon the narratives of my interlocutors as a means to understand the ways in which people imagine themselves. The role that sociologist and postcolonial theorist Avtar Brah (1996) gives to narrative in forming diasporic community as well as to the malleability of this narrative is instructive. She writes:

> It is the *economic, political and cultural specificities linking [disparate] components that the concept of diaspora signifies*. This means that these multiple journeys may configure into one journey via a *confluence of narratives* as it is lived and relived, produced, reproduced and transformed through individual as well as collective memory and re-memory. It is within this confluence of narrativity that "diasporic community" is differently imagined under different historical circumstances. . . . The identity of the diasporic imagined community is far from fixed or pre-given. It is constituted within the crucible of the materiality of everyday life; in the everyday stories we tell ourselves individually and collectively. (1996:181)

If applied to the case of Anglo-Caribbean Cubans, this suggests that significant shifts in Cuba's political and social landscape during the twentieth century might lead them to imagine themselves differently. Settlement in Cuba, working in and around the Guantánamo Naval Base, the rise of revolutionary society, and the crisis that followed the collapse of the Soviet Union all acted as catalysts for such reimagining.

This book is divided chronologically into three sections: the first focuses on the period prior to the 1959 revolution, the second on the experience of revolution, and the third on the Special Period and beyond, to which the lion's share of the text is devoted.

Following the 1959 revolution, the contraction of diasporic space due to the policing of connections with those outside of Cuba, the push for cultural homogenization, and the racial politics of the revolution foreclosed previous routes to and articulations of diaspora. The Special Period crisis, however, created the conditions for both the resurgence of connection with English-speaking Caribbean origin and my presence as a foreign anthropologist conducting research.[58] The experience of the crisis and related ongoing insecurity was the filter through which memories and interpretations of the past occurred.

Drawing upon recent historiography, chapter 1 explores the world from which early twentieth-century Afro-Caribbean immigrants to Cuba came and the one into which they entered. It centers on the trope of respectability, arguing that this was a defense against the predominant economic and ideological assault against people of African descent both at home and abroad. It devotes attention to the secondary internal migration to Guantánamo during the WWII expansion of the naval base. Bringing together the work of postcolonial scholars, diaspora theorists, and analysts of Caribbean migration, the chapter explores their creation of a diasporic space in Cuba prior to the 1959 revolution.

Chapter 2 looks at the impact of the 1959 revolution on Anglo-Caribbean Cuban communities. In the 1950s, people of Anglo-Caribbean origin occupied an ambivalent position in relationship to the nation. Migrating between the United States and Cuba, English and Spanish, ostracism and inclusion, and apathy and involvement, those who remained on the island were negotiating their position as unhyphenated Cubans. Thus the revolution muted articulations of diasporic subjectivity and brought to the fore internal divisions, including those of generation and gender.

Chapter 3 provides a primarily ethnographic rendering of the Special Period's aftermath in order to present a glimpse into the daily realities in which my interlocutors turned to revitalize their Anglo-Caribbean origins. It explores the connections between local and regional efforts to reestablish, establish, and develop ties.

In chapter 4 I relate the experience of heightened racial inequality that emerged during the Special Period with the turn toward Anglo-Caribbean origins. I argue that this move allowed these Black Cubans to contest the growing impact of anti-Black racial attitudes in Cuba. I suggest that the revitalization was a de facto, indirect way of organizing as blacks in a climate where, unlike that in which more recent antiracist organizing is occurring, recognizing racial inequality was still taboo.

Chapter 5 analyzes narratives of social mobility articulated by Anglo-Caribbean Cubans attempting to "rescue their roots" during the economic crisis. In it, I situate Anglo-Caribbean Cuban narratives of social mobility within the sociopolitical context of contemporary Cuba, establishing the central role that narratives play in self-making. To illustrate and further develop my argument, I present selected narratives of my interlocutors, each of whom offers an affirmation and critique of revolutionary society that suggests a more nuanced relationship to heightened political and economic change.

The concluding chapter begins with a "tale of entry and exit" from one of my last field research trips to Cuba, when upon my arrival in the Antonio Maceo airport, I was greeted by a sign intended for tourists that proclaimed, "We multiply dreams." I use this moment as a point of departure to provide a final frame in which the drama of Black subject-making in twenty-first-century Cuba is occurring.

1

British West Indian Migration to Cuba

The Roots and Routes of Respectability

Our parents and grandparents, men and women of strong personality, of high
moral values, devoutly religious, stubborn of habit, respectful and disciplined
citizens, have left us an inestimably rich culture which present and future
generations should know and preserve.

Eixa Croos Valiente and Margarita Lewis, 1996

Citizens. When I came across this passage,[1] I could not shake from my consciousness the use of this word to describe those individuals who were subjects of the British Empire and immigrants in Cuba.[2] Rather than read this
as a creative interpretation of twentieth-century British nationality laws, I
gravitated toward the adjectives that modified "citizens," considering if those
were what rendered "citizen" a valid description of their status, of their claim
to a modern subjectivity. It seemed that these characteristics were what rendered valid their ongoing self-identification as British citizens deserving of
political rights.[3] Nearly all of the *descendientes* in this study echoed Valiente and Lewis in their characterization of those who came before them:
los jamaicanos were literate, well mannered, frugal, hardworking, respectful,
church going, soft spoken, well dressed, responsible, respected (and respectful, particularly of elders), sober, honest, organized (in the sense of community and personal habits), strict disciplinarians, unconcerned with politics,
and proud of being Black.[4]

In this narrative of respectability, what separated the Cuban-born children of jamaicanos from other Cubans was *la crianza* (the upbringing): the
family, churches, English schools, and various fraternal and recreational
associations were the institutions in which "correct" behavior was instilled
and firmly reinforced.[5] Though many of my interlocutors situated this rep-

resentation of Anglo-Caribbean culture in comparison to Haitians as well as working-class Black and mulatto/mestizo Cubans, the narrative of racial respectability is not the sole domain of Anglo-Caribbeans at home and abroad.[6] Imported by the agents of colonial authority, middle-class respectability was negotiated by those under the influence of empire and in some cases deployed as a strategy to challenge accusations of savagery and the related conclusion that non-Europeans are fit for neither full citizenship nor self-government (C. Hall 2000; Banerjee 2010; Rush 2011; Putnam 2014).

Historians exploring themes of race, migration, and Black activism in Latin America in the mid-nineteenth and early twentieth centuries suggest that respectability was a wedge that divided people along class lines (Bourgois 1989; Harpelle 2001; Giovannetti 2006b; Pappademos 2011; Putnam 2013). Although the mass of Black and mixed-race people in Cuba, immigrant or not, were disproportionately working class and poor, the elites and aspiring elites among them hinged upward mobility upon the performance of respectability. In the context of white supremacy, which perhaps found its highest expression in the pseudoscience of race, immigration policies, and the eugenics movement during this time period, distance from Blackness and the African past was largely nonnegotiable in the pursuit of upward mobility.

The cachet of qualities that constitute respectability was most prominently brought under the light of social scientific scrutiny in Peter Wilson's *Crab Antics: The Social Anthropology of English-Speaking Negro Societies of the Caribbean* (1973). He proposed that British Caribbean societies are characterized by a tension between the values of respectability, which references a hierarchical orientation toward social relations and is based in early twentieth-century English middle-class values, and reputation, which places value on individual characteristics such as physical prowess and verbal dexterity. Wilson argues that respectability is the domain of women and the sphere of the household while reputation, a more equalizing orientation and response to the imposed colonial order, is the domain of men and exists outside of the domestic sphere.

This thesis has been soundly critiqued and expanded upon, with its claims around and implications for gender politics in the Caribbean being vigorously debated (Sutton 1974; Austin 1983; Olwig 1990; Trouillot 1992; Besson 1993; Yelvington 1995; Barrow 1998; Freeman 2000, 2007; and Thomas 2004). Feminist scholars in particular have engaged the politics of respectability most interestingly within a neoliberal context. Gina Ulysse (2007), similar to Thomas (2004), argues for the displacement of a politics of respectability, illustrating that Jamaican women who have become successful Informal Commercial Importers "are not interested in investing their profits in pursuit of respectability" (2007:243). In their transgressions of class, in their being "out of place," her interlocutors both challenge and accommodate the binaries of woman:lady, dark skin:light skin, rough:respectable. In her gendered analysis of entrepreneurial experience in Barbados, Freeman (2007) argues that reputation, with flexibility at its core, is more useful for social mobility in the current iteration of global capitalism. In contrast, respectability, which Wilson (1973) conceptualized as in opposition to the counterculture of reputation, is "proving to be more resistant to capitalist globalization" (2007:262). In other words, the qualities required to be a successful businessperson in today's Barbados favor those associated with reputation.

Though a patriarchal family structure was implicated to a certain degree in the realization of racial respectability, which I will touch upon in chapter 2, this is not a gender analysis of respectability. Rather, I am interested in what the discursive deployment of racial respectability reveals about Black subject formation in a moment when Cuba was thrust back into the global capitalist market after a decades-long absence. During the Special Period, the Anglo-Caribbean Cubans involved in resuscitating the ethnic associations, fraternal lodges, churches, cricket teams, and transnational networks of their forebears called upon this enduring trope of Anglo-Caribbeanness.

Confronted by the durability of this trope, I was compelled to wonder why it was this conception of Anglo-Caribbeanness that these Cubans sought to rescue. I'm suggesting that this move constitutes a subject-making practice evidenced in the context of emergent economic and social disadvantage during the reform process.

In challenging the notion that a shared "African past" is the basis of diaspora, Paul Gilroy conceptualized diaspora as a matrix of connections developed in, across, and around the Atlantic Ocean. In his seminal text, *The Black Atlantic: Modernity and Double-Consciousness* (1993), Gilroy theorizes black modernity, using the homonyms of roots and routes as a way to critique the focus on origins (roots) and the exclusion of pathways (routes) out of which diaspora is created. I invoke Gilroy's intervention by using these homonyms in the chapter's title as a way to signal that discourses of respectability emerge out of a particular history of shared racial degradation (roots) and they travel across time, space, and place (routes). In this articulation of diasporic sub-jectivity, respectability becomes the imagined identity that connects people to an Anglophone Caribbean homeland; it signifies authenticity and belong-ing, blurring the line between roots and routes. The principal purpose of this chapter is to provide critical historical context for these subject-making practices from the time of Anglo-Caribbean Blacks' early settlement in Cuba up until the 1959 revolution.

Positioning British West Indian migrant laborers within and between em-pirc and nation(s) and as subjects of multiple postcolonialities, I first draw upon historiography to sketch out contours of the historical landscape of the British Caribbean and Cuba carved out by race and multiple migrations. Then, drawing upon life histories and archival material, I provide a window into the lives that immigrants created.

Black English-speaking Caribbean immigrants brought with them to Cuba their skills, aspirations and ideas, as well as notions of social hierarchy.[7] Their assertions of respectability during this period of violent racial inequal-ity cannot be severed from the class and color politics in their islands of origin or in early twentieth-century Cuba. Circuitous and at times perilous, the journey of late nineteenth- and twentieth-century Anglo-Caribbeans in pursuit of economic autonomy ironically began with freedom.

Frustrated Freedom in the British West Indies and the Production of Respectability

The postemancipation period in the British Caribbean witnessed high un-employment and underemployment caused by the contraction of the sugar industry, a shortage of job opportunities, generally low wages, and popu-lation pressure, particularly in Barbados. Related to the development of industrial capitalism, the severe contraction of the sugar industry in the mid-nineteenth century, a process that was accelerated by the British Sugar Duties Act of 1846, which eliminated the guarantee of a British market for Caribbean sugar, resulted in a lack of adequate opportunities to support a life not marked by destitution. Even with the availability of land for rental or sale due to the dramatic reduction in the number of British Antillean sugar estates from around 2,200 in 1838 to 800 in 1900, the plummeting prices of sugar and general unreliability of the market for tropical raw materials limited the profitability of agriculture. Indeed, remaining estates complained of labor shortages, not simply because the formerly enslaved were unwilling to work on the plantations, preferring to be producers themselves, but because the wages offered were so low.[8]

While the opportunity for African Caribbean people to achieve a greater level of self-determination through land ownership created a peasantry substantial enough to reconfigure the social structure, this route to mobility quickly narrowed through various efforts to wrest land from squatters and undermine formerly enslaved people's attempts to buy land (Mintz 1974; Beckles 2003; Scarano 1989; Craton 1997). Moreover, the importation of Asian laborers, imposition of taxation, implementation of debt peonage, high cost of basic commodities, and the deeply entrenched color/class hierarchy seriously compromised the hoped-for impact of emancipation (Look Lai 1993; Cooper, Holt, and Scott 2000; Rose 2002; Welch 2002; Mintz 1997; Smith 1982; Emmer 2000). The formerly enslaved responded to this onslaught of opposition to their survival in various ways, one being migration abroad.

Interestingly, one of the most significant changes in the postemancipation period was the growth in numbers and prosperity of a middle stratum that was not exclusively from the more privileged mixed race population. In Jamaica, where approximately 75 percent of the immigrants to Cuba originated, land was acquired by freedmen in three ways: squatting, individual purchase, and as members of newly established church communities. In the immediate postemancipation period, leaders of the Baptist and Methodist missionary churches began to buy ruined estates with the intention of resettling parishioners as independent peasants in church communities.[9] Church leaders viewed this as an opportunity to provide greater rewards to those who fully committed themselves to Western Christianity by living in such communities, having officially rejected African spiritual practices as uncivilized and savage. People from these church-founded free villages were reportedly more likely to be literate, thrifty, dependent upon organized Christian churches, and from families marked by legal marriage than were those of the rest of the freedman population (Mintz 1974:171).

Similar to contemporary Caribbean societies, a tension existed between respectability and raunchiness in the late nineteenth and early twentieth centuries, one that Lara Putnam (2013, 2014) highlights in her work on what she terms the "supranational public sphere" created by the Black press and popular culture during the interwar years. Her research as well as that of Jorge Giovannetti emphasizes that British Caribbean immigrants were a heterogeneous group stratified by class, island of origin, and adherence to hegemonic British middle-class colonial culture. Indeed, Putnam argues that the Black internationalists and Pan-African radicals held or adopted the elite stance that dismissed popular culture as vulgar and religion as backward and foolish, refusing to recognize that "religious innovation had long been a vital source of oppositional politics in the British Caribbean, as impassioned individuals spread visions of justice to come" (2013:51). Like Garvey who "denounced the 'superstition' and even 'African barbarism' of popular religiosity" (2013:13), elite leaders were in opposition to the "radical moves" made by those who, like Thomas's (2004) and Ulysse's (2007) interlocutors, might have been less consistently and persistently invested in the politics of respectability. In their mission to "uplift" the race under conditions of segregation, colonialism, and racial terror, the early twentieth century Black nationalist and internationalist elite imagined respectability as racial redemption.

It is therefore quite interesting that, over a century later, Anglo-Caribbean Cubans facing heightened racialized inequality uniformly conjure up this trope of respectability to describe the immigrant communities from which they came. This is in spite of evidence suggesting that they were a diverse group of sojourners: urban and rural, skilled and unskilled, Jamaican and small islander, cohabitating with and without legal marriage, respectable and raunchy. In order to contextualize this discursive move, I first place their journey within the broader regional context and then examine the conditions in Cuba that immigrants and their Cuban-born children faced.

Intraregional Migration: Escape to Cuba, Land of Upheaval and Opportunity

The early twentieth century was a period of great movement within and to the region, and immigrants to Cuba were part of "an expanding migratory field" that began in the mid-nineteenth century (Putnam 2002:11). Although the majority of social science research on Caribbean migration concerns those who travel to Europe, Canada, or the United States, an invaluable body of work exists that explores movement across intraregional national and imperial boundaries.[10] The dawn of the twentieth century in Cuba was overshadowed by the dominant economic and political role of the United States. The grand project of strategic modernization required cheap labor, particularly in the sugar industry, and pulled not only people of (other) Caribbean origins, but also those from Europe and the United States (Cooper, Holt, and Scott 2000).

The extent to which the British West Indian presence was felt in Cuba at different moments changed during a forty-year period that was characterized by surges and lulls in migration and returns.[11] Of the estimated 1.29 million immigrants who entered Cuba between 1902 and 1935, 781,311 (or 60 percent) were from Spain and 311,216 (or 24 percent) were from Haiti and the British West Indies (McLeod, 2000:17).[12] Between 1908 and 1911, 13,685 Antilleans came to Cuba, constituting the second largest migrant group in Cuba after the Spaniards, but this was prior to the real migration boom. Indeed, about half of the total migrants of the first three decades of the twentieth century entered between 1916 and 1920 (75,871) during the Dance of the Millions, when World War I interrupted the production of European beet sugar resulting in an increase in the demand for cane sugar.[13]

The regional distribution of the foreign population is a critical part of understanding the social and cultural spheres in which immigrants negotiated their needs and created communities. In 1907, during the earlier phase of the migration, about half of the Spanish-born were in urban areas and only 16 percent lived in the eastern part of the country (McLeod 2000:41). The majority of Caribbean migrants entered through the port of Santiago de Cuba and remained in Oriente, the eastern province of the island where the population had been more decimated by the independence wars and unskilled labor was needed for the growing sugar industry. Indeed, British West Indians constituted one in ten inhabitants of the region by 1931 (McLeod 2004:41). The demographic picture is complicated when one considers that the Antillean immigrants were initially concentrated not only in the eastern provinces, but also in rural areas. Thus, their small population relative to Spaniards was not necessarily reflected at the local level.

The figures on British West Indian migration also do not speak to the foreign *Black* presence of which these migrants were a part. British West Indians and Haitians who entered the island during this period were both perceived to belong to a larger mass of "undesirable aliens."[14] Their Blackness, cultural traditions, and position as foreign low wage laborers were the basis of this categorization.[15] However, including even the work of Matthew Casey

(2012), which presents compelling evidence that challenges the dominant representation of Haitians as a homogeneous group of unskilled, isolated, lower class people abandoned by their home government and confined to the bottom of the rural labor hierarchy, the historiography positions British Caribbean immigrants in a predominantly privileged position relative to Haitian workers. This placement is based largely on their status as British subjects, their high level of literacy, and their skills.[16] In the discussion that follows, I make the connection between the social and political context of early twentieth-century Cuba and a diasporic subjectivity that engendered the emergence of respectable Blackness.

Cuba at War and U.S. Intervention: Assault on Black Power

> In general the relations between Americans and Spaniards in Cuba were excellent, while those between Cubans and Americans were almost invariably bad. General Young was found speaking of Calixto García's army as "a lot of degenerates, absolutely devoid of honour or gratitude. They are no more capable of self government than the savages." Montejo thought that the "Americans didn't like the Negroes much. They used to shout 'nigger nigger' and burst out laughing." Spanish officers in contrast were greeted as chivalrous brothers in arms.
>
> Hugh Thomas, Cuba, or, The Pursuit of Freedom, 1998

This passage well explains both the lines of imperial allegiance and their racist underpinnings, which amounted to further subjugation of an ostensibly independent Cuba. While economic development was under way, projecting the image of progress and civilization so coveted by Cuban elites, white foreigners continued to hold sway in the political and economic life of a nation that many had sacrificed everything to wrest from Spain.

The Cuba to which Anglo-Caribbean immigrants migrated had recently emerged from thirty years of wars fought for the conjoined issues of independence and emancipation. During the final three months of Cuba's War of Independence (1895–1898), the United States intervened on Cuba's behalf, hastening Spain's defeat by both Cuba and the United States in the Spanish-American War. This marked a new chapter in the fateful relationship between the United States and Cuba in which the United States became a dominant economic, political, and cultural presence in Cuba until the 1959 revolution. In what essentially amounted to a changing of the guard between Spain and the United States, the United States established a provisional government that turned over the reins only after Cubans agreed to the Platt Amendment, which was passed in 1901. This amendment to the Cuban constitution (the constitution being adopted in 1902) put limits on Cuba's ability to enter into agreements with foreign powers and manage its own economy, in addition to giving the United States the right to intervene militarily whenever it saw fit and to hold title to and maintain land used for a naval base in Guantánamo.[17]

Cubans, in fighting for their independence from Spain, had been internally divided regarding the route to and character of this independence. Arguably, this division was one of the reasons that the United States was able to intervene and become a dominant force. Much of the dissent revolved around national identity and the social and political role that people of African descent would play in the emergent republic. At the same time that Cubans promoted notions of racial equality, the African presence continued to be associated with savagery. Fears about Cuba's being forever excluded from the circle of civilized nations due to the failure of its citizens to defend themselves against the threat of dangerous Black foreigners abounded (Helg 1995; de la Fuente 2001b; Giovannetti 2006b). As we shall see, both this issue of national and racial identity and U.S. dominance were central to the Anglo-Caribbean experience in Cuba.

The United States had substantial investments in Cuba prior to the end of the Independence War; however, this economic interest skyrocketed during the period of the "pseudo-Republic" when U.S. businesses and civilians alike took economic advantage of a Cuba reeling from thirty years of war and a displaced labor force. At the turn of the twentieth century when the export boom in Latin America was well under way, Cuban property owners without capital, income, or collateral were forced to sell their land far below its value, creating tremendous opportunities for thousands of Americans (as well as Spaniards) who wanted to escape hard times in their homelands brought on by an economic crisis of the late 1890s (Andrews 1997:11; Pérez 1995:134). U.S. settlers established farms and businesses, sought jobs in the booming public works activity aimed at rebuilding and expanding the country's infrastructure, and pursued investment opportunities.[18] The sugar industry was the primary target of U.S. investment such that by 1908 the entire northern coast of Oriente was owned by U.S. sugar corporations, and within twenty-five years of the founding of the republic, the most salient feature of the Cuban economy was the U.S. dominance of sugar production (Pérez 1999:221).

Relations between Cuba and Spain had continued such that 40 percent of urban property and thousands of businesses were in the hands of Spaniards who were recruited to work and settle in Cuba by the hundreds of thousands (Naranjo Orovio 1997:37; Cervantes-Rodríguez 2010). Many of them left poverty in Spain to become successful businessmen, achieving middle- and upper-class status.[19] Unions, which were dominated by Spanish anarchists during the time that so many Antillean laborers were entering the country, did not admit Blacks and mulattos, least of all foreign ones (Gómez 2005:17). Enjoying white postcolonial privilege, Spaniards, even those who were loyal-ist or loyalist sympathizers and thus were against independence, were given preference over Cubans of color and came to dominate the expanding sec-tors of labor during this period.[20]

Cubans of color were by and large systematically excluded from economic opportunities and subjected to the segregationist practices U.S. occupation forces legitimized and expanded upon on the basis of the ideology of scien-tific racism (de la Fuente 2001b:40). One of the United States' first tasks in subduing the Cuban population was to disband the Revolutionary Army, which had a relatively remarkable level of racial equality, leaving Afro-Cu-ban fighters powerless and jobless as those appointed to government posi-tions were predominantly pro-American conservatives from white elite and middle-class backgrounds (Ferrer 1999). Indeed, people of color, the poor, and nationalists were underrepresented in any positions of authority such as those in the police force and rural guard where applicants had to be liter-ate, have the money to provide their own uniform and horse, and have rec-ommendations from elite pro-U.S. Cubans. This was clearly a racially based exclusionary practice as, according to the census of 1899, only 24 percent of Afro-Cubans could read and write compared to 44 percent of white Cu-bans—by 1907, the rate increased to 45 percent for Blacks and 58 percent for whites; 198 men of color were registered as having a postsecondary educa-tion compared to 8,629 whites (Helg 1995:96, 129). This, in addition to the protection of Spanish properties, the retention of Spaniards in public offices, and the promotion of Spanish immigration indicates that the most salient factor influencing Black and mulatto Cubans' condition was not simply their identity as Cubans in a period of foreign domination but their race in an epoch of triumphant white domination.

The tremendous injustice perpetrated against Black and mixed-race he-roes of revolutionary wars and people of color in general when the United States began its occupation of Cuba would not have been possible had many white Cubans, military and civilians alike, not been averse to (or, in the least, ambivalent about) the notion of racial equality and justice. Those U.S. soldiers, government officials, missionaries and fortune hunters who were steeped in notions of Black inhumanity and believed it their task to civilize all Cubans were effective because they encountered a post-slave society that had a wealth of discriminatory practices upon which to build.[21] Indeed, the postindependence social landscape, in which people of color had limited access to education, particularly beyond primary school, were excluded from jobs in the military, commerce and the professions, and were socially undesirable, was disturbingly similar to the pre-independence terrain.[22] Though a small class of Black and mulatto socially mobile elite certainly existed and had a vibrant presence in Cuba prior to and after independence, people of color were socially marginalized, often subjected to imprisonment and physical brutality, and largely relegated to manual and service jobs such as day laborers, construction workers, gardeners, maids, laundresses, and cooks. Further strengthening white privilege and asserting white supremacy, something that some elites of color participated in due to what Pappademos argues was self-interest and a lack of overt race consciousness, African cultural practices were denigrated, African religions and their practitioners were vilified and persecuted, and Black culture rather than white racism was held responsible for Black people's inferior social position (Moore 1998; Howard 1998; Pappademos 2011).

The wide participation and prominence of people of color in positions of authority in the revolutionary wars had brought about the anticipation of radical social change in which old social relationships would be transformed. Although personal experience of actual upward mobility in the military was limited, the tacit agreement that their decisive contribution in the war would be recognized and proportionately rewarded after independence led to "Afro-Cubans' expectations regarding their position in the future [to] increase dramatically" (Helg 1995:12). It was this expectation of justice and the experience of white betrayal on the part of conservatives and liberals alike that led Black veterans to begin organizing and eventually form the first Black political party in the hemisphere, the Partido Independiente de Color (Independent Party of Color), in 1908. The Party was outlawed by the Morúa Law (named for Martín Morúa Delgado, a man of color), which prohibited race-based political organizations.

In May 1912, the Independientes staged an armed protest sparked by their exclusion from participation in electoral politics. Billed as a Black rebellion, this protest was brutally repressed by rural guards, militia, and the military, and anywhere from 3,000 to 6,000 Cubans were murdered (Helg 1995; de la Fuente 2001a; Thomas 1998; Rolando 2001). Among the consequences of this demonstration of white domination were an increase in racial tensions that was particularly visible in the conflicts over social space and the stimulation of Spanish immigration for the purpose of white colonization (de la Fuente 2001a:78; Naranjo Orovio 1997:39).

The formation of the Partido Independiente de Color and the massacre of the Black population that took place in 1912 are critical events that impacted the world into which immigrants to Cuba entered. It was a world divided, where one segment of what Pappademos (2011) reminds us was a multifaceted rather than coherent Black Cuban political landscape struggled to transform the myth of racial equality into a reality through, among other things, refusing to acquiesce to white power. The Independientes belong to a tradition in which Black resistance is a key to resisting other forms of social injustice. At the same time that their platform insisted upon an end to racially discriminatory practices in employment, social spaces, education, and immigration, their demands included measures that benefited ordinary Cubans regardless of color.[23] In spite of the widespread benefit that such changes would bring, the Party was met with opposition from its inception, charged with racism, and accused of putting race before the Cuban nation. This charge would prove to endure into the contemporary revolutionary period when identifying and discussing racism would be taboo and considered a threat to national unity.

Race, Immigration, and Building the Cuban Nation

Cuba maintained a nationalist ideology that professed racial equality and tended to deny or else minimize systemic anti-Black racism and its social consequences across political and economic regimes. Instances of the social inclusion and/or material success of some people of African descent were used to substantiate a claim to racial equality rather than to exemplify the complexity of power and the workings of racial hierarchy. Indeed, the concept of *adelantar la raza* (improving the race)[24] and the policy of *blanqueamiento* (whitening) were means by which people of African descent could "elevate" themselves: elevation through the severing of perceptible African roots.[25]

The practice of whitening manifested itself at the national level in the area of immigration. The 780,000 Spaniards attracted to Cuba in the first three decades of the twentieth century represented nearly half of the island's population in 1900 (Andrews 1997:13). These immigrants displaced Cubans of color in the urban industrial sector, where Cubans were relegated to the least-skilled, most poorly paid positions.[26] Spanish immigrants by and large did not work, or at least did not stay working, in agriculture (with the exception of those from the Canary Islands), and therefore the problem of labor supply and expense arose (Cervantes-Rodríguez 2010; Naranjo Orovio 1997:68; Andrews 1997:14). The solution sought by U.S. interests was to import Black Caribbean laborers.

The presence of these "undesirable aliens" was a tremendously contentious issue in both official political and popular circles. Cubans were engaged in a furiously passionate struggle over their emerging national identity, and at the heart of this battle lay race and its accompanying band of cultural signifiers. Like other new nations of the Americas, Cuba's racial composition was viewed as the determining factor of its fate. Was Cuba going to be Black or white, a savage colony or a modern nation, "Barbados or Canada" (Chomsky 2000)? European immigration was the solution to this quandary and the importation of Black workers from other Caribbean islands directly sabotaged efforts to whiten the island and thus signaled to some the miscarriage of a modern Cuba.[27] But the interests of the Cuban and U.S. capitalists who needed a voluminous supply of highly exploitable, mobile labor, combined with the conditions on other Caribbean islands in comparison to those in Cuba, guaranteed such a workforce and resulted in the legal and illegal migration of hundreds of thousands of workers to various destinations throughout Latin America (Knight 1985; Petras 1988; Harpelle 1993; Wynter 2001; Putnam 2002, 2013).

If Black migrant workers were at most tolerated during the "Vacas Gordas" (Fat Cows) wartime sugar industry boom when their labor was needed, it is not surprising that they were subjected to scorn, harassment, and deportation in periods of bust. With the reduction of the sugar harvesting season and related economic contractions of the 1920s, Cubans fell on particularly hard times. During the Great Depression, real income decreased 80 percent, unemployment rose to 50 percent of the labor force and the sugar cane crop of 1933 lasted sixty-seven days, half of that in 1926. The salary for farming, when paid, was twenty cents a day until nightfall. A can of coffee collected

paid five cents, often in kind (Chailloux and Whitney 2001:55). Many immigrants were destitute and were viewed as a menace to Cuba's fragile social
and economic status.[28]

Though Black men were entitled to vote and thus politicians at least took
Black Cubans into consideration as a decisive voting bloc, Black foreigners
had no leverage within the political system. The only recourse for English-
speaking Caribbean immigrants was to appeal to the British Consul as subjects of the Empire. Apart from this largely inadequate or at least inconsistent
protection,[29] they had no formal defense against Cuba's deeply entrenched
fear of Black foreigners, a fear that had bloody consequences for people of Af
rican descent, "native" and foreign, on more than one occasion (de la Fuente
2001a; Chomsky 2000; Naranjo Orovio 1997; Helg 1995; Giovannetti 2001).
Indeed, much of the historiography relies upon the correspondence between
immigrants, the British Consul, and the metropole concerning the question
of repatriation and redress for wrongs committed against foreign laborers.
These exchanges have provided insight into how the immigrants viewed
themselves vis-à-vis empire and their strategic use of British subject status
(Giovannetti 2006b). It also is a window into divisions among islanders as Jamaicans were entitled to repatriation funds due to the Emigration Act of 1904,
which required a permit to emigrate, the fee for which (in theory) contributed
to the cost of relief or repatriation (Whitney and Chailloux Laffita 2013). This
only applied to Jamaicans, leaving "Small Islanders" with less recourse.

As a whole, Black immigrants not only were held responsible for the economic crisis gripping the nation in the '20s and early '30s, but also, in the
minds of some, were associated with and blamed for any revolt or disorder
that took place (Giovannetti 2001:74). This was particularly so if the unrest
had to do with Black Cubans' asserting their right to full citizenship within
the political sphere. The Liberal Revolt of 1917, during which anywhere from
14 to 50 British West Indians were executed and many more beaten, robbed,
and humiliated, was a particularly vivid example of the revival of the racial
fears that had led to and clearly persisted after the 1912 massacre. The economic crises and forced deportations that followed the crash in sugar prices
in 1921 and the stock market crash in 1929 were other instances in which
Black immigrants were held responsible for Cuba's hardships and targeted
for abuse (McLeod 1998; Gómez 2005). Thus, for some, their dream turned
into a nightmare as they were maligned, beaten, jailed, deported, and even
murdered.

This evidence indicates that the world that Caribbean immigrants walked into was in many ways a hostile one. In spite of the fact that wages tended to be higher than those received in their islands of origin,[30] they were subjected to low and inconsistent remuneration, artificially inflated prices of basic consumer goods, media campaigns portraying them as dangerous savages, brutality and imprisonment by Cuban police and rural guards, ridicule and harassment by the Cuban peasantry, and abuse at the hands of officials and employers who "believed that British subjects were 'aggressive,' 'arrogant,' and more 'troublesome' than Haitian and even native-born Cuban workers" (Whitney and Chailloux Laffita 2013:8).

The World That They Created

The institutions of the Anglo-Caribbean immigrants provide a window into the experiences, values, and beliefs of this population and an indication of what it is that Cuban descendants refer to in their mission to "rescue their roots." Confined within the pages of marriage and baptismal records, meeting minutes and pamphlets, as well as photographs of families, coworkers, and events is a record of the "official" legacy. Such documents declare what particular members of the community found noteworthy, wanted to record, and had the resources with which to do so. Order, self-improvement, financial responsibility, and Christian morality are among the characteristics most strongly represented.

For Anglo-Caribbean Cubans, connection to their origins is fundamentally through family. I began many conversations and most interviews with questions about family who migrated to Cuba. When people learned that I was interested in the experiences of anglófonos and descendientes in Cuba, those who had documents and photographs brought them out to share with me their foreignness. From the prerevolutionary period, there were old black-and-white, mostly studio photographs of stone-faced patriarchs dressed in suits, either standing next to their new brides or seated and surrounded by the children who would come from a legal union. Others, sepia colored and crumbling, featuring determined-looking women, sometimes with young children at their sides and on their laps, documented the family before their passage. One wedding photograph features the bride, three bridesmaids—gloved hands clutching bouquets and necks adorned with pearls—and three flower girls

Figure 1.1. Mr. and Mrs. Skelton, founders of the British West Indian Welfare Centre, Guantánamo, Cuba, ca. 1940.

seated on the studio floor with their hands folded across their laps, and the groom, in tuxedo and sparking white gloves.

Such images and imaginings are partially indicative of the high rates of endogamy among British West Indians and their descendants (Espronceda Amor 1999; Chailloux and Whitney 2005:78).[31] Of the civil marriages between immigrants in Santiago, 77 percent prior to 1940 were between immigrants

Figure 1.2. Wedding photograph of Jamaicans marrying in Cuba, ca. 1940.

Figure 1.3. A young woman and her children before leaving Jamaica bound for Cuba, ca. 1920.

Figure 1.4. Jamaican wedding party, ca. 1940.

of the same nationality.[32] Records from the All Saints' Episcopal Church in Guantánamo indicate the dominant presence of British West Indians in this church as 88 percent (185 out of 210) of the marriages performed between 1902 and 1940 were between two people from the British West Indies (McLeod 2000:178).

While these data provide important information regarding the race/color and national identity of individuals getting married, this bias toward legalized marriage reflects an exclusion that is potentially quite significant. Common law marriage, consensual unions, and cohabitation were the more dominant forms of heterosexual coupling among the African Caribbean working class during the early decades of the twentieth century (Barrow 1998; Smith 1996). Yet there is little record of the details of such arrangements; indeed, it is in this way that those who do not conform to practices sanctioned by the state have been erased from the historical record. One exception to this that I found was in the minutes of a fraternal lodge in Santiago that rejected a man's application for membership based on the fact that he was not legally married to the woman with whom he lived, suggesting that such institutions played a role in enforcing a particular moral order based upon the matrix of respectability.[33]

In addition to family, English schools were an institutional locus for the (re)production of Anglo-Caribbean identity. Perhaps due to the late nineteenth-century fledgling campaign for universal primary school education in the British West Indies, establishing schools was a priority for the immigrants. The proliferation of private English primary schools points to the importance placed on language and basic literacy.[34] The following excerpt from my field notes is but one example of how descendientes represented the role of English schools in their upbringing:

> We stopped by several people's homes, mostly women, all descendants, all somewhat willing to participate in the research. In the first house, there were two women, mother and daughter. The mother has twelve children, all went to university [she explained]. . . . Her parents moved to Cuba from Jamaica. She emphasized the discipline with which they were raised, saying that the discipline was a beautiful thing and that it began in the classroom. She then recited word for word [in English] what must have been how each day began in the English school: "Good morning students, good morning teacher," and the rest was the teacher telling them how they had to behave.[35]

Indeed, participants in their sixties and seventies, all of whom went to English language schools, were animated in their recollections of incidents of misbehavior and the punishments they constantly received at the hands of Ms. or Mr. So-and-so. As Winton, a Guantanamero in his seventies exclaimed, "¡Cómo nos daban golpes!" (How they beat us!) and "¡Pero duro, ay mi madre, qué fuerte eran los jamaicanos!" (Tough! Oh my Mother, Jamaicans were strong!).[36] Jorge Smith, who was taken care of by three different English teachers after his Jamaican mother suffered a mental breakdown, was seventy-six years old when we first met in 2001 and recalled their strict behavior with equal clarity:

> My parents came from Jamaica, from St. Catherine in Jamaica, and they came to Cuba and had me. My mother, when I was four years old, went crazy and they took her to Mason [an insane asylum] and she died there. So, my father raised me. . . . I lived with a teacher, here in

Santiago. Her name was Ms. Daly. From there, I went with Ms. Johnson, another teacher. Then from there I went to Ms. Watts. They were
English teachers. I was boarded, I didn't have siblings and my father
left me with her so she could take care of me since he worked in the
fields. . . . So the teachers were the ones who took care of me and my
father paid them. . . . [They were] strict, very strict! And gave blows
like crazy! That Ms. Johnson wasn't easy. . . . After this, at almost twelve
years old, my father got together with a Jamaican woman and I went
to live with them."[37]

Such oral testimonies suggest the interconnections between the English
schools that the immigrants established and the reproduction of a particular construction of Anglo-Caribbeanness. However, while the value
of education is part of the matrix of respectability associated with people
from the Anglophone Caribbean, it was clearly important to Cubans of
color as well as to other diasporic populations. Cuban public schools were
open to students of color, and the attendance and literacy rates of Black
Cubans increased significantly during the second and third decades of the
twentieth century. Indeed, the racial gap in literacy for the island nearly
disappeared by 1931, but it was at this point that public school registration
sharply declined and the number of segregated private schools rose (de la
Fuente 2001a:141).

Perhaps it was the precariousness of public education in Cuba at that
point that inspired immigrants to create their own schools. It was most certainly the importance of being able to communicate in English, since this not
only enabled the connection of children to their families, but also, with the
U.S. and British economic presence, gave them an advantage in a competitive
labor market. Thus, it was not only receiving an education, but an education
in English that was critical to the immigrants. Furthermore, by maintaining
their own educational institutions, they did not have to confront the racial
discrimination that permeated the Cuban public schools where students of
color were barred from activities that involved representing the school in
public events and were consistently given lower grades than whites (de la
Fuente 2001a:148).

Church was another ubiquitous institution in Anglo-Caribbean communities.[38] The variety of churches available included Episcopal, Baptist,
Methodist, Catholic, Pentecostal, Salvation Army, and Seventh Day Ad-

ventist.[39] Here, Edward, whose St. Kittsian grandfather was a Seventh Day Adventist, illustrates the interconnection between religious practice and respectability:

> No one drank or smoke around my grandfather. I was the first grandson and very close to my grandfather. Every Friday night, I go over to his house, spend the night, go to church on Saturday and return home at sundown accompanied by my grandfather. On one occasion, I remember running ahead of my grandfather as we rounded the corner of my street. When I entered the house, I found my father shirtless, in shorts and smoking a cigar with a buddy in the living room. . . . As soon as I entered, my father, knowing my grandfather was soon to follow, disappeared into his room and emerged fully dressed and without the cigar. No one knows what he did with the cigar, but it was clear that even as a full grown man in his own house, he abided by my grandfather's expectations of behavior. [My father and uncles] revered my grandfather; he was like a god to them. He commanded a level of respect simply by his presence, there was something divine about him. His departure in 1965 was very difficult.

Edward went on to show me letters that his grandfather had written him in 1970 and 1971. One explained how he had to leave, that he would have starved had he remained in Cuba (a predicament that I will explore in chapter 2). Both letters illustrated a bond and concern for his grandson's spiritual health. In one, he said that it's fine to plan to be a doctor or lawyer, but the most important thing is to be a person of God, to remember that there is a God in the sky who sees and knows all.[40]

Not only was church attendance a recurrent theme in narratives of life in Anglo-Caribbean communities, but the predominant religiosity was evident in the overlap between church and other institutions. For example, Reverend Derrick, one of the first and most revered leaders of the British West Indian Cultural Centre and grandfather of the incoming president of the Young People's Department when I met him in 2001, was also an ordained minister. Membership to the fraternal lodges required a belief in God. Ceremonies, events, and meetings of the associations were opened and closed with prayer and it was not uncommon for the English schools to be housed in a church.

Another aspect of immigrants' lives that revealed the routes and roots of respectability was their positioning within the labor force. As discussed earlier, the majority of English-speaking Caribbean immigrants entered Cuba as unskilled laborers recruited for the sugarcane harvest. However, some experienced upward mobility within the agricultural sector as well as movement from the rural areas to towns and cities where they found steady employment during the dead season.[41] Embedded within the narrative of their mobility is the matrix of respectability, described here by labor historian Barry Carr:

> Jamaicans performed low status field work, but their higher literacy and political nous earned them the respect of employers and, therefore, promotion to higher paying jobs. . . . Due to their superior personal hygiene and education, British West Indians and Puerto Ricans were frequently given the most highly prized jobs both in the sugar yards, or *bateyes* (where they were employed in skilled and semiskilled jobs such as sugar dryers, stevedores, and guards), and on the railroads (where they worked as mechanics and electricians). Large numbers of British West Indians, especially women, also worked as servants for the foreign managerial elite, where their English was much appreciated by overseas managers. (1998b:88)[42]

This depiction of Anglo-Caribbean immigrants is repeated throughout the historiography of this mobile labor force in Latin America.

This relatively privileged position among the working class was linked to their status as British subjects who, in theory, had a right to the same treatment and protections as white subjects. However, time and time again, they confronted the reality that the British Empire's rhetoric of racelessness was hollow. Their persistent appeals to the British Consul and even to the king himself to intervene on their behalf in response to the harsh conditions in Cuba, particularly following the end of World War I, were often rebuffed. Rights were indeed not race blind, causing them to question whether they were British subjects or objects (Whitney and Chailloux Laffita 2013; Putnam 2013; Giovannetti 2001, 2006b; Charlton 2005). Thus, with regard to the color/class hierarchy existing alongside the rhetoric of equality, the world from which immigrants came and the one that they found in Cuba were strikingly similar.

Respectable Blackness and Defending the Race: The UNIA

> The UNIA was to find itself largely a migrant forum in Cuba and, for that matter,
> in the other Latin American countries, a forum through which the cultural ties of
> the English-speaking Caribbean could be maintained, and the economic problems
> of the migrants' marginal situation could be aired, addressed, and improved. In
> those forums an identity and unity of purpose and achievement would come
> gradually, and not without difficulty, to supersede narrow insular identities and
> petty rivalries over island size, and to provide a psychological bulwark against
> racial discrimination in the Eurocentric value-orientations of Latin American
> societies.
>
> *Rupert Lewis*, Marcus Garvey: Anti-Colonial Champion, *1988*

More recent work on native Black participation in the Universal Negro Improvement Association and African Communities League (UNIA-ACL) in
Cuba (McLeod 1998, 2003; Guridy 2003) and the Dominican Republic (Muñiz and Giovannetti 2003) challenges the perception that it was an organization of foreigners with no appeal to Spanish-speaking people of African
descent. However, the first part of Rupert Lewis's assertion holds true.[43] The
majority of the Garvey Movement's base in Latin America was comprised of
those Afro-Caribbean migrants who left the British West Indies to confront
racism and xenophobia in their host countries.[44]

Although the extent to which these conditions dissolved island identities
is debatable, the belief in racial solidarity and Black pride was embedded
within community discourse and manifested itself in the proliferation of
UNIA chapters in Cuba. Cuba had at least 50 UNIA divisions, second only
to the number in the United States, and Garveyism in Cuba continued to
thrive into the late 1920s, after it had gone into decline in the United States
(McLeod 2000:127).[45] Perhaps because of this decline, the UNIA was not
prominent in my interlocutors' narratives of community. Nonetheless, the
challenge to racial subjugation woven through the ethnic revitalization that
I discuss more fully in the following chapters suggests that the UNIA's strong
albeit relatively brief presence in Santiago and Guantánamo left a mark on
those institutions that did endure.

One reason that the proliferation of the UNIA in Cuba is relevant to this
project is that it exemplifies two related processes of Anglo-Caribbean subject formation. One concerns the development of diasporic subjectivity and
the other the complexity of the politics of respectability. The genesis of the

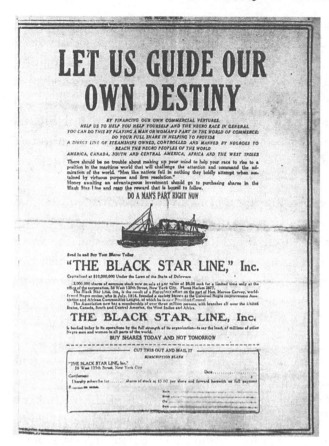

Figure 1.5. United Negro Improvement Association poster, soliciting financial support for the Black Star Line shipping company.

Garvey Movement was Marcus Garvey's realization, based on his experiences in Jamaica, the United States, and as a migrant laborer in Limón, Costa Rica, that people of African descent were subjugated based on their Blackness no matter their national origin, geographic location, or occupation. While this was not the first articulation of Black nationalism or of the belief that people of African descent shared the common experience of oppression or of the desire to return to Africa, the widespread appeal of the message and participation in the movement signifies a watershed moment in the genesis of African diasporic subject formation. While Garveyism was indeed a defense against the virulent racism in host countries, and, as Garnes argues, thrived in part due to the "acculturation and uprootedness" that characterized the West Indian experience (2009:134), it simultaneously reproduced the same Eurocentric values that it sought to undermine.

This emphasis on "improving the culture and education of black people" must first be understood within the context of constant accusations of Black immorality and ignorance as evidence of inferiority used to justify discrimination. In addition to hygiene, Black sexuality was targeted in the campaign to malign both British West Indians and Haitians.[46] They were pathologized as promiscuous and the women were held responsible for the rise in prostitution in spite of evidence that some Cuban women worked as prostitutes in the areas where migrant laborers congregated (Gómez 2005:16).

The language of improving culture and nurturing Christianity signals that part of the UNIA's mission was to cultivate respectability as a defense against such accusations, accusations that were racially based. This was at least in part successful. Consistent with Chailloux's claim that British West Indian migrants were the aristocracy of the working class, members of the UNIA were described as *de buena posición* (people with a measure of social and political status) rather than common plantation laborers (Guridy 2003:127).[47]

As noted earlier, this characterization of British West Indian migrants must be situated within those of other Black populations. While viewed as Black, Anglo-Caribbean migrants were perceived as distinct from Haitians; this difference lay in their education, skills, diligence, discipline, religiosity, knowledge of English, etc. They were considered to be *negros finos*, a categorization that I explore in depth as it applies to English-speaking Caribbean migrants and their descendants in chapter 4. In the Dominican Republic, they were referred to as *negros blancos* (white Blacks) in order to more accurately categorize them, which Muñiz and Giovannetti interpret to signify "the acceptance of the West Indian population within Dominican society" (2003:170).

However, while their status as *negros finos* (or *negros blancos* in the Dominican case) distinguished Anglo-Caribbean people from other groups and might have signaled their social incorporation, it also was a tool of enforcing certain exclusions within the group. The case mentioned above of the man who was denied membership to one of the associations due to his not being legally married to the woman he lived with is one example of this. Furthermore, based upon my interlocutors as well as those who appear in Rolando's *Hijos de Baraguá* (1996) and those Giovannetti resurrects through his historical research, the notion that island identities completely dissolved does not entirely hold true. In particular, those not from Jamaica were at times adamant about asserting their small island identity.

Some evidence can also be found that education or sophistication, more than island of origin (though the two were certainly related), informed some class and status distinctions within the migrant population. As one of my interlocutors, Teresa, reflected, "The immigrants came here looking for their fortune and all they found were coffee and sugar plantations, bad conditions in the *barracones*, and exploitation . . . and not just by the owners, but also by the smarter Jamaicans. . . . The smarter ones took advantage of the poorer, less educated ones who relied on them for help with the British Consulate. . . . They charged them a lot so they could make a profit. . . . 'El vivo vive de los bobos'" (The smart or cunning live off of fools).[48]

The distinctions in status and possibility within the Anglo-Caribbean immigrant communities that Teresa alludes to are further elaborated upon with the next wave of movement: the migration to Guantánamo. One of the most significant migrations of people from the Anglo-Caribbean was internal; with the wartime expansion of the U.S. Naval Base that began aggressively in 1939, workers moved to Guantánamo in search of better conditions.[49] As a result of this migration, some immigrants and their Cuban-born children not only achieved a measure of economic mobility but also developed transnational connections indicative of the formation of diasporic consciousness.[50]

Diasporic Subject-Making in a Transnational Social Field: Guantánamo in Focus

> In a general meeting on 14 of July of 1946, they [the British West Indian Welfare Centre] received a visit from Mr. Eric Johnson from Boston, U.S.A. [from The National Federation of British West Indians in Boston]. In this meeting they also adopted the quota for sick benefit. On this day, they made an agreement to open a branch of the Centre in the Central Hermita in Costa Rica. . . . In [another] meeting, Mrs. Bobby . . . spoke about the problem of the Black race and how the Centre had to defend our race . . .
>
> *Author interview with Edward, August 11, 2004, Guantánamo, while reviewing Centre archives*

As Edward guided me through the pages of the British West Indian Welfare Centre's minutes from its early days, we moved across Spanish and English,

Figure 1.6. British West Indian Welfare Centre leadership in front of the Union Jack, ca. 1950.

the Caribbean and the United States, his family history and mine. His grand-parents' migrations placed him in Guantánamo; in a way, my grandparents, having migrated from Montserrat to Boston, had done the same, for it was my experience in the United States that pushed me to answer Cuba's call,[51] to investigate those rumors of racial justice that led me to "discovering" my Cuban counterparts. Indeed, we had both been born somewhere other than our parents had, and our parents had been born somewhere other than their parents: diasporic connection was created through the ongoing experience of movement.

And move they did. The details relayed in Edward's commentary are in-dicative of the ample evidence in the institutional records and the family histories of my informants that the Cuban branch of the African Anglo-Caribbean diaspora was indeed a part of that highly mobile, transnationally expanding migratory field. The route from the British Caribbean island of origin to Cuba was often an indirect one, including stops in Central America, the United States and England. Some interlocutors' families had made the expected stop in Panama—indeed, one of my elder interlocutors was born in Panama to Jamaican parents, and another's Barbadian grandparents met while working in the Canal Zone before migrating to Camaguey in 1935.[52]

For others, the journey to Cuba was more circuitous. For instance, Elton's father migrated from Grenada to New York to Guantánamo where he met and married Elton's mother, the daughter of Jamaicans.[53] Smith's parents migrated directly from Jamaica, but his wife's mother had been born in Puerto Rico to Jamaican parents, moved to the Dominican Republic, and then to Cuba where she met her Jamaican-born husband, who had just arrived after a stint in the Dominican Republic as well.[54] Winton told the tale of his Jamaican grandfather sending the family, including Winton's mother, to Cuba before he migrated to England, eventually joining the family in Boquerón.[55] The founding director of El Centre, Mr. Skelton, had himself migrated to Banes from New York, but his family had left Jamaica for Panama before arriving in the United States.[56]

For nearly all of my interlocutors, their family's story of migration and separation continued with the advent of the 1959 revolution, which will be addressed in the next chapter. Here, however, I am highlighting another migration, an internal one that brought immigrants and their Cuban-born children to Guantánamo during World War II due to the expansion of the Guantánamo Naval Base. Prior to, and for some, even after the 1959 Cuban revolution, Anglo-Caribbeans were a part of a transnational social field that included their island of origin (as part of the British Empire), the wider Caribbean, Central America, Republican Cuba, and also the United States, not only as a geographic destination but also in the form of the agro-industrial business enterprises such as United Fruit Company and military installations such as the Guantánamo Naval Base. These plantations and the base were racially and ethnically diverse as the United States' rapidly growing imperial enterprises brought together people from disparate locations.[57] Like the company towns described earlier, the naval base was racially segregated and people of color were relegated to lower status positions; nevertheless, jobs on the base were prized given the limited options for stable, well-remunerated employment and the ubiquity of the racial hierarchy. For some, employment on the base provided a route to realizing the dream of upward mobility, thus racial abjection sat alongside opportunity. The need to "defend" the race persisted, as did racial respectability.

Indeed, Guantánamo's El Centre, a site of the reproduction of racial respectability, thrived in the context of the social mobility that some members experienced, and transnational connections were quite active. At the same time, by the mid-twentieth century, one generation had been born in Cuba, and after the expulsions of the '20s and '30s it became increasingly clear to those who remained that Cuba would be home. However, for those in Guantánamo, "Cuba" existed at the intersection of Cuba, the United States, and the African Caribbean world. Their subjectivities were constituted by the particularities of the transnational social field in which they operated.

Migration to Guantánamo: Expanding the Transnational Social Field

In addition to being the site of a primary school and a gathering place for social events[58] as well as providing mutual aid, medical consultations, and legal advisement,[59] the Centre was a space of connection to the larger Anglo-Caribbean world. The minutes from their executive board meetings indicate that they received visitors from a parallel institution in Boston, hosted a reception for a cricket team from Jamaica,[60] provided disaster relief after a hurricane in Montserrat,[61] and even donated money for the building of a hospital in Jamaica.[62]

This financial and emotional investment in their islands of origin coexisting with and in many ways being dependent upon their building a life in their place of residence exemplifies the sorts of practices that social scientists in the 1990s popularized as transnationalism. Basch, Glick Schiller, and Szanton Blanc (1994) theorized that what they observed in their research with contemporary immigrants from the Caribbean and the Philippines was a departure from sociological models of immigrant assimilation and incorporation. Instead, they observed that immigrants are remaining embedded in the economic, political, and social world of "home" while simultaneously developing roots in their "host" country. They argued that this necessitates a new theorization of the nation-state that reflects the apparent permeability of its boundaries.

In the two decades since the publication of Basch, Glick Schiller, and Szanton Blanc's 1994 work, substantial expansion of and critical engagement with their analysis has occurred (Kearney 1995; Robotham 1998; Portes, Guarnizo, and Landolt 1999; Smith and Guarnizo 1998; Mahler 2001; Mahler and Pessar 2001; Pessar and Mahler 2003; Vertovec 2009; Walderinger and Fitzgerald 2004; Itzigsohn 2000; Faist and Bauböck 2010; Duany 2012). However, with few exceptions, these studies on transnational practices are based upon those migrants/immigrants/transnational subjects whose lives are lived between a capital-rich metropolitan center and someplace "other." Here, I must echo and elaborate upon postcolonial theorist Shalini Puri's (2003) question and ask what kinds of transnational identities, conflicts, and alliances might emerge when we consider those formations that occur as a result of the circulation of people, ideas, capital, et cetera *within* the Caribbean?

Thus far, we have seen the ways in which early twentieth-century British West Indian migrants have carried with them the ideology of respectability in the process of their settlement in Cuba. Now, as we look more closely at the community in Guantánamo, we see that this experience raises interesting questions about the decreasingly discrete worlds in which transnational subjects circulate and how asymmetries of power between those worlds might come to bear upon transnational practices. To this end, I take up the notion of the transnational social field, a concept that Glick Schiller and Levitt developed, which refers to the social networks that exist across the borders of the nation-state in which individuals are embedded and can *choose* to consciously engage (Levitt and Glick Schiller 2004, emphasis mine).

One critique of transnational theories, along with processes of diaspora and globalization, has been their tendency to be ahistorical (Mintz 1997; Foner 1998, 2006).[63] A consideration of the transnational social field of these early to mid-twentieth-century immigrants and their Cuban-born children reveals that some transnational subjects navigate a more circuitous route than others. In this case, not only are we dealing with the question of how a place's status as a colony or territory comes to bear on formulations of trans*national*ism but also with the impact of the U.S. military presence.[64] For Anglo-Caribbean Cubans, the United States, in the form of the Guantánamo Naval Base, acted as a third player on this field prior to and through the revolutionary period. The U.S., Cuban, and British colonial governments policed the physical as well as symbolic borders people of Anglo-Caribbean origin traversed. However, the connections that were established, the ways in which these borders were clandestinely breached, and the more covert reconnections that have occurred since the 1990s continue to certainly complicate any model of society that gives primacy to one or even two nation-states. National borders undoubtedly act as mediating factors in the movement of bodies, goods, and ideas, but they shift and reconfigure themselves under the pressures of the particular political and economic moment.

People in and around Guantánamo's Anglo-Caribbean community, some of whom worked on the naval base and all of whom felt its economic and social influence, built social fields that linked their islands of origin, Cuba, and the United States. People in Guantánamo were transnationalized not only because of the ties they maintained to their islands of origin while residing in Cuba, but also because of their connection to the base.

The naval base, established in 1903 with the signing of the Platt Amendment and expanded considerably during World War II, is under the jurisdiction of the U.S. government. Like most large military bases, it is a miniature U.S. city complete with golf courses, bowling alleys, clubs, medical facilities, financial institutions, residential subdivisions, schools, and, most recently, fast-food restaurants. However, at the same time that it is very much an "American" space, it is also a transnational one, as historian Jana Lipman contends (2009:5). At its height in the early 1940s, it employed 13,000 people and, after the war, had a civilian workforce of approximately 3,500. Workers from the English-speaking Caribbean were often preferred to Cubans, which was the source of discontent among non-Anglo-Caribbean Cubans who wanted equal access to the more stable employment that the base offered (Lipman 2009:6, 47). As people who lived and/or worked in this replica of the United States in Cuba, Anglo-Caribbeans and their Cuban-born children were traversing (at least) three social worlds: that of Cuba, the United States, and their home country, whose status as a British colony calls into question the extent to which some were also embedded in yet another social world: England the Motherland.

People of Anglo-Caribbean origin who worked on the base physically crossed the border between nations each time they left it, moving between the social, material, and political worlds of Cuba and the United States. With the thousands of workers armed with their *chapas* (badges those living in Cuba received once hired on the base) who made the daily commute across the *frontera* came currency, goods (pilfered and bought), ideas, and cultural experiences. Their salaries were a form of remittances: money earned in one nation that was sent to and spent in another—both Cuba and their islands of origin.[65] Their identification badges might be likened to passports, and the carrying of shoes, toys, food, liquor, and other material goods from the base to give to their loved ones living off the base is akin to today's practice of sending barrels or suitcases containing goods back home. During the Cuban revolution of the 1950s, base workers smuggled supplies to the rebels in the Sierra Maestra, thus demonstrating involvement in political life.

Many of the more recent immigrants are identified as transnational actors because they earn a living in U.S. or other metropolitan areas while their social, spiritual, financial, and political lives are based in their home country. In essence, those base workers were earning money in America—represented by the U.S. Naval Base—that supported their lives and the lives of their loved ones outside of America.

This question of the inclusion of the United States in the transnational social field is clearly relevant to other Latin Americans of Anglo-Caribbean origin, particularly when we consider areas in which the United States has had a dominant military and/or economic presence.[66] For instance, in the case of Panama, the Canal Zone was located within Panama but was initially controlled and operated by a commission appointed by President Theodore Roosevelt. This commission established a racially segregated enclave that attempted to replicate the social divisions characteristic of the American Deep South, where most of the project managers were from (Newton 1984).

A similar dynamic existed in agricultural enclaves set up by U.S. companies, the most influential being the United Fruit Company. Like those individuals who lived and worked in the Canal Zone, employees of "the Company" when it operated solely on Central America's Atlantic Coast were spatially, socially, and economically isolated from the country in which they worked. In the cases of Costa Rica and Nicaragua, it was not until well into the middle of the twentieth century that populations in these areas began to become incorporated into the nation (Gordon 1998; Harpelle 2001; Purcell 1993). Thus, the United States was as much if not more an influential player than was the official "host country" in the transnational social field in which Caribbean immigrants and their children operated.

Movin' On Up to Guantánamo

I was born on a hot and humid summer morning, in the rigidly segregated, poverty ridden sugar plantation community of Banes, northeastern Cuba. Although my family were [sic] among the fortunate few in our community, we were by no means not an integral part of the overall picture; it was just less blatant, less painful. My grandfather—Pappy—had a year round, six days a week, $0.50 per day job as an orderly in the United Fruit Company Hospital. My grandmother—Mami—worked as a cook from 6 a.m. to 8 p.m., six days a week, at the home of one of the Big Bosses of the Co., for $6.00 or $7.00 dollars a month. For the few youngsters in our community that could afford not to go early off to the sugar harvesting, the only other option for improving themselves was by learning a "Trade." The most frequently available trade was as an auto mechanic, baker, tailor, musician, jeweler or barber. . . . No other option was really available for people from our neighborhood. . . .

My first awareness of WWII may have happened during our evening dinner, in which I heard my grandfather share with us the horrific news coming out of the war zone. . . . At the same time, most people in our community kept talking about the great news coming out of Guantánamo, where lots of jobs were being created by the huge expansion that was taking place at the United States Naval Base. Hundreds of unskilled workers, especially those who understood English, were being hired for a host of jobs. Many people in our community fit the required profile, which led to a massive human migration from tens of similar plantation communities in northern Oriente to Guantánamo in the south.

It may have been either 1943 or 1944, very early in the morning, my mother, my brother and myself, left our modest home in La Guira, Banes and walked the dark trail to the train station and boarded a Gas Car at 5:30 a.m. Full of hopes, we were elated by the news that had been coming our way describing the better life that awaited us in Guantánamo. . . . When we arrived at the home our grandfather had rented, we were thrilled, delighted. . . . Our living conditions had improved a million percent. . . . Those fortunate to be employed became "different" overnight.

Alberto Jones, "Guantánamo Remembered," 2001

Jones's experience of the shift in living conditions and status was not unique among my interlocutors. Given the potential for this kind of social mobility, English-speaking immigrants and their Cuban-born children from all over the island responded to the naval base's call for workers. Jobs at the base were highly coveted as they were potentially secure, relatively well-paying positions, and some even provided a pension. Though many of the jobs available were for domestics and unskilled laborers, such as restaurant, commissary and warehouse workers, the skilled tradesmen (mechanics, blacksmiths,

electricians, carpenters, and masons) among the Anglo-Caribbean community also found opportunities in Guantánamo. There were even opportunities for Anglo-Caribbean immigrants and their Cuban-born children to
work in offices, retail stores, and recreational facilities. As Jones goes on to
explain, in order to get onto the base to be assessed for employment, workers
needed a pass that could only be given by those already on the base. Thus,
hiring occurred through social networks and securing a job on the base was
dependent upon community ties or an ability to obtain a pass clandestinely
from Cuban officials who sold them (Lipman 2009:42).

Of my interlocutors, three had worked on the base and twenty-three were
children, spouses, or grandchildren of base workers who had migrated to
Guantánamo and surrounding towns (Caimanera and Boquerón primarily),
usually from another location in Cuba, to join someone in their social network who had been willing to embark on a reconnaissance trip. For instance,
Isabel's Jamaican grandfather was a blacksmith whose older brother, a me-
chanic, had brought him onto the base. Lester's grandfather, another blacksmith, who had learned his trade in Barbados, bought his own tools, and
worked for himself rather than for U.S. companies in Camagüey, did not mi-

Figure 1.7. Office work on the Guantánamo Naval Base, ca. 1950.

grate to Guantánamo. However, his son, Lester's father, unable to find decent employment, left Camagüey in 1945 at the age of twenty-five and worked on the base in the Naval Exchange's photography department until retiring in 1989.[67] Winton, who pointed out that not all jobs on the base were created equal, that there was something of a hierarchy among Anglo-Caribbean base workers that was organized around the skill level, stability, and pension associated with the job, recalled that his father, mother, aunt, and uncle worked on the base in low-level positions.[68] Smith's father got him a job on the base first as a dishwasher, then as an orderly, when he was seventeen years old. Indeed, it was Smith whose comments about his experience as a base worker shone a light on particular elaborations in the transnational social field for those connected to the base.

In reminiscing about how much he enjoyed his time on the base in part because there was such an active social life, he commented on the presence of African American soldiers and their relationships with the Cubans, smiling slyly and chuckling as he recalled his amorous engagement with a Black American woman who lived on the base as the wife of one of the enlisted men.[69] Similarly, Lester recalled that his father enjoyed working on the base, attributing this in part to the fact that there were workers from all over the world, not just the Caribbean, a point that I will return to below.

Though still constrained by racial and class discrimination and relegated to the lower level of the labor hierarchy, these interlocutors reiterated the perception that those who worked on the base or were connected to someone who did were privileged. Lester, a physician in his fifties, summarized this sentiment when he remarked that "there is no doubt that the base workers and their children were better off than others; there wasn't a huge difference, but you could see that the salaries were better, they dressed better, for instance. The morals and behavior and social development of this group was better in the society. People saw us from this point of view so there was a certain difference."[70] Other informants joined Lester in this assessment that employment on the base increased the status of Anglo-Caribbean Cubans, which at times created a division between themselves and those who did not have similar opportunities.

According to Jones (2001a), this economic success did not go unnoticed by local Cubans who, particularly in the case of Guantanameros, were heavily influenced by the presence of the English-speaking Caribbean community. As living conditions in Guantánamo were difficult for those without

Figure 1.8. Quinceañera celebration for the daughter of a Cuban-born Anglo-Caribbean naval base worker.

access to the base, and access was constrained by association and common "ethnic" identity, "other citizens in Guantánamo with no such connection were left frustrated, segregated and bitter, with occasional frictions within the community" (Jones 2001a). This was echoed by my interlocutor Elton, who reasoned that "the antillanos in a certain way were more educated/cultured, had more privilege and there were class differences between the jamaicanos and cubanos because the work at the naval base allowed jamaicanos to improve their status in the economic sense. They discriminated against jamaicanos. For example, in the Cuban schools, I was looked upon badly and teased—*jamaiquinito, inglesito*—because I was well dressed and had nice shoes."[71]

It does indeed appear that those people of Anglo-Caribbean descent who obtained stable employment on the base were able to move closer toward what could be considered a middle-class lifestyle, the key to which is not only material comfort, but also the ability to plan for the future, one that was increasingly likely to take place on Cuban soil. The wooden houses that they built for their families in the late '30s or early '40s could be reconstructed with more durable materials; the ever-present entrepreneurial efforts—in which women participated considerably—could be expanded; they could afford to save for a child's higher education in the hopes of having a professional in the family; and, of course, they could consume, bringing themselves both pleasure and status.

Edward's family story is but one that illustrates the route to social mobility. His grandparents came to Cuba from Montserrat and St. Kitts, living and working in Banes, a town in the present day province of Camagüey. His grandfather worked as a carpenter while his grandmother was a homemaker with nine children. In 1941, his uncle left for Guantánamo and, once he secured employment at a photography store on the base, sent for his other siblings one by one, the oldest males being the first to venture out. His grandfather, who had joined his sons in Guantánamo, remained employed on the base until 1965 when he left for Jamaica. His father began working, eventually securing the position of golf course manager, exiling on the base in 1970[72] and remaining in that position until he retired and moved to the Dominican Republic. From his experience working on the base and his exposure to U.S. military personnel, specifically white men of privilege and power, his father proclaimed that he would never live in the United States.

With the money he made on the base, Edward's father was able to buy land and build a house in a more affluent part of town while paying rent on the apartment his family lived in. He was also able to invest in a cockfighting business, raising the animals and benefiting from the winnings they earned. As evidence of his economic success as well as adoption of Cuban cultural practices, he held a *quinceañera* for his daughter for which he had special clothes made, cars rented, and elaborate meals prepared, in addition to celebrating for a month beforehand with food and a room full of drinks for neighbors and friends. He had plans for my interlocutor, his son, and his eldest daughter. They were to be a lawyer and doctor respectively and, at the time of the revolution, he was contributing money to an educational fund for that purpose.[73]

Melvina tells a similar, though perhaps less ostentatious tale of upward mobility. Her parents both came to Cuba from Jamaica. Her mother was the daughter in a humble family where the father was a stable hand who came to Cuba with his boss and where the mother was a laundress who got paid a pittance to clean the dirty laundry of Americans in Banes. The family lived in Banes until one brother got a job on the naval base and they moved to Guantánamo. Her father came to Cuba as a young adult with his mother. He first worked as a blacksmith and then found work on the base. After meeting and marrying Melvina's mother, he moved the family to Santiago and built a wooden house in one of the Jamaican neighborhoods, commuting between Santiago and the base.

Indeed, while the English-speaking Caribbean community thrived in Guantánamo due to its proximity to the base, we see that Santiago residents were also carried along in this wave of improved opportunity. Money earned on the base could go directly into a household in Santiago. Some participants living in Santiago reported that they themselves or their family member who worked on the base worked during the week and came home on weekends. Or else they had a rotating schedule in which they worked and lived on the base for a number of days and then were off for a number of days, during which time they were free to return to Santiago to spend time with their families. Also, extended family, regardless of location, benefited in more casual, indirect ways from having a stable wage earner in the network. In this way, the prosperity that emerged was experienced in the surrounding areas.

As mentioned, such was the case in Melvina's family. Her father worked at the base during the week, coming home on weekends with food, bags of clothes, shoes, and toys for his children and the less fortunate neighbors. He owned a car and the house that he eventually rebuilt with his earnings from the base. His mother, who worked as a cook and baker for wealthy Cubans in Vista Alegre, also had a small business baking Jamaican sweets that she sold to Anglo-Caribbeans and Cubans alike. Melvina's father had his own shop in Santiago and could afford to take his family on excursions to various points of interest on the island. Melvina recalled that they entertained frequently and were always impeccably dressed, that her father always wore a suit and insisted on the children looking neat so that they wouldn't be disrespected. As she commented, "they weren't professionals, but they had the feel of being professionals."[74]

Memories of Misrecognition: Prerevolutionary Racism and the Politics of Respectable Blackness

Race and discrimination were ever present in these discussions of English-speaking Caribbean culture and social position. With the exceptions of Eugenia—who migrated to Cuba from Jamaica as a child, joining her grandmother in 1955, and who insisted that class difference was the only basis of any discrimination that existed in Cuba—and Ricardo—who pointed to their selling their labor for less money as the root cause of discrimination against Black immigrants—my interlocutors perceived the social order of the time to be racist.

Racism unquestionably shaped the contours of Black immigrant life. Examples that participants gave to support this claim include segregation in social life and public places such as parks, restaurants, and clubs; a racialized labor hierarchy characterized by brutal economic exploitation; employer comments about disliking but being dependent upon "niggers"; the humiliating racism of belligerent navy personnel from the American South for whom immigrants and their children worked on the base; the random beatings meted out by Cuban law enforcement; the verbal insult of *jamaiquino de mierda* (shit Jamaican) that flew out of the mouths of children and adults alike; and the recognition that Black people had to "remain in their place" in order to avoid conflict.

While acknowledging the racial hostility of the prerevolutionary environment, my interlocutors insisted that their foreparents were proud of their Blackness and that a lack of shame about their Blackness is part of their inheritance. In a context where the presumed inferiority of Blackness was reflected in nearly every aspect of social relations, according to this narrative, jamaicanos emerged relatively psychologically unscathed. As Teresa put it, she has always been proud to be Black and jamaiquina. Remarking that she looks for the quality of the person, not the color, she adds that she has never had a complex about being Black, jamaiquina, cubana, or anything. Such attitudes indicate that while upwardly mobile Cubans and other Latin Americans of African descent were presumably pursuing the strategy of whitening "adelantar la raza" (to better the race), a least some workers from the English-speaking Caribbean created and occupied a space in which Blackness and respectability were conjoined.

In the narratives of their descendants, English-speaking Caribbean immigrants' own self-respect and "correctness" allowed them to garner the respect of the larger Cuban community. Racism, most often articulated in terms of petty verbal assaults and structural constraints to economic mobility, was mitigated by the culture of English-speaking Caribbean people. In discussing the bettering of their condition prior to the revolution, language, literacy, and knowledge of a trade were named as important factors, but so too was the set of values and traditions elaborated upon above. For instance, Melvina felt that their cohesion and separatism buttressed the effects of racism:

> They always looked for racial unity, they never tried to integrate with white people. They spoke badly about whites because the whites were hard and exploited them. They exploited them but when there was a holiday, they gave presents and took care of their employees. The exploitation manifested in the low pay for the work and they were racist of course. My mother worked for a woman who said that she can't stand niggers but she can't live without them. She took care of children in Banes who would say "look at the *cuco*," which is a ghost. Children were afraid of Black people. The Americans would pay my mother and grandmother next to nothing for all of the work they did, also they would watch her because they thought she would steal. Americans didn't permit the workers to have wood houses, only tin regardless of whether they had the money.[75]

In this narrative, jamaicanos worked within these constraints and managed to apply their cultural knowledge and values to assist their daily confrontation with racism and even propel themselves forward. Ricardo made a connection between the strict way of bringing up children and an increased marketability for women seeking employment as domestics in the prerevolutionary period. Like their English, this background was valued by the middle- and upper-class employees. Pablo insisted that his older siblings were able to go to university before the revolution because their father was serious, hardworking, abstained from alcohol and tobacco, and valued education. Deunes was under the impression that his great-grandmother's knowledge of natural healing and willingness to help others diffused racial and xenophobic discrimination.

One implication of this perceived relationship between culture and racism is that Black people are at least in part responsible for any mistreatment they experience. Caridad, who taught English to wealthy Cubans, recalled that they treated their mostly Black Cuban servants poorly but treated her well because she was a teacher, suggesting that one's occupation, not one's race, determined social experience. Smith echoed this when he said, "Racism existed in Cuba, but I valued my color. There were *blanquitos* [little whites] who wouldn't hang out with Black people in school. The treatment depends on your presentation and character; many Black people are to blame because they don't value their color."[76]

Carlitos expressed a similar sentiment in his response to the question of whether his parents or grandparents suffered discrimination: "No [they didn't] because they could take care of themselves and didn't have to ask anyone for anything. My grandmother raised her children in this same way. Both she and my mother commanded respect so they didn't suffer racism."[77]

Eugenia, who does not believe racism exists in Cuba, neither before nor after the triumph of the revolution, identified the behaviors that do elicit discrimination: "Yes, for me here racism doesn't exist. And why people may say that racism existed is because people in Vista Alegre [a formerly upper-middle-class neighborhood in Santiago] were rich and they lived separate from Black people because Black people caused an upset wherever they went.... It's not that they rob, it's that they form a *bulla* [quarrel, commotion, uproar, ruckus] and there's a *revuelta* [disturbance] that follows. They break up everything."[78] Thus, a combination of the conduct, *educación*, values, and race pride of jamaicanos, and presumably their lack of conformity to stereotypical Black behavior such as rowdiness, mitigated prerevolutionary discrimination.

Conclusion

In this chapter, we have seen that many people of Anglo-Caribbean descent, faced with deeply entrenched Negrophobia and an anti-immigrant hostility that was particularly forceful against Black foreigners, attempted to protect themselves within their insular communities by upholding the moral high ground upon which they, in their role as civilized Christian subjects, stood. Through both the documents that English-speaking Caribbean immigrants created to record the daily life of their organizations and the oral testimonies of their children and grandchildren, respectability and Christian morality emerge as major underlying themes.

This respectability was inextricable from the principles of racial pride and uplift that people of African descent, "native" and immigrant, practiced in order to defend themselves against white supremacy. The UNIA and other organizations that they supported were dedicated to enforcing standards of morality and discipline that refuted common accusations of savagery. In addition, these organizations served to connect their members to each other across national and imperial boundaries. As we see in this case, the expansion of the naval base changed the contours of diasporic connection. Those living within its orbit had access to material and social privileges, which included those that derived from having the United States included in their transnational social field. The respectability that was rooted in the postemancipation British colonial identity was elaborated upon, reinforced through this connection to the United States. While they continued to see themselves as a part of a larger Black world, they were transitioning from transnational British subject to U.S. laborer and Cuban citizen and, for some, from working to middle class.

With the 1959 revolution, seismic shifts in Cuba's political, economic, and social landscape occasioned the contraction of diaspora space and a re-imagining of belonging. The policing of connections with those outside of Cuba, the push for cultural homogenization, and the racial politics of the revolution largely foreclosed previous routes to and articulations of diaspora. As we will see in the following chapters, the reimagining had less to do with a shared past and more with an uncertain future.

2

Get Out or Get Involved

Revolutionary Change and Conflicting Visions of Freedom

In a 1995 interview, Alden Knight, a Cuban actor of Jamaican descent, proclaimed that he will no longer perform Nicolás Guillén's poem "Tengo" (I Have)[1] because it represents what had been achieved in Cuba for Black and poor people that has now been lost. He reasoned, "When 'I Have' can again in all honesty be performed, then we shall have achieved again what we had by the late 1960s, which were years of poverty but equality" (quoted in Pérez Sarduy and Stubbs, 2000:134). He is not alone in his expression of dismay at the changing tide of racial equality in contemporary Cuba. Anglo-Caribbean Cubans who were going about the business of rescuing their roots echoed Knight's nostalgia, filtering the past through the present moment. Those who spearheaded this revitalization were children and young adolescents in the late 1950s and 1960s, a watershed moment in the lives of all those in Cuba, immigrant and native. Hierarchies of race, class, gender, and nationality were being upended. The *Hombre Nuevo* (New Man) was to emerge out of the ashes of the anti-neocolonial struggle, casting off the cloak of social inequality that had burdened Cuba for centuries. Che Guevara's New Man, motivated to work for the common good rather than payment and prestige and to sacrifice all for *la patria* (the fatherland), was to be the new modern subject (Bowles 1971; Guevara 1977; Pérez-Stable 1999; Newman 2005; Guevara and Castro 2009; Cheng 2009). A change in the possibilities of the space one could occupy as a Black person, as a woman, and as a person with neither capital nor connections was at the heart of popular narratives of the revolution. Indeed, this was one reason that Black and mulatto Cubans were overwhelmingly in support of it: the revolution was to deliver their long awaited "rightful share."[2]

Cuban society was undergoing a process of intense transformation from which perhaps no one was spared. Along with conflict with the United States, of which the 1960 Embargo, Bay of Pigs invasion of 1961 and Missile Crisis of 1962 were emblematic, an estimated 717,000 people left Cuba between 1959 and 1974.[3] While the overwhelming majority of those people who left Cuba during this time were white and of upper- and middle-class origins, there were of course Black and mulatto Cubans across the class spectrum who also did not foresee benefiting from the country's political and economic reorientation. Anglo-Caribbean families were among them, being divided by conviction, perceived opportunity, and circumstance. The community institutions that they had spent decades building disintegrated. Revolutionary Cuba rejected the United States' economic and political presence in Cuba that was in large part responsible for Anglo-Caribbean migration and upward mobility. Thus, at the same time my interlocutors expressed a longing for the early revolutionary period and the erosion of certain barriers to equality, their nostalgia was complicated by the upheaval, chaos, uncertainty, and loss characteristic of this rupture with the United States.

Taking the lead from my interlocutors, I explored tensions both created and intensified through this moment of revolutionary change as they proved to be critical to Black Anglo-Caribbean-Cuban subject formation. Migrating between English and Spanish, among British Empire, the United States, and Cuba, and between ostracism and inclusion, apathy and involvement, those who remained in Cuba through the waves of out-migration from the 1960s to early 1970s were engaged in the process of negotiating their position as increasingly unhyphenated Cubans. In spite of the persistent challenges that they faced upon inclusion in a state-controlled nationalistic society under siege, challenges that included a rejection of transnational connections, the possibility of participating in the nation as full citizens proved to be a powerful incentive for becoming Cuban. Articulations of diasporic belonging were therefore muted in the post-1959 period due to both the pressure and the desire to participate in the revolution's nation-building project.

My interlocutors' experiences complicate the conflicting narratives of widespread unconditional, uncritical Black and mulatto support of the revolution and forced compliance with its agenda. In this chapter, I use their recollections of this time period to illustrate that people of Anglo-Caribbean origin occupied an ambivalent position in relationship to the nation, a position that often shifted at the intersections of generation, gender, and class. The 1959 revolution was certainly not the first moment in which Anglo-Caribbean immigrants and their children were faced with the decision to assert a distinct and perhaps irrevocable position in relationship to the Cuban nation. Indeed, Whitney and Chailloux Laffita (2013:39), in their inquiry into "how, why, when, and under what conditions did some people become Cuban while others did not" prior to 1960, cite economic crises and expulsions of the 1920s and 1930s as moments in which British Caribbeans "became Cuban (or not)." Here, I am suggesting that, given the flexible, situational, and fluid nature of identity—including a Cuban national identity—there is a way in which they could *both* become Cuban *and* not. Being Cuban, as does being Anglo-Caribbean, has multiple mediated meanings. The discussion that follows explores how the revolutionary process acted as a powerful force shaping the politics of belonging, and argues that, ultimately, it served to undermine expressions of collective Anglo-Caribbean identity, particularly in family and associational life.

"No se Meten en la Política, Pero . . ." (They Don't Get Involved in Politics, But . . .): Jamaicanos on All Sides of Revolution

> Well, my grandparents really, the old folks, you know that the jamaicanos were very reserved and they had always stayed away from politics, they respected the police and the laws of the country. But my parents, they were Cubans and they were more involved in what was happening.
>
> *Carmen, granddaughter of Jamaican and Barbadian immigrants*
> *to Cuba, interview with author, June 29, 2005, Guantánamo*

> At the beginning of the fighting, a microbrigade of Batista came and my grandmother, she told them, "This house is the house of a Jamaican, and what's more, this is a house of God," and they respected houses of religious people a lot before and also foreigners. She said she would go to the Consulate."
>
> *Eugenia, self-proclaimed "last Jamaican to come to Cuba,"*
> *interview with author, June 16, 2005, Santiago*

> Subject positions, political ideas, and social roles have no necessary logical and linear relation. . . . They can be arranged in innumerable ways and negotiated such that coherence can be claimed for almost any combination, and that the combinations that emerge have everything to do with the historical meaning they have acquired in specific conjunctures and power relations.
>
> *Edmund Gordon,* Disparate Diasporas, *1998*

Initially using a broad brush to paint the picture of their immigrant communities, many of my interlocutors proclaimed that los antillanos did not get involved in politics. They were in Cuba to work, too concerned about daily survival to risk suffering the consequences of challenging the racial and economic status quo as Black foreigners. However, as people began to fill in the details of their families' stories, it became clear that they were indeed involved in various forms of activism. From their arrival in the early twentieth century through the 1959 revolution, they exercised their political will in a number of ways. In addition to applying pressure on the British Consulate to protect its darker subjects in a foreign land and furthering the spread of Garveyism, they also joined and formed trade unions, smuggled supplies to rebels attempting to topple the Batista government, became rebels themselves, worked to keep their institutions afloat, and either gave up their jobs or exiled themselves on the U.S. Naval Base in 1964 when "GTMO officials offered workers a blunt choice—Cuba or the base" (Lipman 2009:183).[4] Thus, a key question concerns not whether people of Anglo-Caribbean origin were politically engaged, but rather what the strategies that they pursued to effect change reveal about processes of subject formation across time and space.[5]

Figure 2.1. A Cuban-born Anglo-Caribbean man gathers with fellow members of the Communist Party, ca. 1950.

Outlets of this activism changed over time and generation, reflecting a shift in the positioning of people of Anglo-Caribbean origin and allowing us to see the way in which they pivoted among class, race, and diaspora-based identity politics. A clause in the 1940 constitution granted Cuban citizenship to all those born on Cuban soil. Because one of the primary roles of immigrant institutions was to protect the rights of foreigners, immigrant children occupied an intermediary position. They were culturally and socially connected to the Anglo-Caribbean community, but their legal status as Cubans meant that their ownership over Anglo-Caribbean institutions was dubious.[6] Their shift away from diasporic practices and identity was under way. As I will suggest in the next chapter, their revitalization of roots during the Special Period is the most recent iteration of organization and activism.

Fighting the Revolution

Fulgencio Batista, a light-skinned mulatto military man from Oriente, had been in power directly or indirectly since leading a sergeants' revolt in 1933. In 1952, he led a coup and then won the election of 1954; by then, people of Anglo-Caribbean origin were situated between the world they or their parents left behind and one that was rapidly becoming politically tumultuous.[7] Throughout the 1950s, political tensions erupted in violence, particularly after Fidel Castro and his followers attacked the Moncada Garrison in Santiago in 1953. Though they were defeated, jailed, and exiled, the movement to overthrow Batista continued. Students were at the forefront of the struggle, organizing a clandestine movement (Directorio Revolucionario) and rural insurgency in response to government repression. In the midst of this, a group of young revolutionaries, led by Castro, set out for Cuba with the intention of deposing Batista. Their boat, the *Granma*, arrived in southern Oriente in November of 1956. Government forces ambushed the revolutionaries, but the eighteen who escaped into the Sierra Maestra waged war against the Batista regime, recruiting thousands of fighters from rural and urban areas.

The revolutionary struggle was in part fought by an urban underground movement that coordinated acts of sabotage in the cities and was popularly referred to as El Clandestino.[8] The Batista government responded to this movement with indiscriminate and widespread torture and murder meant to intimidate the population (Pérez 1995:294).[9] While a disengagement fueled by fear of reprisal and general disinterest in the affairs of a foreign land may have characterized some segments of the Anglo-Caribbean communities, it became clear as my interlocutors revealed their stories that they had a much more dynamic response to revolutionary struggle. Indeed, there was a contrast between the discursive identity of los anglófonos and the actual experiences that they themselves recalled.

For instance, people in the community responded to the injustices they witnessed by getting involved in the clandestine movement. Josefina, whose father migrated to Cuba from St. Marteen and whose mother was born in Cuba to Jamaican parents, emphasized that there was no difference between groups in the level of participation in the movement. She recalled, "Oh, people of whatever nation went, whoever felt moved by the cause went to fight in the mountains: . . . children of Gallegos [Spaniards from the Galicia region], Haitians, Jamaicans, whoever. My brother went to the mountains. He was the president of the FAU, the Federation of University Students at the University of Oriente and when there was the chaos over there [at the university], he fled."[10]

Melvina, who was in primary school at the time of the revolutionary struggle, also recalled the involvement of young people who were joining the movement, even going to the hills to become "Mau Mau,"[11] due to violent government repression: "Everyone wanted to be involved in this because there were so many abuses and they were killing so many young people." She recalled that a friend's brother was part of the clandestine movement and was going into the Sierra Maestra when Batista's soldiers murdered him. Her own older brother was also part of the movement, but survived to become second in command at a large prison.[12]

Tío Richard, an octogenarian shoemaker born in Cuba to Jamaican parents who was still practicing his trade at the time of my fieldwork, recounted how he risked his life and came close to being killed on two occasions because he used his street corner business to smuggle messages, clothing, shoes, and even arms to rebels. He said that he witnessed the abuses of the Batista regime, the murder of young people, and had to act.[13]

One of the most poignant tales of involvement in the clandestine movement came from Eugenia. Rounding the corner from Calle Doce onto Calle del Oro, I sometimes would hear Eugenia's morning music blaring from the closed metal-slat windows of her casita. Her door would be wide open, revealing her walking about mopping feverishly or engaging in some other domestic task. I would climb the three steps onto her tile porch and call her name a couple of times before she heard me over the music and said, "Ay, Andrea, pasa, pasa" (Oh, Andrea, come in, come in). Eugenia identifies herself as an *espiritista* (spiritist), and hanging in her living room above her couch were three framed pictures that complicate understandings of the revolutionary as atheist and the immigrant as apolitical. The large one in the center was a print of Camilo Cienfuegos, the revolutionary hero most often pictured in his green military fatigues with a large straw-colored hat, a beaming smile, and eyes that project warmth, compassion, and humility. To the right of this was a picture of Jesus in soft blues and pinks revealing the fuchsia Sacred Heart that comforts and forgives all believers. To the left was a large black-and-white photograph of Pope John Paul II and Fidel shaking hands. On the bookshelf was another framed picture of Jesus and on the coffee table an artistic rendition of Caridad del Cobre sitting upright in its thick glass frame.

The vibrant complexity of the salsa music that energized Eugenia while she did her chores provided a sharp contrast to the material humility of her home. While the cassette player might have been among the belongings that she treasured, Eugenia also counted among her valued possessions a car, watch, television, and a letter she received from Raúl Castro himself as reward for being a whistle blower at a factory where she worked as an accountant in the 1980s. In spite of being an exemplary worker, she had been fired from her position due to her unwillingness to ignore corruption. She decided to appeal her dismissal, setting off an investigation that became quite public. According to Eugenia, after reporting on her superiors, she was blacklisted because no one in Cuba wants an honest accountant. She was out of work for twenty-six months and survived through the kindness of neighbors and former coworkers as well as by selling household items and goods from the *tarjeta* (ration card).[14]

By the time we met, her car was more often than not in a state of disrepair and the television and watch were a decade and a half old. She was particularly upset by the fact that she would never be able to visit Jamaica again because they now charged dollars to renew passports, and she could not afford the fee given her very modest pension. Eugenia believes in the revolution and respects its heroes, but says that she disagrees with a lot that happens in the country, blaming the corruption on those who surround Fidel.

Perhaps shaping these views and certainly defying the perception that immigrants did not get involved in the political affairs of their host country, Eugenia's formative years were spent steeped in the revolutionary movement. Following her mother's death in Jamaica, she arrived in Santiago from

Westmoreland in 1955 at the age of eleven to live with her brown Jamaican maternal grandmother who had migrated to Cuba in 1924.[15] Her grandmother taught organ and English classes at home, and was very active in the church and community, but definitely did not remain outside of the affairs of the Cuban nation. Though Eugenia was fourteen when the revolutionaries marched into Havana and did not participate directly in the revolutionary struggle that had gripped the country, she grew up in an activist immigrant household. It was in 1958 that Eugenia realized her grandmother was a revolutionary:

> Well, I realized that she had packets of clothes and soap from the church and I never asked her what she did with this. . . . She gave classes to children and had begun to give classes to older people to hide revolutionary activity so when people saw revolutionaries in her house, they would mistake them for her students. She was a graduate and trained in teaching English classes. . . . [One day] my grandmother's nephew, the nephew of her husband . . . came in with a revolver, wanted to [keep it here], and then left. . . . I don't know where she had hidden them [referring to the nephew with the revolver] but within a few days, he had

Figure 2.2. Jamaican immigrant and revolutionary grandmother, 1986.

left the country. . . . She would [pass messages] and give [messengers] money and then automatically burn the messages.

She met Fidel in person when he was young. My grandmother was very revolutionary. . . . After the triumph of the revolution, she always talked about Fidel. She died talking about Fidel. Her life was Fidel.[16]

According to one of the articles about Eugenia's 1984 struggle in the factory, Eugenia's grandmother greeted the triumph of the revolution like "un baño de rosas" (a bath of roses).[17] In this article, Eugenia's immigrant background and that of her grandmother were highlighted. Mentioning this story to me to familiarize me with the Jamaican-Cuban population in Santiago, a local scholar recalled that Eugenia's identity as a female immigrant of color was used to dramatize the significance of her defiance of the factory bosses. She was portrayed as a humble Jamaican immigrant and exemplary revolutionary who was being victimized by those in powerful positions who betray the revolution.

During the revolution, Eugenia's grandmother used her status as a foreigner as well as a prominent member of the religious community to conceal her clandestine activities. According to Eugenia, her grandmother's belief in Fidel Castro was what motivated her to participate in the struggle. There was no contradiction between the official atheism adopted soon after the triumph of the revolution and her own deeply felt religious beliefs because "many of the things in the Bible, Fidel did or wanted to do." Eugenia's protest against unfair treatment at her workplace was an effort to press individual power brokers as well as the revolution itself to remain loyal to the ideals that her grandmother died believing in. Furthermore, this case and others that testify to the participation of people of Anglo-Caribbean origin in revolutionary activity illustrate an investment in the soil upon which they stood.

Making, and Making It Out of, the Revolution

The months and years immediately following the rebel victory on January 1, 1959, were dominated by intense emotions. This was not simply due to the overthrow of Batista by a band of revolutionaries that had become increasingly popular, but because, upon seizing power, these revolutionaries set about reconfiguring the country's social and economic structures.[18] It was a chaotic time, one of possibility, confusion, joy, apprehension, and fear, as the

Figure 2.3. Children in "el monte" (the wilderness). People were sent to rural areas to teach young and old how to read and write during the 1960 literacy campaign.

various decrees, reforms, and mobilizations took shape. The young people were forming militias, being offered scholarships, and going off to work in the countryside as agricultural laborers and teachers. According to some of my informants, all young people at the time wanted to join the Young Communist League as it was a source of pride and "like a fad."

A word often used to describe the environment of this time is *lindo*, which can mean pretty, beautiful, or fine, and when used by participants, it also implied a kind of spiritual quality that came from a sense of solidarity and invincibility. As Leticia, the granddaughter of Jamaican immigrants, described:

> [It was] an environment of revolution and nothing more. . . . [In] the years of the '60s and '70s, they were creating everything. The sports institute they created in '62. . . . In '62 or '61 they had the Agrarian Reform when they gave land to the peasants, and they had the literacy campaign and they educated everyone to read and write. It was explosive and beautiful because it was for everyone. . . . It was a time when everyone loved the revolution and was helping, doing everything here. . . . You looked forward to when you were fourteen or fifteen to be in the Committee in the Defense of the Revolution [CDR]. . . . It was a very beautiful time, a time of rebirth.[19]

Everyone was called upon in the uprooting of the previous system, placing social pressure on families to relax constraints on the youth, particularly young women, as I discuss later in the chapter. As might be anticipated, generational divisions were exposed and deepened, especially in the reportedly strict households of the Anglo-Caribbean communities. Like the young people before them who at times migrated to Cuba or other destinations against the advice and will of their parents, some Anglo-Caribbean descendants hid their plans to pursue opportunities created by the revolution from their parents. While their parents might have been "outlooking" to their Anglo-Caribbean roots (Charlton 2005:4), these youth sought out their sense of connection within the boundaries of the Cuban nation.

Elton, a Guantanamero whose father immigrated from Grenada and whose mother came from Jamaica, deceived his mother into believing that he was studying in Santiago when in fact he had been recruited by the national judo team. His mother only found out about this when a neighbor said that her son's picture had appeared in a newspaper article featuring the judo team's victory in France![20] Carlitos, now in his early fifties, recounted that he too went against his mother's wishes by signing up to work and study in Camagüey. He was fifteen, not yet at the age to enter the military, and was recruited to study and work in another province. He told his mother that they sent out a call for this opportunity and, against her wishes, he got on the bus to Camagüey. Somehow, his mother had gotten word of his plans and went to look for him. She found him on the bus and spoke with someone in charge, telling him that he didn't have permission to leave. She was told that the people in charge of the mobilization were now taking care of him, he was about to complete a mission, and she should go home. He recalled that this was the first time he was separated from his mother and that this was the beginning of his long journey in pursuit of an education.[21]

The other, perhaps more pressing conflict that jamaicanos had with the revolution emerged with the growing tensions between Cuba and the United States. After initially backing the rebels, the United States quickly withdrew its support of the revolutionary government, and an escalation of hostility ensued, which has been maintained for over 50 years. The budding trade relations with the Union of Soviet Socialist Republics (USSR), which began with the purchase of 170 thousand tons of sugar in 1959 and the nationalization of sugar *centrales* and oil refineries, were followed by the United States' cancellation of Cuba's sugar quota. This, in turn, was followed by the expropriation of all U.S. property. These events, occurring in the first half of 1960, led to the imposition of the U.S. embargo on all imports from Cuba, the nationalization of major foreign banks in October of that year, and the United States' severing of diplomatic relations in January of 1961. The Bay of Pigs, a military invasion carried out by CIA-trained Cubans who had fled the country and were intent upon ousting the revolutionary government, occurred in April of that same year. Later that month, Castro declared the socialist nature of the revolution, and a year and a half later, Cuba's strategic position in the Cold War became apparent during the Cuban Missile Crisis, in which President John F. Kennedy demanded the withdrawal of Soviet troops and arms from Cuba, imposing a naval blockade that was withdrawn a month later.[22]

People of Anglo-Caribbean descent, particularly those who lived in Guantánamo, were caught in the middle of this military, ideological, and economic crisis. One particularly poignant example of this occurred in 1964 when, after Cuba cut off the base's water supply in retaliation for the U.S. Coast Guard turning over thirty-eight Cuban fishermen fishing seventy miles from Key West to authorities in Florida, U.S. Navy officials fired the majority of local hires in a wave of layoffs. During this year, some two thousand "Cuban" employees, some of whom were of Anglo-Caribbean origin, were faced with the choice of staying on the naval base and cutting all ties to Cuba—that is, being "exiled"—or remaining in Cuba and losing their jobs and pensions. Faced with the prospect of being separated from their families for an indefinite period of time, approximately 1,500 chose Cuba. Ultimately, 448 workers chose the base and 750 were allowed to commute (Lipman 2009:183).

A steady stream of violent and nonviolent incidents also occurred between Cuban and American personnel across the border with the base. In 1976, a U.S soldier killed a Cuban soldier on the frontier, not the first such occurrence, and, after attending the soldier's funeral in Guantánamo, Raúl Castro announced that no workers on the base could participate in any revolutionary organizations.[23] This is indicative of the suspicion with which those who worked on the base were regarded.

Even for those who did not work on the base or depend on it for their livelihood, the nationalization of businesses, the attack on U.S. dominance, and the flight of elite and middle-class Cubans dependent upon the United States' presence had immediate and dire consequences to economic and social life.[24] For the nearly 150,000 Cuban employees of American enterprises,

the expropriations were traumatic. From middle managers to clerks to lawyers, this particular group and all of those people and industries that were
dependent upon their higher salaries were affected by the immediate decline
in their standard of living.

With the increase in state control over the private sector, political beliefs
came to have a determining effect on employment. As historian Louis Pérez
Jr. remarks, "Those Cubans who opposed the revolution, no less than those
who showed insufficient ardor for the revolution, were now enormously vulnerable. . . . They were dismissed by the thousands, and their positions filled
by loyal supporters of the revolution. Almost seven hundred employees of
the Cuban Electric Company were fired and replaced by militants. By 1961,
every senior administrator of the 161 sugar mills was a revolutionary. Indeed,
between 1959 and 1961, that was the case in nearly 75 percent of the administrative positions of all sugar mills" (1995:329).

As these positions were eliminated, so too were the working-class positions occupied by people of Anglo-Caribbean origin who serviced these
middle- and upper-class employees.[25] But the consequences went beyond
the material. Fidel's strict edict, announced in a June 1961 speech directed
at intellectuals, was "Inside the Revolution, everything. Outside it, nothing."
There was no room for challenging the direction of the country mandated
by revolutionary leaders.[26] Anyone who demonstrated or was suspected of
harboring sentiments that questioned this direction was sanctioned. People
of Anglo-Caribbean origin were forced to take a stand. The deepening pen-
etration of the revolutionary government into daily life and the environment of polarization that developed did not allow for a policy of nonalign-
ment.

Under these conditions, and in spite of the boom in educational opportunities and significant movement toward resource redistribution, there began
what some described as an exodus of anglófonos. Though this included both
the Cuban-born and immigrants, the latter were foreigners even if they had
lived in Cuba most of their lives and were the first group to leave the island
since they could do so with relative ease, at least logistically.

There are several reasons why it is nearly impossible to identify the number of people of Anglo-Caribbean origin who left. The first concerns the
disjuncture between official categorization and group affiliation. The Cuban-
born children of Black immigrants are Cuban regardless of their cultural or
linguistic practices and self-identification. Those born in Cuba are included

in the "Black" or "mulatto" category and those who are not are categorized by region and phenotype. A related but perhaps not as predominant an issue concerns the fact that this was a highly mobile group and thus their birthplace, whether in Costa Rica, Panama, or the Dominican Republic, did not necessarily reflect their national identity. Furthermore, no census was taken in Cuba between 1953 and 1970, years of tremendous turmoil that had a significant impact on birth, death, and emigration rates.[27] The manner in which people left, as well as the sensitive nature of the topic of exile, in particular the departure of those Black and working-class people who were supposed to be the greatest beneficiaries of the revolution, make accurate numbers of these departures exceedingly difficult to ascertain.

Of the participants in this study, eleven had immediate family members who left Cuba during the first fifteen years of the revolution, either by migrating to another Caribbean island or the United States or by exiling on the base. The Cuban government interpreted leaving Cuba as a betrayal, and those who attempted to leave but were unsuccessful were punished. Indeed, Winton, the Guantanamero in his seventies who had worked on the base but chose not to exile, had attempted to leave Cuba through swimming onto the base. He was caught and jailed for three years as a result.[28] Pamela, whose father was Jamaican and whose mother was the daughter of Jamaicans, recalled that while a teenager in the early 1960s, she was denied the opportunity to go to school and was sent to perform agricultural labor when her family initiated the process of trying to emigrate.[29]

Thus, as with native Cubans, Anglo-Caribbean immigrants and their families faced the choice of dispersing or remaining on the island in a polarized society that was becoming increasingly unpredictable and politically demanding. They too took serious risks and endured painful separations that in many cases proved to be permanent. While there had always been some migration out of Cuba,[30] the circumstances under which these leavings took place were quite trying as they brought to the forefront both ideological and familial divisions. This was a difficult period for the community during which families were separated and community institutions disintegrated.

Edward provided one poignant example of the pain that some people endured as a result of this polarization. One of his uncles, who had been a fireman on the base prior to the revolution, joined the Communist Party and began working for the Ministry of the Interior in the early 1960s. He earned a political science degree and moved up to a senior position in the Ministry, which required that he sever ties with some family members. As Edward explained, "Certain relationships, including with your own family who were not [revolutionary], were prohibited. . . . For example, my uncle, after entering the Ministry of the Interior, he separated from our family. Why? Because my father, his brother, worked in the naval base, [and] my aunt, his sister, was religious . . . so he separated from the family. He was over there and the family over here."[31]

Edward went on to describe the trajectory of his father and uncle's relationship in a manner that conveyed both his belief in the power of the revolution to polarize families and communities and his faith in a Higher Power to which even the revolution and its combatants must submit. His father, who had been one of those who was able to be a commuter, had finally exiled on the base in 1972. From there, he moved to Puerto Rico. When he returned to Cuba for a visit in 1980, the uncle who worked for the Ministry of the Interior saw him in the street and avoided him because it was prohibited for him to have contact with people from abroad. According to Edward, this was quite painful for his father who said he did not approach his own brother because he "didn't come here to cause problems for anyone."

The next time Edward's father returned to Cuba was in the mid-1980s when his daughter, Edward's sister, died. In this instance he unexpectedly ran into the same brother while in Havana. Edward recalled that "The two of them stood like this [gasp] and so what to do? What to do? I was struck still too, we all stood like this and my uncle said 'my brother' and they hugged each other. . . . God is great. . . . God made the way to find him." The ultimate reunion occurred when this same uncle, who had renounced his religion and separated from his family, returned to the church after he retired and fell ill. Upon his death, there were combatants on one side and church people on the other in the funeral home. Edward interprets this as evidence that "God's power is immense."[32]

At the same time that people were leaving, so too were some people becoming more deeply entrenched in the revolutionary process due to their own social convictions, the educational opportunities that became available, and the subtle and not-so-subtle coercion enacted by the limitation of choice. Indeed, the line between enthusiastic and obligatory participation for those who were active in the Cuban mass organizations, the educational process, and mobilizations was not as clear as one might assume. The climate of the country was one in which educational and employment opportunities were closely linked with political participation, and the "political" saturated public and private spheres. Because neutrality and inaction were close to impossible for the majority of the population, it is difficult to discern whether such participation exemplified and nurtured revolutionary fervor or actually obfuscated doubts, discontent, and disappointment. To obtain a job, to be promoted, to get access to coveted material goods, to be successful in society, one had to emerge favorably in evaluations not simply of job performance but performance as a revolutionary and contributor to revolutionary society.

Furthermore, in a society where foreigners and those connected to foreigners or people who left Cuba were suspect, the Cuban-born descendants of Anglo-Caribbean immigrants who remained were under added pressure to demonstrate their loyalty to the revolution. In addition to contributing as participants in the clandestine movement and the mobilizations of the early 1960s, they also were present in Cuba's mass organizations as trained professionals, including holding positions in the Party. Eugenia, for instance, was the director of a zone that included seven CDRs, organized campaigns to control the mosquito population, directed neighborhood beautification efforts, and managed other projects of this nature. Melvina was the block secretary for the FMC for years, which entailed collecting the dues of seventy-five centavos every three months, assisting in the publication of a newspaper that responded to concerns affecting Cuban women, and making sure that the needs of people with problems from employment to teenage pregnancy to spousal abuse were addressed. Carmen became the coordinator of her residential zone, which includes twelve CDRs, in addition to holding a position in the FMC where she was in charge of fourteen blocks, and being a delegate of the Poder Popular (Cuba's legislative parliament) for almost six years. Edward was the general director of CDR district 1 in 1972 and 1973, the secretary of the union in the teachers' sector in the mid-1970s, and the ideological secretary of the Juventud until he was obliged to leave when he reached the age of thirty-one.[33]

With involvement in mass organizations, the departure of Anglo-Caribbean immigrants, and pressure from the revolutionary government, community institutions deteriorated. Indeed, pressure to disband began prior to heightening tensions of the 1960s and 1970s. After the attack on the Moncada in 1953, Batista's government initiated a crackdown on some Anglo-Caribbean institutions. My research in the Santiago municipal archives revealed concerted efforts throughout the 1950s on the part of police to close lodges, recreational clubs, and other cultural institutions in order to exert tighter control over society as a whole, a move that was repeated under the revolutionary government. Santiago municipal archives contain letters addressed to various ethnic organizations requesting documentation that they would be unlikely to produce, such as membership and financial records dating back decades. Internal police department memos confirming closure of the organization frequently accompanied letters.[34]

Upon coming to power, the revolutionary government eliminated race-based associations. For Cubans of color, this meant that the structures they had in place to challenge racial discrimination and build diasporic connections were dismantled. Ethnic associations also fell prey to this drive to eliminate potential hotbeds of counterrevolutionary activity, to consolidate power, and to subjugate ethnic and racial difference in the interest of national unity. The Anglo-Caribbean institutions were by no means singled out; rather, they were simply another corner of Cuba's social landscape whose presence did not support the refashioning of civil society. Eugene Godfried, a journalist and activist from Curaçao who worked as a radio broadcaster in Cuba for several years, observed, "The official position which over-emphasized the 'Cuban' citizenship of the citizens has estranged the immigrants of 'white' color as well as 'black' color as is the case of Haitian, Jamaican and other Caribbean and African nations" (Godfried 2000). This top-down project of homogenization contributed to the diminished distinction among Cubans of various immigrant origins.

As a segment of the population closely associated with the United States and its presence in Cuba, Anglo-Caribbean immigrants and their Cuban-born children were under more pressure to demonstrate commitment to Cubanness, which precluded strong bonds with their Anglo-Caribbean diasporic identities. Most of the younger generation ceased speaking English, going to church, and participating in associations. They were busy taking advantage of educational opportunities and building and being incorporated into revolutionary society's emergent mass organizations. At the same time, many of the older generation of original immigrants began returning to their islands of origin, to other Caribbean islands, or to the United States, as Cuba and its neighbor to the north became increasingly polarized.

However, in spite of the position held by people of Anglo-Caribbean descent in Guantánamo, the British West Indian Welfare Centre remained one of the few ethnic associations that did not meet its demise with the revolution. Its membership did dwindle, and during one period in the late 1970s, the leadership decided to accept non-Anglo-Caribbean Cubans in order to prevent the institution from completely collapsing. As Violda Carey recalled, "In 1974 we almost lost the Centre. I was the President from 1979. I broke away from the regulations. . . . I let the Haitians become members. They, too, were foreigners and they wanted to be members. It was a battle to be able to enroll their descendants" (quoted in Chailloux, Whitney, and Claxton 2006:147). Edward told a similar tale, but included the detail that it was not only Haitian descendants who were allowed to join the Centre, but also Cubans with no other Caribbean origin. The Centre became a gathering place that was not exclusive to ethnic identification.[35]

While the institution did not close, the connections to family and friends who either left the country or exiled on the base were stigmatized. Illustrating the pivotal role that the state plays in regulating transnational connectivity, and in the case of revolutionary Cuba nearly torching the transnational social field, communication between people on and off the island was silenced for political reasons. The erosion of their institutional infrastructure and polarization of the society no doubt encouraged the departure of many community members. Many of their livelihoods had always been dependent upon Americans, and they were less amenable to becoming further incorporated into Cuban society.

This climate was one in which anyone who was not opposed to the United States and in clear support of the socialist agenda was looked upon with suspicion. As people who spoke English, were employed by people from the United States, and had family abroad, some Anglophone Caribbean Cubans, particularly those in Guantánamo who had such a close connection to the base, found themselves on the defensive, having to prove where their loyalties lay both within and outside of the family. Leonarda—her mother a Jamaican immigrant and her father the Cuban-born son of Jamaican immigrants—migrated from Banes to Caimanera with her parents who sought employment on the base. Her father worked in a nightclub and her mother was a housewife who, in more difficult times, worked as a laundress. They had eight children; her father died at a fairly young age and her mother remarried another Jamaican descendant who had a job on the base. She recalled:

I was young, nine when the revolution triumphed. The first school I went to was the English school with Ms. Odein. She was *de madre* [really difficult or hard]. I was in a private school with her so that I could be prepared to do well in the Spanish public school. . . . It was very important for us to be able to communicate because [my mother] insisted on one thing. My mother was accustomed to when she called us, we answered in English and if everything wasn't in English, she hit you. . . . But also the English language at that time was important, and later [after the revolution] it was a little . . . well, people said "English, for what? English, for what?" . . . When my mother called me, I preferred to get hit than to answer in English. When I was inside the house I answered in English, but outside I didn't speak English.[36]

Leonarda's experience demonstrates not only divisions along generational lines but also the way in which language continued to be a marker of allegiance. Prior to the revolution, it had distinguished them as British subjects and then, for the Cuban-born, as people who worked in the offices, bars, warehouses, kitchens, and fields of the Americans. Connection with this dominant group secured their economic niche. However, while speaking English might have placed them in a relatively advantageous position, racial subjugation within the confines of the plantations, on the naval base, and in the urban centers was ubiquitous. In a labor force that was racially stratified, where it was common policy to have a different pay scale pegged to racial identity and geographic origin, any advantage they enjoyed was within these economic and social constraints.

Even those who managed to prosper were not immune to the vagaries of the racialized social hierarchy. Purcival, the son of Jamaican immigrants who was fifteen years old when the revolution triumphed, was initially excited and involved in the revolutionary process throughout the 1960s and '70s, founding his local militia. He explained that prior to the revolution, his father and maternal uncles worked for the base and lacked for nothing. The local *guardia* during the Batista era was even kind to him and other neighborhood children, but as a Black person, he couldn't enter the central park. Nor could he and his siblings use the beautiful sports center facility in Vista Alegre because it was reserved for whites. With the revolutionary victory and subsequent unsettling of the racial hierarchy, for some the dissolution of community institutions and stigmatization of English was a small price to pay.[37]

"Fidel Tiró la Ley": Race and Revolution

"Fidel threw out the law": this statement was made by the main protagonist in the film *Cuban Roots/Bronx Stories* (Sporn 2000), who was a child when the revolution triumphed and who recalled that the urban reform law saved his family from being evicted. Likewise, the interviews in this section focus on my interlocutors' experiences of prerevolutionary Cuban society and the beneficial changes they experienced as a result of the revolution.

In her sixties, Carmen is a retired teacher who lives in Guantánamo. She is also the granddaughter of Jamaican and Barbadian immigrants whose family has been involved in the revolutionary struggle. She has continued in this tradition and was very active in revolutionary society. Indeed, she was difficult to catch up with due to her full schedule. Sitting in the living room of her house in Guantánamo, she shared with me boxes of photographs and memorabilia she had collected over the years. In addition to studio photographs of her grandparents, of herself in an elaborate first communion gown and again with friends in white dresses worn for her *quinceañera*, there were also pictures that document her family's and neighbors' participation in the political life of the country. For instance, she showed me photos of her father among a group of fellow communists gathered in a house and a bar, of the rural children she taught during the literacy campaign, of a young neighbor in army fatigues who was to go fight in Angola, and various activities of her CDR, of which she was a leader.

During the interview, she revealed that her Cuban-born father joined the Communist Party in 1948 and was active in the 1950s in spite of the tremendous risks involved in simply being found in possession of their newsletter, *Obrero*. Carmen suggested that her father's political activism was rooted in the belief that communism was the way to bring an end to racial injustice. In naming members of her family and other jamaicanos who supported the revolution, she insisted, "They were defending the Black class, the poor. . . . They were fighting against racial discrimination and social discrimination, to end the abuses, the misery and corruption and all of this. They had to support it." She focused on the segregation of public space, describing in detail instances in which her family entered but were not served at restaurants and the age and race restrictions that governed access to the central park just a few blocks from her home. She recalled the impact that this had on her family and reflected on generational and social differences across time:

"They suffered, they suffered, my parents. . . . I was young and I didn't understand. . . . Families then were very reserved. There were a lot of things that I
didn't know when I was little. Children didn't know a lot, not like now when
they know everything, everything. It wasn't like that. My cousin had to tell
me that we, because of our color, couldn't go in that part of the park. Look at
that, the government prohibited us from going into the park because of color,
only the younger children could go in and play. How hard, how hard. . . .
Now everyone is in the park. There's white, Black, Chinese, Japanese, Jamaican, everyone, young and old. But then, the children of color [could enter]
but the older no, only whites."[38]

Through these statements as well as her ongoing involvement in mass
organizations and engagement in the local community, Carmen espouses
the national ideology of racial equality and has carried the torch of political activism within the confines of revolutionary society. As we see in her
remarks and as I elaborate upon in chapter 5, embedded in the narrative of
Anglo-Caribbean Cuban community is a social transformation that is not a
simple lionizing of the revolution. Carmen makes an unsolicited comparison
between racial politics before and after the revolution, finding the latter to
be more just. However, in her statements, she also hints at the deterioration
in families' ability or inclination to protect their children from hurtful information and experiences in the current moment. That there are generational
differences in social mores is far from revelatory. What is intriguing is how
individuals interpret and articulate the relationship between such differences
and the revolutionary project.

As illustrated by Carmen's narrative, Cuba, in the years leading up to the
revolution, was racially stratified. It was a society characterized by conflict
and contradiction and one that continued to be deeply ambivalent about the
role of Cubans of color in the nation. Economic growth and development
sat alongside instability, corruption, and "vast inequalities in the distribution of goods, services, and opportunities" (Fagen 1969:23). Although few
ethnographic studies have been focused on how race and revolution were
lived, there are historiographies of republican Cuba that provide significant
contributions to our understanding of the economic and social landscape,
including the position of Cubans of color (Helg 1995; Pérez 1999; de la Fuente
2001b; Bronfman 2004; Pappademos 2011). They indicate that rural Cubans,
Black and mulatto Cubans, and those from the middle classes were not far-
ing well during Batista's second term.[39]

Upon coming to power, Fidel asserted that the four main battles of the revolution were against unemployment, poor living standards, the high cost of living, and racial discrimination at work centers (Fidel Castro, quoted in de la Fuente 2001b:263). The initial strategy to eliminate racial stratification included publicly denouncing racial discrimination and constructing it as counterrevolutionary, outlawing segregation in public places, and eliminating the private social institutions where discrimination was widely practiced. Furthermore, in 1960, the government changed hiring practices such that all new employees were hired through the Ministry of Labor, thus subverting discriminatory hiring practices (de la Fuente 2001b:274).

However, the campaign against racial discrimination waned after 1962 when the official discourse promoted the idea that the revolution had solved the problem of race discrimination. The leadership proclaimed that the elimination of extreme class differences by making institutions of higher education, employment, and medical care accessible was sufficient to achieve racial equality. Discussions about race and confronting racism became taboo and "if openly racist acts were deemed to be counterrevolutionary, attempts to debate publicly the limitations of Cuba's integration were likewise considered to be the enemy's work" (de la Fuente 2001b:279). Though there is some debate concerning its origins, pervasiveness, and persistence in the private versus public sector, by now there is ample evidence that the revolution did not solve the problem of racial discrimination.[40]

Becoming Revolucionario

Perhaps most important for Cuban-born Anglo-Caribbeans, at least some of whom had basic literacy skills, was that the revolution transformed the character and content of higher education. Addressing both the scarcity of institutions of higher learning as well as the inaccessibility of such opportunities to Cubans living in rural areas, the number of universities increased from three in 1959 to forty in the 1980s, and enrollments expanded tenfold. Before, educational programs most relevant to the national economy were inadequately subsidized and not promoted due to the reliance on foreign managers, technicians, and specialists and on those Cubans educated abroad. University curriculums introduced during the 1960s and 1970s reflected the need for people educated in the most strategic sectors of the national economy rather than in the humanities, social sciences, and law, preparation principally for positions in government and public administration (Pérez 1999:360).

The elimination of racial as well as economic barriers to accessing higher education had a tremendous impact on the lives of working-class people. It was a radical shift from the exclusivity and inaccessibility of a university education that marked the experience of my interlocutors' parents and grandparents who, as a result of the system of race/class/origin discrimination, faced multiple obstacles to propelling themselves into positions of such prestige. Though in some instances one person in a family or community was able to attend university through much sacrifice, mass access to education was unprecedented. In most instances, after children received an elementary education in the English schools and perhaps some exposure to what would be the equivalent of junior high school in the Cuban schools, options for further education were limited and young people began their working lives full time.

The revolution presented an unparalleled opportunity. During this time, much of Cuba's professional class was fleeing the country, opening up positions for those who were inclined to take advantage of this situation. The country desperately needed highly trained personnel to work as professionals, technicians, administrators, and managers in order to stabilize and develop the economy. Those Anglo-Caribbean descendants who had attended English and Cuban schools, and in whose community the importance of education and self-discipline were reportedly stressed, were in an optimal position to take advantage of such opportunities. Becoming a professional not only furthered one's personal middle-class aspirations, but it was also viewed as a contribution to the revolution.

The resources that the revolutionary government invested in the educational system combined with a policy of antidiscrimination prepared the formerly excluded to fill the professional void left by middle- and upper-class exiles. Those who remained in Cuba and aligned themselves with the revolution were able to access these opportunities.[41] During this period, the descendants of British West Indian immigrants confronted a predicament due to their association with and reliance upon the United States' presence in Cuba. For some Cubans, as illustrated by Leonarda, Pamela, and Edward's cases, speaking English, having family abroad, and having a family history of being brought to Cuba to work for Americans were grounds to distrust those with Anglo-Caribbean backgrounds. However, the world that they occupied rapidly became very different from the social, economic, and political world of their parents and grandparents. For many, there was a shift from being the elite of the working poor to being part of the educated professional class. This mobility was a source of pride and status. Though they continued to face racial barriers to betterment and in most cases lost the institutional base of the British West Indian community, the opportunities provided by the revolution appeared to overshadow the ongoing discrimination and daily struggle to create a material life that was commensurate with expectations based on educational status.

However, as I remarked at the outset of this chapter, their relationship to the Cuban nation in revolution shifts with the intersections of gender, class, race, and ethnicity. The remainder of this chapter focuses on the way that gender framed individual and familial readings of the revolution as a force of liberation. It suggests that much like black intellectual and activist Walterio Carbonell and the branch of Black *fidelistas* who sought what Jafari Allen would call a "larger freedom" by articulating a truly radical project of social change (Guerra 2012), first-generation Cuban-born West Indian women used the revolution to break through the boundaries of respectability.

Becoming (More) Cubana: West Indian Daughters, Cuban Women

"¡Jovenes rebeldes, Patria o Muerte! ¡Jovenes rebeldes, Patria o Muerte!" (Rebel Youth, Fatherland or Death!) Melvina and Leticia, the Cuban-born daughter and granddaughter of Jamaican immigrants, chanted in unison and in remembrance. Stirred by my questions about their experience of revolution as Jamaican Cubans, they recalled how the streets rang with the marching of local militias composed of young Cubans declaring their readiness to defend the revolution. Integral to the narratives of immigrant daughters and granddaughters who came of age during the revolution was the way in which the lives of girls and women transformed. For some, participation in revolutionary activity was a monument to a long-relinquished adventuresome spirit. For others, it was a time in which they were confronted with the impasse between the call for female participation in revolutionary society and their family's plan for them as young women.

Cuba's effort to have a "revolution within the revolution" in which all women were to achieve full equality with men was an opportunity to chal-

Figure 2.4. Revolutionary woman. One of the stated aims of the revolution was to eliminate gender inequality, to have "the revolution within the revolution."

lenge race- and class-based barriers to educational and occupational opportunity as well as the gendered constraints imposed upon them by their immigrant families. Yet another way in which some immigrant daughters experienced this tremendous social transformation was as a loss of economic autonomy at the hands of the socialist system.

Here, I am concerned with how Anglo-Caribbean Cuban women's memories of the early years of the revolution assist us in exploring how the turn from an identity rooted in Anglo-Caribbean origins was a gendered process. I examine how these women's recollections reflect the tensions among personal autonomy, familial responsibility and expectation, and nationalist projects. For these young women, connection to a Cuban rather than an

African Anglo-Caribbean diasporic identity offered greater opportunity for self-realization, autonomy, and mobility.

On December 6, 1966, at the closing of the Fifth National Plenary of the Cuban Women's Federation (FMC) in Havana, Fidel stated, "Arriving here this evening, I commented to a comrade that this phenomenon of women's participation in the revolution was a revolution within a revolution. [Applause] And if we were asked what the most revolutionary thing is that the revolution is doing, we would answer that it is precisely this—the revolution that is occurring among the women of our country! [Applause]" (Stone 1981:48). In 1959, about 9.8 percent of Cuban women held jobs, and while some were secretaries, nurses, and teachers, the overwhelming majority— over 70 percent—were domestic servants and the rest agricultural workers. Women carried much of the burden of Cuba's underdevelopment because they were the ones who did all the household chores without benefit of electricity and running water. Women also had the highest rate of illiteracy (Stone 1981:6).

Historically, conditions for Black and mulata women were worse than those for men or white women. Most were excluded from the few areas of the economy outside of domestic service that were open to white women, such as the communications and commercial sectors. For instance, the telephone company, where 40 percent of the labor force was female, did not hire Black women, nor did retail establishments. Indeed, it was not until 1951 that educated mulata women were hired as clerks in upscale Havana stores, and that only occurred as a result of Carlos Prío, Cuba's president, intervening in response to pressure on the part of a Black middle-class organization. Furthermore, many of the women who had been hired were fired after the Christmas season (de la Fuente 2001b:118–20).

As with the Cuban wars of independence in which women were among the *mambises* (Cuban guerrilla soldiers) in the nineteenth-century encampments from which they waged their anticolonial wars, women were integral to the armed struggle to oust the Batista regime. Indeed, Celia Sánchez, Haydée Santamaría Cuadrado and Melba Hernández, all of whom fought in the Maria Grajales platoon,[42] are among the most celebrated revolutionary heroines. In the construction of revolutionary society after 1959, women continued to cross gender boundaries by being incorporated into the militia, participating in the literacy campaign as both teachers and pupils,[43] becoming physicians, engineers, technicians, bus drivers, sugar mill workers, and serving in other formerly male-dominated jobs. Those members of the so-ciety who "questioned the 'morals' of women who dressed like men, wore pants, and carried guns" resisted this challenge to the gender hierarchy and were known to greet the militia women with rocks when they went out to drill (Stone 1981:9).

The conflict between the professed national project of social equality and the deeply entrenched ideologies of inequality (and the practices that are their reflection) more often manifested itself in less public domains such as interactions between family members. For Anglo-Caribbean immigrant families experiencing revolution, this more intimate place of belonging was a battleground upon which the continued struggle against inequality oc-curred. The following are sketches of five women with whom I worked and whose stories point to the gendering of this struggle. In them we see that the revolution opened up a space for belonging that conflicted with certain patriarchal norms predominant in both Anglo-Caribbean and Cuban house-holds.

Beth: "I Was Brave"

Beth is the granddaughter of immigrants from Nevis. Now in her late sixties, she has had problems with her "nerves" and confesses to be afraid of every-thing. She says, "When I was young, I was brave, not like now." Participating in the clandestine movement that was critical to the success of the 26th of July Movement, Beth stored bullets, carried messages, assisted rebels who went into hiding, sold 26th of July bonds to U.S. soldiers while working on the Guantánamo Naval Base, and was at the point of going into the Sierra to join the rebels when the revolution triumphed. Beth hid her involvement in the clandestine movement from her family. "My mother had nothing to do with it, only me." She repeated, "Only me."[44]

Esperanza: "The Revolution Will Take Care of Me"

Esperanza's parents were Jamaican, and her father left Cuba when she was young. Her stepfather, the father of her younger sister, was from Barbados. All worked on the naval base. Her aunt was one of the pillars of the com-munity in the '40s and '50s and ran the English school at the British West In-dian Welfare Centre in Guantánamo. Esperanza was trained to teach English before the revolution and decided to participate in the literacy campaign by teaching at one of the nearby *centrales*. However, she did not go on to further her education; instead, she married another Anglo-Caribbean Cuban. She recalls that her husband and mother decided that she would stop working and she complied. Esperanza's sister, on the other hand, defied their mother's wishes by leaving to study in Santiago and then Havana. As Esperanza recounted, "[I married] with a jamaiquino from Guantánamo who worked on the base. He and my mother agreed that I couldn't continue working so I stopped working and lost this opportunity [to study]. My sister didn't, she was braver than I, and even though my mother didn't want it, she went and began school at the Escuela de Superación and she began to get ahead. Now she is a neonatologist and she has even been abroad. For three years and eight months, she was in Botswana. . . . She said [to my mother], 'Fine, you don't want this, well, the revolution will take care of me.'"[45]

Caridad: "Everything Died"

Caridad is the daughter of Jamaican immigrants and was in her late twenties when the revolution triumphed. At that time, she was making a good living teaching English to wealthy Cubans in Vista Alegre, an upper-class neighborhood in Santiago. She recalled giving one-hour classes twice a week, being paid twenty-five dollars per student by Cubans with money who wanted to learn English. She explained, "The family I worked for had cars and a farm, a beautiful garden, a gardener, but," she stated flatly, "after the triumph of the revolution, there was no garden and everything died." Caridad recalled that they treated their servants poorly—most were Black and Cuban—but treated her well because she was a teacher. As a young woman who spoke English and lived in an urban centre, she had a tremendous amount of autonomy. With the revolution's turn from the United States and the flight of the upper and middle classes, Caridad's more comfortable lifestyle disintegrated.[46]

Leticia: A Young Woman Alone

Leticia's paternal grandparents came from Jamaica. She was nine years old at the time of the triumph of the revolution. She was sent to a school for athletes established in 1961; when she was sixteen she participated in a national competition and was selected to go to Havana to be trained as a professional athlete. I asked her how her parents reacted to this opportunity and she responded, "[My father] didn't like for his children to leave without supervision, to be away from home alone without anyone, to go to Havana?! They had to fight a lot to get him to let me go to Havana. My grandfather, who had more awareness and a larger vision, he fought with my father. My sister also [had an opportunity], my sister would have studied nursery science in Havana and my father didn't let her go. . . . She wasn't eighteen yet."[47]

Melvina: The Ten Million Harvest

"In '70 here in Cuba there was no carnival, there was no anything, because [of] the Ten Million Harvest. I met [my husband] in the harvest of the Ten Millions. . . . He was here [in Santiago] in the university and everyone went to go harvest. The men cut cane and the women collected it. So, in July and August everyone went to the countryside. It was like a party. We were really happy, forming congas, singing, it was a healthy life, a healthier life than now. . . . [I felt] happy, outside of the gaze of my father. . . . With the freedom, not the freedom, but with the new system, the system that Fidel put in place in the country," she reflected, "the children of jamaicanos were liberated a little. . . . When I first went to the countryside in '68 for forty-five days to pick coffee, collect cane, and harvest oranges, . . . it was great. I learned a lot that I never learned at home. . . . I was more free. I felt freer outside of the house and the dominion of my father, and many were like me, who felt freer."[48]

Melvina had a very domineering Jamaican father and paternal grandmother. Whether it was her father being against her going to the countryside, or the break between her father and sister when her sister married a Cuban (non-Jamaican) and joined the Communist Party, points of conflict between her father's desire to control their family and the social changes under way were frequent in her narrative of the experience of revolution. In spite of the fact that her sister had the opportunity to study medicine under the revolution, becoming a specialist, her father was against the revolution and ultimately returned to Jamaica.

While individuals' acceptance or rejection of the revolution is clearly complicated, what seems apparent in these cases is that the disruption of patriarchal control certainly has been a factor in the ever-evolving relationship between individuals and revolutionary society. Stuart Hall, in a short reflective piece entitled "Minimal Selves," admits that the real answer to the question always asked of migrants, "Why are you here?" is that he left Jamaica to get away from his mother. He writes, "Isn't that the universal story of life?

One is where one is to try and get away from somewhere else. That was the story, which I could never tell anybody about myself. So I had to find other stories, other fictions, which were more authentic or, at any rate, more acceptable, in place of the Big Story of endless evasion of patriarchal family life" (1987:44). For these Cuban-born Jamaican women, the Cuba that the revolution created was their migratory destination. However, this movement, this reimagining of position and possibility that access to educational and occupational opportunities opened up for them, did not foster unequivocal support of the revolutionary program, in part because, as was the case with Melvina and Leticia's fathers, loss of control over the female members of the household threatened patriarchal norms. These fathers resisted a strong state stepping in and fulfilling this role, yet as we saw in Leticia's case, the state opened up opportunities previously out of reach for most and provided an additional step towards becoming Cuban.

However, following Louis Pérez's (1999) argument, we must complicate what it means to "become Cuban" by recognizing that cultural elements of Cuba's neighbor to the North are embedded in Cuban national identity. As I described in chapter 1, this was particularly true for Anglo-Caribbean Cubans who moved within a transnational social field that included the United States, Cuba, and their islands of origin. Although the revolutionary period of the '60s and '70s witnessed the torching of that social field, the blaze did not engulf these connections entirely, and, I argue, these connections allow us to elaborate upon the relationship between diaspora and the state.

The Revolution, Soul Train, and the Creation of Diaspora Space

In this chapter, I have been concerned with various experiences of the revolution, including the impact of the presence of the U.S. Naval Base on the lives of my informants and their families following the 1959 revolution. I have argued that those of Anglo-Caribbean origin occupied divergent and dynamic positions in relation to revolutionary Cuba, positions that were mediated by several factors, with gender being but one. In the remaining section, I explore how this shifting relationship to the state and revolutionary government comes to bear upon articulations of diaspora.

Avtar Brah wrote that diaspora space is "the intersectionality of diaspora, border, and dis/location as a point of confluence of economic, political, cultural, and psychic processes . . . [and] where multiple subject positions are juxtaposed, contested, proclaimed, or disavowed" (1996:208). I use this conceptualization of diaspora space to assess the extent to which these economic, political, cultural, and psychic processes, which necessarily change over time, lead to changing articulations of diaspora. As we will see, far from being emblematic of a severance from the state, as notions associating diaspora with extraterritoriality suggest, the occupation of diasporic space occurs in part due to the state's role in mediating transnational connections. The case of Guantánamo, in particular, illustrates the importance of attending to the specificities of place in considerations of how race and diaspora are made—and unmade (Patterson and Kelley 2000).

Born in Guantánamo in 1955 and remembering the global distribution of music in the '60s and '70s, Lester reflected on the impact of the transnational connections that the naval base afforded even after the 1959 revolution: "We had the privilege of being able to watch the channel from the base so we saw musical groups and watched *Soul Train* every week.[49] The youth at this time wanted to leave class to watch this show. There was also *Soul of the City* but the most memorable was *Soul Train,* and this had a lot of impact in Guantánamo from the point of view of the styles and dances. . . . This was a privilege because we were the first to get access to Black American culture."[50] Apparently, the "Soul Train" made a stop in Guantánamo!

This fascinating detail of daily life in the early revolutionary period came up again in a casual conversation I had with Edward when we were discussing our favorite musicians while waiting in the living room of another descendiente to whom he was introducing me. In speaking about his love of Luther Vandross and other Black American R&B singers, he recounted how, every Saturday morning during the 1970s and into the 1980s, he and other people in his neighborhood would crowd around a television and watch *Soul Train.*[51]

Ironically, at the same time that there was a strict severance of transnational ties with the advent of the 1959 revolution in Cuba and resulting hostilities with the United States, for people in Guantánamo, the proximity of the U.S. Naval Base led to the unexpected movement of information and cultural material. As it turns out, unlike other Cubans, residents of the city could access the American television programs broadcast on the base. Taking full advantage of this lapse in media control, they listened to the music and practiced the dance moves of Black America. *Soul Train,* as a result of the United States' dominant global position, was broadcast to an international market and therefore exemplifies the movement of cultural material across national boundaries, even in the case of Cuba where those boundaries were particularly rigid.

This unanticipated breach of the border that divided Guantánamo the U.S. Naval Base from Guantánamo the city was by no means a singular episode. Exchanges between the two spheres occurred on a daily basis with the physical movement of personnel from their residences in Cuba to their jobs on the Base, which was and continues to be a space that is the legal, economic, and cultural domain of the United States. The fact that many of these workers were of Anglo-Caribbean descent makes this border crossing particularly interesting when considering the social, cultural, and political circuits between the Caribbean and various mainlands.

My discovery that people in Guantánamo had access to *Soul Train* in the 1970s and '80s brought up questions that concern the processes and politics around the creation of diaspora space. One way that scholars have thought about diaspora is as an event: geographic dispersal, which was a traumatic event followed by hostility and rejection in the host country, sense of connection to others due to belief in a shared origin, and centrality of homeland, including longing for, involvement in, and/or desire to return to that homeland. This is a predominant, popular interpretation of this term. Another way to think about diaspora is as a conceptual framework through which to look at various articulations of displacement and belonging. Diaspora decenters the nation-state as the basis of connection. It relies on the imagining of a shared past and a shared experience of degradation and is produced through recognition as against misrecognition (Hintzen and Rahier 2010).

The *Soul Train* revelation was one of those moments of mutual recognition. I identify this moment of connection around what was a particularly powerful breakthrough in Black popular culture (i.e., *Soul Train*) as one that opened up a diaspora space. Rather than have diaspora space exist through the presence of those who come from elsewhere, it is created. This does not negate the kinds of entanglements and asymmetries of power that are often ignored in understandings of diaspora. As Nassy Brown (2005) argues, power differences across nation and gender mean that everyone doesn't access or experience diaspora equally. If diaspora is used to create belonging and challenge misrecognition and racial abjection, Nassy Brown asks, does "everyone partake in the privileges of membership to the diasporic community with impunity?" (Nassy Brown 2005:42) The answer is clearly "no." Indeed, access to *Soul Train*, itself a rupture in, rather than a typical feature of, the cultural landscape, was uneven. In the following chapters, I continue to explore the processes and intersections that stratify, create, and foreclose diaspora space. In the proceeding discussion, however, the crisis known as the Special Period, rather than the 1959 revolution, is the event that initiated a seismic shift in Cuba's economic, political, cultural, and psychic spheres.

3

Special Identities in Cuba's Special Period

Race, Region, and Revitalization

But, more than the guarantee of success for a cultural initiative in our quotidian work of the promotion of ties of friendship, cooperation and solidarity between the peoples of Cuba and Jamaica, that which we valued in this project was perhaps the start of a stage of more profound work which leads us to the necessary deepening of our cultures, idiosyncrasies and common features which constitute the germ of our necessary integration. . . . There are many challenges which our small insular nations face as a result of globalization. It is because of this that we are obligated to globalize our knowledge in particular, our mutual knowledge. This will make us stronger through our culture, as is expected in today's times.

José Francisco Piedra Rencurrel, Cuban ambassador to Jamaica, 2002

We from the Anglophone Caribbean understand [the persistence of racially motivated discriminatory practices against those of visibly African ancestry] well. Our history was forged in the same circumstances of plantation slavery that created Cuba's own society. We know firsthand the experience of being discriminated against and marginalised because of the colour of one's skin, despite personal emancipation and freedom from the obscenity of slavery. It was precisely this experience that gave rise to the struggles of Marcus Mosiah Garvey, who captured the imagination of Blacks all over Africa and the Americas, including Cuba where he had more branches of his Universal Negro Improvement Association than anywhere else except the United States of America itself, with his message of racial pride and equality. . . . So, Your Excellency, we do understand. The Cuban Revolution may well have liberated the structural exploitation of the Cuban people, Black and White, but the attitudes, some overt, some subtle, that have sought to justify the centuries of enslavement of Black Africans do not yield so easily.

Rex Nettleford, Barry Chevannes, Rupert Lewis, and Maureen Warner-Lewis,
"Letter from Jamaica," November 26, 2009

There has been considerable recent public controversy over "the *negro* problem" in Cuba, marking a shift away from the staunch position that the revolution has solved racial discrimination. This debate has been ongoing between Cubans on and off the island and across the racial spectrum, as well as within and between Cubans of color and other diasporic groups. For instance, in 2009 a group of sixty prominent African Americans joined Afro-Brazilian intellectual and icon of Black activism in Brazil, Abdias do Nascimento, in declaring their support for the Afro-Cuban population in its struggle against racism in a document entitled "Acting on Our Conscience."[1] Those Anglophone Caribbean leaders quoted in the opening of this chapter joined them in criticizing the state's unwillingness to allow for independent dialogue and protest of racial discrimination. This public criticism of Cuba was unique in that it marked a departure from what has for the most part been a supportive stance toward the Cuban Revolution. It was met by a flurry of responses, including a counterdeclaration by other African American artists, intellectuals, and activists entitled "We Stand with Cuba!" (Azikiwe et al. 2009) and a "Message" from prominent Afro-Cubans who strongly objected to Cuba's characterization as a racist nation (Morejón et al. 2009). The primary evidence that the Afro-Cubans provided in defense of their nation is Cuba's dismantling of the structures of inequality as well as support of Africa and the Caribbean through technical and humanitarian aid. For them, any assessment of Cuba's "*negro* problem" must take into consideration national and foreign policy.

A more recent incident that set off a maelstrom of commentary occurred in 2012 when the *New York Times Review* published a severely distorted version of an article submitted by Roberto Zurbano, then editorial director at Casa de Las Americas, who was dismissed from his post after the article's publication. In his article, originally entitled "The Country to Come: And My Black Cuba . . . ?" but changed by the *New York Times* editor to "For Blacks in Cuba, the Revolution Hasn't Begun," Zurbano argues that "in the last twenty years Black Cubans have suffered a reversal or paralysis of the great social mobility that propelled them from 1959 to 1989" and explains the predicament in which Blacks find themselves, highlighting the uncertainty of the role that they will play in the nation's future (Zurbano 2013; West-Durán 2013). Unfortunately, as a result of the inaccurate translation, the article failed to communicate this more nuanced perspective of the predicament of Cubans of color and provoked an avalanche of both criticism and support of Zurbano.[2]

These more recent public debates reinforce what I found in my fieldwork among Black Cubans of Anglo-Caribbean descent whose lives were marked by the Special Period, namely that, in addition to the economic deprivation, Cubans of color have had to grapple with the erosion of that "space of dignity" around racial equality that the revolutionary project provided (Allen 2011:81). This is a point of conjunction between Black Cubans who are and are not of Anglo-Caribbean origin. This erosion of gains made toward containing racial discrimination, coupled with the relative weakening of the state's ability to provide even minimally adequate support for the entire population, surrounded efforts to invigorate the Anglo-Caribbean connection. While Anglo-Caribbean Cubans shared the challenges of the Special Period with other Black Cubans, thus illustrating the erasure of the boundary between them, they depart from their Black and mulatto compatriots in the pursuit of particular strategies to navigate the crisis. As I will argue, at a time when conversations about racism on the island were still taboo, Black Cubans of Anglo-Caribbean origin used the guise of ethnicity to challenge economic, psychological, and moral assault.[3]

Unveiling Cuba's precarious position within the global economy, the Special Period intensified tensions between socialist ideology and daily survival, between the rhetoric of racial equality and reality of discrimination. For Black Cubans of Anglo-Caribbean descent, it also created an opening for both the reinvention and reassertion of connection beyond the boundaries that the revolution had demanded prior to the 1990s. The revitalization of Anglophone Caribbean associations, strengthening of transnational ties facilitated by the state's investment in certain forms of diasporic connections, continuity and disjuncture across generations of immigrant families, and assertions of respectable Blackness occurred under the cloud and then in the shadow of the Special Period.

As I will describe, this reconnection has a highly functional component: these "lifelines" are a source of potential economic support and offered some relief from the deprivations suffered by the severe shortage of key resources and consumer goods. However, for those who are passionate about the "rescuing of their roots," the reward for attempting to rebuild their cultural institutions is more complicated than actual or potential material gain. As the children and grandchildren of Black English-speaking working-class migrants who had been closely associated with the U.S. presence in Cuba, their emergent identities reveal a "critical Black subject" whose analyses of post–Cold War Cuba are articulated not through hip-hop lyrics, Afro-Cuban religions, or erotic practice, but through the Black experience of social mobility and racial discrimination in revolutionary society.

In this chapter, I first convey some of the contours of daily life during the Special Period in order to contextualize the revitalization and its intersection with personal, community, national, and regional alliances. I go on to discuss the community's efforts to establish connection with the Anglophone Caribbean, paying particular attention to how this is situated within Cuba-CARICOM (Caribbean Community)[4] relations and thus folded into the agenda of the state. This is an example of the convergence of personal, local, national, and regional agendas; however, the reasons for investing in these connections at a national level differed from those at a personal level. Then, through the cases of two Rastas of Anglo-Caribbean origin, I explore generational differences in articulations of diasporic connections.

Echoes of the Special Period

Although there is considerable debate regarding when and whether the Special Period ended, by the time that I began my research in 2001,[5] the worst years of the crisis were over. Nevertheless, it inserted itself into this project both by providing a reason and context for the resurgence of Anglo-Caribbean identity and by serving as a marker of the most dramatic transition that has occurred in the lives of all Cubans. What emerges from accounts of experiences in the early 1990s is how all-encompassing the crisis has been as well as the gravity and traumatic nature of the situation. The food and water supply was severely reduced, there was no gas to cook with, and public transportation practically disappeared. Clothing was scarce, soap and toothpaste came every few months, and sanitary products not at all.

When such consumer goods began to become more available in the second half of the 1990s, inflation was astronomical. According to one university professor with whom I worked, people at all levels of society suffered from problems resulting from the inability to maintain personal hygiene. She relayed to me a discussion she had had with a neighbor in which the neighbor talked about the bug infestations and skin rashes people developed because of the ineffective soap substitutes that were widely used, denying that she herself experienced these conditions. My interlocutor reasoned that many have suppressed this and other memories of the worst period of the crisis.[6]

To explain the extent of the scarcity, women were particularly vocal. They talked about having to cook the little food there was without oil and the desperation with which neighbors fought for water during its infrequent delivery. With no gas for the stove, people dismantled each other's fences as they scavenged for wood to burn so that they could cook their meager meals, only to find themselves with no means to clean their bodies of the smoke's sooty residue.

The only people who remarked that they did not suffer from the loss of food included one who works as a clerk in a produce store and could pilfer goods for his family, and another who lives in a more rural area further north where they had livestock and could grow their own food. The other exceptions were those who had family members who worked on the naval base and had more resources with which to acquire the little that was available on the black market. These cases were clearly the exception, and thus the majority of people were forced to endure material deprivation and the psychological consequences of insecurity.

The importance of the Special Period's deprivations is revealed in how often the topic emerged, even in conversations whose beginnings were seemingly innocuous. For instance, what started out as a casual inquiry about Hortencia's relationship with her Jamaican grandmother, who was then ninety-two, took a turn toward the deprivation of the recent past. She recalled that her grandmother used to be strong, but with the lack of food during the Special Period, her stature diminished. Having seen photographs of her grandmother at different periods of her life, I now questioned my assumption that time itself was the culprit of her visible deterioration. Saying that her grandmother was not one to complain, Hortencia remembered detecting the toll that the lack of nutrition and the worry exacted. She recalls that they went hungry a lot during this time as there wasn't meat, rice, or any of the food upon which they had relied. Consequently, they often ate cornmeal porridge with beans. According to Hortencia, this lasted for five years, as things began to get a little better by the late 1990s.

"Thanks to nature and the Holy Spirit that we survived," Hortencia stated, to punctuate the recollection of her grandmother's decline and to introduce stories of her own suffering and humiliation. At the onset of the crisis, Hortencia was a young teenager and attending high school away from home where she recalls being fed rice with candy at times. She said that she cried daily and, when home for the weekends, begged her mother to allow her to stay home as she had to guard the few items in her possession at the boarding school because theft was rampant. These were dark days for her, the intimate details of which she clearly recalled with pain. She confessed having to use, wash, and reuse old cloth for sanitary napkins and remembered with particularly acute humiliation comments made by strangers about her ill-fitting undergarments and by cousins about the condition of the two pairs of underwear she owned.

Hortencia's *quinceañera* was illustrative of both the attempt to cobble together a life that had some resemblance to the one lived *antes* (before) and the anxiety produced by the absolute fragility of distorted facsimile. In spite of the hardships they endured, Hortencia's family was actually one of the more fortunate ones because her aunt was working abroad on a mission and able to help. One of the instances in which her aunt gave assistance was Hortencia's *quince* in 1993, which was the peak of the crisis. Again, it was in the process of casual conversation that the harsh details of the Special Period revealed themselves. While showing me pictures of herself when she was younger, the few shots from her *quince* appeared and I remarked on the thinness of her older brother, whom I knew as a tall, rather burly man. She corrected me when I mistakenly attributed this to his youth, reminding me that this was during the worst part of the Special Period.

Indeed, upon closer inspection, I noticed that all of the faces I had become accustomed to seeing were slightly sunken, displaying forced smiles, their bodies swimming in ill-fitting clothes. Hortencia explained that, though her aunt provided the food, clothes, and money for the photographs (considered to be essential for even the most minimalist of *quinces*), there was still the problem of electricity. She recalled her distress at the prospect of having one of the frequent blackouts arrive as an unannounced and unwelcome guest. Without music and light, the party would have been over, the lack of electrical power a metaphor for the powerlessness felt by Cuban families across the island in the face of this sudden and ominous disconnection from material resources.[7]

Melvina relayed an instance in which the assistance of family abroad provided rescue from a more dire situation. With the shortage of food, the near disappearance of the public transportation system, and the mandate that as many people continue to go to work as possible, people were left with no choice but to either walk or ride the bikes hastily supplied by the government as a solution to the lack of gasoline. While maintaining as many job centers as possible and providing some form of transportation constituted the government's attempt to stem the crisis of unemployment and fuel scarcity, this action created other problems. The low caloric intake combined with the increase in exercise was responsible for people's significant weight loss. Melvina, whose health has never been good, had to walk several miles to her job and fainted in the street one day. She was taken to the hospital and it was discovered that she needed major surgery. At that time, it would be generous to say that the hospitals were low on supplies, and thus her sister, the physician on a mission, had to bring all the necessary materials for her operation—from anesthesia to gauze to antibiotics.[8]

Another grave incident was relayed to me during my stay with Pamela and her mother Mabel in Guantánamo, providing me with a window into the worst consequences of the Special Period as well as the toll that the lack of resources on a regional level can take on a family in spite of connections abroad. Mabel, whose son lives in the United States, spoke of the economic situation in Guantánamo with a tone of disgust and bitterness. During one of our conversations, some of which were dominated by either allusions to or direct details of the trials that they were going through ("¡No hay nada aquí!" [There's nothing here!] she would say), she began talking about how the transportation in Guantánamo was so horrible. She said that there were no cars or buses or anything that came by the house at certain times of day and that if someone was sick, they could call an ambulance but it wouldn't come for twenty-four hours. "What do people do?" I asked. "They die," she said, then proceeded to tell me of how her second husband got up in the middle of the night with pain and they ran out to the street, trying to get a car to take him to the hospital, but the drivers of the cars they found were all drunk and there was nothing and no one to help them. So her husband died in the house of a heart attack. She believes that his life could have been saved had he gotten to the hospital in time—but there was nothing they could do, so they sat and watched him die.[9]

The day after Mabel shared this with me, Pamela told me that her Cuban stepfather had taken care of Pamela's severely handicapped son Michael as his own and was a tremendous help around the house. Mabel and he had been married for five years and she was in bad shape after he died. I was staying with them on the seventh anniversary of his death and was shopping with Pamela when she bought the white candle that sat burning on the table next to a glass of water throughout the day. At some point in the morning, Pamela, a practitioner of Lukumí, the Yoruba tradition in Cuba, opened the small door under the stairs to reveal an altar that contained several *orishas*.[10] She cleaned the space and the steps at the top of which sat another *orisha*, lit more candles, and put out rum. It was when I asked her why she was doing this that she told me the significance of the day, saying that she set out the candle to remember her stepfather.

I thought that perhaps he would have died even if there had been some way to get him to a hospital but that the spirit of the house would have survived. As it is, the household has an undercurrent of death and impatience and waiting. Pamela's daughter, Yanet, seems to be waiting for an opportunity to build a kind of life different from the ones she sees her mother and grandmother living. Pamela is waiting too, for her time to travel that will come in her sixties, she says, after two trips to Havana and two denials of her requests in spite of all papers in order. Mabel may have given up on waiting for a change in government or for something that will bring back days less burdened by empty stores and her life as a widow. And maybe they're all waiting and dreading a moment when Pamela's handicapped son Michael will need an ambulance that might only come when it is too late.[11]

The muted desperation and heaviness of dormancy that settled in during and in the aftermath of the Special Period stood in direct contrast to the dynamism of the revolutionary past. In memory, the Special Period marked the decline in active and enthusiastic participation in the mass organizations. As Melvina reminisced about the festive environment of the countryside during the mobilization, singing the songs and recalling how she and the man who would become her husband met during the Ten Million Ton Harvest, she mused about what a happy time it was, how it was a healthy life, healthier than now. At that time, she recalled, the revolution needed the support of the masses so there were a lot of parades and meetings, unlike now. When I asked her when this changed, she says, "This was after the fall of the socialist bloc when we were in the pure, pure, pure part of the Special Period and everything ended. A lot of tourism came in and it was very different, a lot changed, drugs came in, tourism, the people with family abroad began having contact with them, they began to come, singers and performers could come, before no foreign artists came to sing, and now there were more artists from abroad. It's totally different. Before, it was more pure."[12]

Eugenia elaborated on the impact of the economic crisis on the revolutionary activities, holding the measures taken during the Special Period responsible for the lackluster approach to activities that before were examples of solidarity and revolutionary vigor. She specifically identifies the rise in inequality that has come about due to the depenalization of the dollar and implementation of the dual economy as the culprit:

I belong to the FMC, the CDR, before I belonged to the militantes, the people who do exercises for combat. . . . The activities aren't the same as before, they've fallen a bit. . . . Now there isn't unity in the blocks. People have a lot of problems and . . . like when you're going to do an activity, the CDRs decorate the block beautifully, and all of them aren't equal. [This began] with the problem of the divisa [foreign currency], the chopping [colloquial term for "stores"]. It was totally different. Those who have divisa can go to the stores; those who don't, can't. . . . Everything has changed because not everyone receives divisa. Some businesses pay in divisa, some don't. The tourists give money and people can earn fifteen dollars to ten dollars a day in tips. Everyone can't. Some people rob. Here if you wear a chain, they take it because of greed. . . .

Those who leave the country, it is not because of the revolution, it's ambition—they're looking for money. . . . Those who are doing missions earn fifty dollars a month over their salary and the money in the country they're in. They bring televisions, washing machines, refrigerators, CD players. We're not all equal, we can't be equal. . . . Since this began, we're not the same. . . . I'm a revolutionary. . . . Everything I have, the television, the car, was given to me by Raúl, by the revolution.

The people want more. The more they have, the more they want. For example, the military workers, they retire at forty-five and have their pension of 450 pesos, then begin to do another job, they travel . . . they don't leave jobs for others. . . . Here there is too much greed; everyone wants more and more and more and more. In this country, a [great] control over things exists. In my house, I live alone, and in others, ten people live on one tarjeta. . . . I love Cuba and the revolution, but I want to travel [and] everything is in divisa. . . . Now there is the division of the divisas.

There are kids who go to school with a backpack, with their uniform, and there are others who have old uniforms or don't have school shoes. Before, everyone was the same, they had the same pair of shoes. Now they go to school with a watch, with this, with that . . . while others don't, and I say that things aren't like before.[13]

For Purcival, the deprivation and desperation of the Special Period brought him to a place of bitterness about the failure of the revolution to bring about prosperity. Considering the enthusiasm of the 1960s, which he reasoned was the result of his naiveté and inexperience, his sense of betrayal as well as frustration with life in the revolution as he began his sixties was more palpable and overtook any nostalgia about past involvement in the revolutionary process. Indeed, the hard times of the '90s seem to have diminished if not erased the value of prior successes and opportunities, such that he initially represented the change as occurring prior to the Special Period. He recounts:

The triumph of the revolution came and it seemed like it was a beautiful thing. I thought . . . I would have been abroad now because my father was going to send me to Jamaica to study, but I didn't want to go because it was so beautiful. . . . At that time, it looked really beautiful; we were fooled a little, things changed a lot. . . . It wasn't like I thought. From '80 on, I had more experience and was older and could think more. . . . The things changed in '80, well, really in '90 with the Special Period. It's not the same. There wasn't oil, there wasn't anything. You didn't find anything. I ate very little. There were always blackouts, like the ones you see that we have now, it was worse then. We spent twenty-four hours without electricity.

I got very skinny. . . . In the early '90s there wasn't any food that I liked. I like meat but there wasn't any; everything was bad, bad, and I didn't eat. You had to invent something to eat. There wasn't chicken, meat, [and] people began raising animals in their backyards, like pigs, in order to feed themselves. . . . I remember that when I began to work I earned 176 pesos and things were cheap. I was married and had a daughter and my wife didn't work and I gave her money. Things were cheap, not like now. A beer that costs ten pesos was sixty cents then. The price started going up: first it was sixty, then eighty, then one peso, and now it costs ten.[14]

As Purcival went on to discuss his frustrations around other changes, such as the elimination of overtime, he revealed that the volunteer work that he performs, such as hurricane repair work in Havana, is not truly voluntary; rather, it's what he and others refer to as *oblivoluntario*, obligatory labor under the guise of volunteer work. The consequences of not participating are such that participation might as well be mandatory. He indicated that a certain unspoken coercion was exercised in achieving mass participation in the revolutionary process as a whole because employment depended upon it. Perhaps Purcival was disgruntled prior to the economic crisis, but the events after 1989 hammered the last nail into the coffin of his revolutionary zeal.

For Carmen, whose father had belonged to the Communist Party of the 1950s and whose family was known as revolutionary, the Special Period did not lead her to cease her activism. On the contrary, it seems that as a community leader, she was in the thick of things, trying to find solutions for the many problems that became increasingly bleak. She recalled:

> Yes, things were very difficult and a lot of people didn't understand how to resist. They abandoned the country in rafts, swimming, though there are sharks in the sea, because they felt desperate. . . . It was difficult. There wasn't anything to eat. We washed our clothes with salt and baking soda and a plant called *mabita*. A moment arrived when there was so much need that there wasn't soap, shampoo, things to wash clothes and our bodies. . . . I was the delegate of the Poder Popular and had to talk a lot about what was happening, about the population. . . . We had to learn how to invent. It was really, really hard . . . [but] I had a lot of faith in the government.[15]

However, not everyone is as committed and energetic as Carmen. As *la lucha* (the struggle) has challenged *conciencia* (consciousness) to a duel in the daily lives of so many Cubans, the speeches, rallies, volunteer work, and posts in the mass organizations now seem to have little genuine appeal to most. For those who came of age during the Special Period, who have memory of neither the harshness of prerevolutionary inequalities nor the effervescence of revolutionary society in rapid transformation, the activities and organizations that captivated their parents' generation are met with apathy and disaffection if not contempt.

While people all over the world struggle every day against scarcity and deprivation, what appears to be unique about the Cuban case during the Special Period is the suddenness with which this occurred and the contrast of this situation with the kind of lives people lived *antes* when the deprivation was not as intense and they were, as Alden Knight, the Cuban actor, remarked, poor but equal (quoted in Pérez Sarduy and Stubbs 2000). The trauma lies not solely in the absence of consumer goods, but in the intense anxiety that resulted from being confronted with their own, and perhaps the revolution's, vulnerability and insecurity as well as the humiliation that accompanies such a fall. When the government adopted market-oriented strategies to save the economy from utter disaster, what some would argue as the inevitable did indeed occur. In exchange for being able to put hunger, if not some nutritional deficits, behind them, Cubans have had to contend with social transformations such as the reassertion of inequalities and erosion of the safety net provided by government subsidies.

More Critical Context: The Rise of el Extranjero

The resurgence of the tourism industry has had a monumental impact on Cubans' everyday life, most notably in cities that are popular among foreign visitors [*extranjeros*],[16] especially Havana and secondarily Santiago. The development of the tourism industry during the Special Period was a way to bring in much-needed foreign investment and currency, which introduced more lucrative employment and played a decisive role in economic stratification among Cubans.[17] It also revived a dormant social division emblematic of the colonial/neocolonial era: that between native and foreigner. Most Cubans are in a disadvantageous position vis à vis foreigners as, like other tropical tourist destinations, the contrast between the material world of tourists and those of Cubans is stark. What makes Cuba unique is that the desperation to acquire foreign currency sits in stark contrast to nationalistic revolutionary ideals and rhetoric.

Jineterismo, which as we noted in the introduction refers to prostitution strictly speaking and hustling more broadly, is the most often cited example of the social impact of tourism, but there are ways in which those not directly involved in the tourist industry feel the preferential treatment given to the foreign presence. I observed this one night when Lidia, a non-Anglo-Caribbean mestiza friend, and I went to the Culture House in Santiago, a club where Cubans used to go to enjoy art exhibits and performances such as live music and poetry readings. When we approached the entrance, we were told that they had instituted a policy whereby nonmembers could not enter unless accompanied by a foreigner, regardless of whether they could pay the entrance fee. Membership is available only to a select group of people in the arts and thus others who want to attend must find a foreigner to accompany them, which clearly encourages jineterismo. Lidia was furious. The Culture House, like many other clubs, restaurants, and places of entertainment, was populated by older white foreigners accompanied by young Black and brown Cubans. Though this changed in 2008, during the time of most of my field research many of the venues previously enjoyed by Cubans were turned over to tourists and the Cubans who accompanied them.[18]

Along with tourism, the depenalization of the dollar in August 1993 transformed everyday life in Cuba.[19] Although the rationing system was still in place during the time of my fieldwork,[20] relatively few goods provided at significantly subsidized rates appear on the *libreta* (state-issued ration card) or are available with any regularity. Furthermore, people frequently complain that these basic goods, such as rice, beans, sugar, oil, and cigarettes, are only enough to last for half of the month. Meat, poultry, fish, and vegetables are even less available, and most people have to find a way to supplement what the government provides with what is available through the black market and bartering (Scarpaci 1995).

A legal means of procuring goods that expanded during the reform process was through the government-controlled dollar stores, increasing the variety of consumer goods available to purchase in dollars. However, the peso exchange rate with the U.S. dollar has hovered around 25 to 1 since 1995. While this is a marked improvement from the astronomical inflation at the beginning of the crisis, when the rate was as high as 200 to 1, it still makes surviving on a peso salary next to impossible (Alonso and Lago 1995 Kildegaard and D. Fernández 1999). Given this reality, combined with the state's declining ability to provide essential goods, Cubans rely on mechanisms outside of state-controlled distribution to find the necessary commodities (Fernández, 1994). Therefore the informal economy and officially illegal activity, such as pilfering goods from work centers and participation in the black market, also flourished during the Special Period (Pérez López 1995; Mesa-Lago 2001; Ritter 2007).

The Cuban government has allowed for an expansion of the non-state or private sector of the economy, particularly self-employment or "trabajo por cuenta propia" (Pérez López 1995; Henken 2002; Corrales 2004). Countless examples of this activity existed in my daily life in Cuba. Activities ranged from people selling fruit on the sidewalks or out of horse-drawn carts, to the more hidden door-to-door peddling of goods, such as cigarettes and special diet items that appear on the *libreta* (like milk for young children and elders), to the more risky selling of stolen cigars. Indeed, this last example illustrates how such illegal activities supplemented legal ones as well as the new routes to advancement and roots of rising inequality: the white Cuban who had a job at a hotel and made money from selling stolen cigars to tourists, including those who stayed at the *casa particular* that he and his wife ran. Thus, it can be the case that one foreign-currency-earning endeavor supports others, deepening the chasm between those with access to CUC and those without.

This has had a particular impact on educated Cubans. In 2005, professionals who spent years of their lives achieving advanced degrees and training earned at most between 500 and 700 pesos per month, a healthy salary in the days before the collapse of the Soviet Union. When converted to dollars (now CUCs), this twenty to twenty-eight dollars fell quite short of an income needed to maintain their previous standard of living. As Zimbalist notes, "In Cuba's perverse economic environment . . . hard-currency rewards are useful in mitigating the distorted incentives that enable hotel chambermaids, bellhops, taxi drivers, prostitutes, and others working in the dollar-based economy to earn several times more than engineers, doctors, or manufacturing workers" (1994b:19). While this dynamic has moved many professionals to seek employment in the tourist industry or some form of self-employment, some are able to use their position to acquire foreign currency.[21]

Another option for accessing foreign currency and consumer goods that is available to Cubans is being sent on a mission abroad. Cuba is well known for its internationalism as well as its skilled workforce, and taking advantage of these strengths, the government exports professionals to countries in need of such expertise, especially in health care. The majority of the participants in this research had close family members, friends, neighbors, or coworkers who had been or were currently working outside of the country.[22] The cash and consumer goods that they sent and brought in upon their return, as mentioned by Eugenia above, were critical to alleviating material deprivation. Symbolizing survival, comfort, and possibility, el extranjero, both in the form of individual visitors and trips abroad, occupied a seat at the head of the table.

The Rescuing of Roots: El Centre and Beyond

As an extranjera attempting to avoid that categorization, I found that travel-ing between Santiago and Guantánamo in transportation reserved for Cu-bans was a bumpy and often stressful ride. Bad roads, close quarters, and fear of discovery meant that I arrived at my destination more exhausted than one would expect after a relatively short journey, something that my hosts usually remedied with the offer of a limonada and a seat at the kitchen table.

But when I made it to Pamela's house one late morning after taking a *bici-corre*, a bicycle carriage powered by young men whose worn T-shirts I would watch darken with sweat as they brought me to my destination, Pamela told me to put down my bags and go with her. There was an activity at El Centre. A group del extranjero was there. When we walked the half dozen blocks to the building, I was shocked to find that this was not a delegation of visitors from Jamaica or Barbados or St. Lucia in Guantánamo for their own rescu-ing of roots, but a group of Americans! While this might be fairly normal in Havana, Oriente sees far fewer extranjeros, particularly those from the U.S. And Guantánamo?! Olvídate! (Forget about it!)

In this case, Guantánamo was a stop on the route of a group of study-abroad students from the University of Massachusetts led by a Haitian-born professor whom I had initially misread as the Cuban *responsable* (an official guide) for the group. I would be hearing and speaking English for the after-noon as he enlisted me to give an impromptu talk on my research. They were there to learn about "the Cuban people" and the Centre was meant to expose them to one facet of "de dónde son los cubanos" (where Cubans are from). (This is also the title of a book examining Cuban origins.) Mine would be one presentation in a scheduled itinerary that included a lecture on the history of the migration and settlement in Cuba that emphasized the professional accomplishments of Anglo-Caribbean Cubans, as well as performances by a youth group's choreographed dance to soca[23] rhythms and a reggae singer singing along to a recording of Bob Marley's "Redemption Song."

The moment was made possible by the Centre's concerted efforts to estab-lish connections with el extranjero. The Young People's Department began in 1993 with 206 members and increased to over six hundred within four years. This activity not only stimulated the development of other associations throughout the island and the formation of a national network of Anglo-

"SUEÑO Y REALIDAD"
II SIMPOSIO INTERNACIONAL

" LA PRESENCIA DE LA CULTURA DE
LOS PUEBLOS ANGLOPARLANTES
EN CUBA "

Cine Teatro Guaso
Jueves 19 de nov. 1998 (a)

British West Indian Welfare Centre 34
Young People Department

Brindis por el 1er. Aniversario del
Departamento de Jóvenes
Descendientes.
Domingo 10 de Julio de 1994
Lugar: Centre
Hora: 5.30 P. M

PRECIO: 10'00
OK (b)

British West Indian Welfare Centre
GALA ARTISTICA POR EL DIA DE LA
CULTURA CUBANA
LA CULTURA CUBANA COMO CULTURA
UNIVERSAL"
Domingo 17 de Octubre de 1993
19
ENTRADA

Lugar: Teatro Guaso
Precio: $2.00 (pesos)

Nº 493 7 pm (c)

Figure 3.1. Mementos of revitalization: (a) flyer for the Sueño y Realidad (Dreams and Reality) Symposium held in 1998; (b) ticket for a toast to the Young People's Department of the British West Indian Welfare Centre on its first anniversary, 1994; (c) ticket to the Artistic Gala for Cuban Culture Day, "Cuban Culture as Universal Culture," held by the Young People's Department in 1993.

Figure 3.2. El Centre welcomes guests to discuss ties with the Caribbean Community (CARICOM).

Caribbean associations,[24] but also established the link with the Caribbean American Children's Foundation, the humanitarian organization founded by Alberto Jones, a Jamaican Cuban living in northern Florida.

Although the Cuban state approved of and monitored activities of the British West Indian Welfare Centre, it is a nongovernmental organization and as such is not sustained by government funding. Thus, in addition to the social, educational, and mutual aid activities of the group, El Centre performed outreach to the international community as a way to fund the programs that were being developed. Emblematic of such collaboration, Jones organized two African-American trips to Cuba that were hosted by Anglo-Caribbean organizations, and he initiated projects that targeted donations to schools and organizations in Santiago and Guantánamo, ensuring that some of those who will most likely benefit are of Black British West Indian descent.

The renewed interest in an Anglo-Caribbean origin was inseparable from the desire for material benefits. This ranged from something as basic as access to food at the events sponsored by the associations, to being eligible to receive donations such as badly needed hygiene products, medicines, and writing supplies, to the potential for contact with foreigners and travel abroad, experiences which in turn might lead to an alleviation of economic hardships.

One story of migration that appeared in the May 27, 2007, Jamaica Sunday *Gleaner Outlook Magazine* speaks directly to this link between personal and national or regional agendas. It featured Norma Ming, a Cuban whose grandparents were from Jamaica. Entitled "Norma Ming Connects with Her Roots," the story chronicles her 2003 "adventure to find her roots" after setting out for Jamaica with no known relatives, but having been helped by "a committee of Jamaican descendants [that is] set up with the aim of making contacts with relatives."[25] This story ends with Ming becoming a naturalized Jamaican citizen and working as a Spanish teacher in St. Thomas parish.

From this starting point of transnational collaboration, the Young People's Department of the Centre founded an international relations department in 1995 in order to build relationships with institutions and personalities from the countries represented in the membership of the Centre. With this objective in mind, they organized events at the Jamaican embassy in Havana as well as establishing a link with the University of the West Indies. There were plans to develop an exchange program between the UWI system and the University of Guantánamo, as the number of Cubans of Anglo-Caribbean descent and the existence of the Centre made Guantánamo the perfect site to anchor a bridge between Cuba and the English-speaking Caribbean. Edward, while president of the Young People's Department, traveled to the UWI campuses, meeting with leaders and intellectuals such as the late Rex Nettleford, Barry Chevannes, and Rupert Lewis, three of the four signatories of the letter to Fidel Castro quoted at the beginning of this chapter, about developing institutional connections with eastern Cuban educational institutions. During his presidency, Edward had visions of Guantánamo being the main hub in the communication and relationship between Cuba and the Caribbean, with Guantanameros of Anglo-Caribbean origin playing prominent roles in the interchange.

Although the initiative that would have built a bond between educational institutions in eastern Cuba did not develop into fruition, this connection between UWI and the Centre was maintained through the annual Intra-Caribbean Migration conference hosted by UWI Mona (Jamaica). Begun in 2000, this seminar series was coordinated by the Latin American-Caribbean Centre, and featured the "Cuban Connection" in 2001. Several members of the leadership of the Centre participated in this event, presenting papers, which were published by the Latin American Caribbean Centre from 2000 to 2006 and eventually an edited volume.

This seminar series was both example and outcome of the heightened interest in intraregional cooperation in Cuba after the collapse of the Soviet Union. In the early 1990s, this regional integration was noted to increasingly take the form of organizations that sprung out of civil society as an alternative to ties developed through formal political parties, signifying a widening of transnational relations in the region (Serbin 1994). David Lewis, Chief of Party for the Caribbean Policy Project of the Organization of Eastern Caribbean States, proclaimed that exclusive schemes in regional cooperation and integration were obsolete as civil society is taking a prominent role in a move toward cooperation that regional actors cannot afford to take (Lewis 1995:25). This desire for increased connection and its manifestation in the realm of grassroots organizations and NGOs is clearly reflected at the local level in the efforts of Anglophone Caribbean Cubans. Indeed, this desire would not likely have been able to bear fruit had there not been support at the national level.

Since the collapse of the Soviet Union, the formation of the European Union (EU), and the transition of North America and the Pacific into distinct trading blocs, the Caribbean faces the risk of greater marginalization. The result has been a renewed commitment to regional integration. Indeed, immediately following the watershed moment that signaled the momentary disappearance of any rival to U.S. global hegemony, one of the shifts that occurred was a move for the prominent Latin American powers at the time—Mexico, Venezuela, and Colombia—to become key actors in the geopolitical drama of English-speaking Caribbean states who were rapidly losing their already tenuous economic foothold in the world market (Serbin 1991). This transition would challenge the deeply entrenched linguistic, racial, cultural, and political barriers that have been held responsible for the balkanization of the region, boundaries that have notably been traversed by migrant laborers since the late nineteenth century (Serbin 1991; Giovannetti 2006b; Jackson 2006).

The intensification of Cuba-CARICOM relations was also emblematic of and a response to the global restructuring of alliances, of which NAFTA and the EU are key examples. Both of these alliances were seen as threats to the Caribbean's economic future due to possible erosion or termination of preferential treatment in trade and economic assistance (Núñez and Verba 1997:85). Thus, the greater integration of the Caribbean and Latin America has been one facet of a larger process of regional bloc creation (Cotman 2006).[26] New political realities such as the growth of regionalism and re-imposition of U.S. hegemony in the region drove integration at the national level (Basdeo 2005). The 1990 CARICOM Summit marked the beginning of establishing cooperative projects with Cuba; the general secretary of CARICOM made his first visit to Cuba that year. Although CARICOM refused Cuba's overtures to be admitted as a member, in 1993 it established a CARICOM-Cuba Joint Commission to assess the implications of changes in Cuba's economic position in the region. Furthermore, while a reintegrated Cuba is projected to have both trade-creating and trade-diverting effects on its neighbors (D. Lewis 1995), CARICOM countries have consistently advocated for Cuba's inclusion into the larger regional and international community.[27]

CARICOM and Cuba formalized their interest in strengthening their economic and diplomatic ties with the 2000 signing of the Cuba-CARICOM Trade and Economic Cooperation Agreement (renegotiated and signed in 2005), the convening of a triannual CARICOM-Cuba Summit (the first of which was in 2002), the establishment of December 8th as CARICOM-Cuba Day, the 2005 signing of the CARICOM-Cuba Cultural Cooperation Agreement, and the 2006 opening of Cuban embassies in Antigua, St. Vincent, and Dominica.

One facet of this relationship—articulated as based in "common cultural ties" and a similarly vulnerable position in the geopolitical hierarchy—involves the exchange of Cuba's significant human capital for CARICOM's pledge of economic cooperation and solidarity. At the 2005 CARICOM-Cuba Summit, Fidel Castro said that 10,502 Caribbean citizens had received free medical treatment as a part of the Operation Miracle ophthalmic program, 1,142 Cubans were performing voluntary service in CARICOM countries, and nearly 2,000 students were studying in Cuba, with 3,318 having completed their studies there, some on scholarships offered by the Cuban government (Bennett 2005). Cuba is reportedly also helping CARICOM countries to observe better energy conservation practices by donating energy-saving light bulbs that have saved the region US$193 million.[28] In addition, with the CARICOM-Cuba Cultural Cooperation Agreement, Cuba and CARICOM states pledged to continue and expand their connections—particularly in the areas of health, sports, engineering, education, culture, and the fight against the spread of HIV/AIDS.[29]

It is this aspect of Cuban foreign policy that Nettleford and colleagues (2009) acknowledge in their cautious critique of Cuba's silencing of antiracist activists on the island. In their challenge of the government's handling of dissent evident in the allegedly unjust jailing of a peaceful antiracist activist, they write, "As long standing supporters of the Cuban Revolution and its government who have always upheld Cuba's right as a sovereign nation to live free of foreign interference and admired its progress in health and education for its people, we are deeply concerned that the well-known director of the Juan Bruno Zayas Health and Human Rights Centre . . . was arrested, beaten and imprisoned since July 2009 on a charge of stealing two bags of cement" (Nettleford et al. 2009). Approaching this critique from a place of solidarity, this letter relies upon the foundation of subjugation that Jamaica and Cuba share, identifying the freedom of expression as the point of departure. If Jamaica had prohibited public assembly and protest, there would be no Bob Marley, they argue, and in so doing allude to the complex relationship between the state and subject formation.

Racism and Revitalization: Converging and Diverging Personal, National, and Regional Agendas

People of Anglo-Caribbean origin have certainly not been alone in searching out linkages outside of Cuba. Indeed, this was an individual and national strategy to survive the crisis and continues to be indispensable. One of the most significant consequences of the reforms has been the intensified movement of people, material goods, and ideas between Cuba and the non-Soviet world, including most notably those Cubans in diaspora. The opening mandated by the economic crisis offered an opportunity for reconnections that was seized by Cubans laying claim to Spanish, Chinese, and Jewish identities. The work of Kathy Lopéz (2009, 2013) and Martin Tsang (2014) on the revitalization and reconfiguration of Chineseness in contemporary Cuba as well as Ruth Behar's (2002) hauntingly beautiful documentary on Jews in Cuba are among the few investigations that approach the question of ethnic identity in the contemporary period. The Jews of Cuba whose religion "has been kept alive in Cuba through the efforts of Jews in Canada, Mexico, and Argentina" experienced a revival as a result of the influx of humanitarian aid and interest on the part of American Jews (Behar 2002; 2007). Similarly, Havana's Chinatown, once the largest in Latin America, has been transformed into a thriving neighborhood and tourist destination due to foreign investment facilitated by the Cuban government, with some Chinese Cubans reaping remarkable economic rewards as a result (Tsang 2014). In both cases, those who have laid claim to Chinese and Jewish ethnic categories are also of African descent. Indeed, Tsang's research focuses on what he terms African and Chinese diasporic cross-fertilization in the religious sphere, and Behar's documentary depicts Jewish Cubans across the color continuum, featuring a brown-skinned boy anxiously awaiting migration to Israel that is facilitated by the Israeli government (Behar 2002).

Similar to Chinese and Jewish Cubans, Anglo-Caribbean Cubans are the product of "continued diasporas and intercultural adaptations," and assertions of connection occurred in the context of crisis and opportunity. While the Anglo-Caribbean Cuban revitalization had not enjoyed the same success by the early years of the twenty-first century, it did offer an alternative, and a complement for some, to the more visible and often illegal, stigmatized activities available to other Cubans. These activities have been racialized, providing a new arena in which old, enduring associations between Blackness and criminality have been empowered (de la Fuente 2001a; Blue 2007).

In this context, at the personal and local level in Santiago and Guantánamo, there were several related reasons for the reinvigoration of this connection between Cuba and the English-speaking Caribbean. The early period of the crisis generated an intense sense of insecurity, desperation, and uncertainty that was based upon material deprivation as well as a questioning of the ideological foundations upon which Cuban society had been built since 1959. In response to this vacuum, people needed to come together around something that provided a sense of strength and history in addition to, if not beyond, Cuban revolutionary history. Related to this is the importance of the mutual aid tradition of ethnic associations.[30] Members of the resurgent associations pooled their resources and helped people of English-speaking Caribbean origin who were in more dire need, such as the elders of the community who suffered considerably from the ravages of the Special Period. Given that the Cuban state's ability to provide sufficient material support was seriously compromised, stepping in and doing what they could to help seemed to be somewhat empowering.

Blue Mountain Association in Santiago, also founded during the Special Period, existed as a separate entity but collaborated closely with the British West Indian Welfare Centre. Of the association's founding, one if its leaders, Melvina, recalled that when she went to an event honoring dedicated community members of the previous era at El Centre in Guantánamo, she saw the name of her grandmother as one of the honorees. She took pride in this legacy and was inspired to spearhead the establishment of an association in Santiago.[31] She contacted everyone she knew and word spread throughout the community. Initially, different people in the organization were responsible for the descendants in each neighborhood of the city, and these representatives reported back regarding who was ill, and who needed what.

However, with the rise of the associations and their ties to el extranjero, it became difficult to separate the rescuing of roots from the rescuing of one's standard of living. As Melvina recalled, "Some people who had not been raised as jamaicanos and only wanted things and came from poor neighborhoods to join the association . . . [and] people who were unknown were investigated. . . . People after the third generation were not accepted into the association."[32] Initially, the people who were known members of the community formed the association. But after the call was put out more broadly through the media—a radio program in the case of Blue Mountain Association—the process of selection ensued. Those who were not known had to bring in a passport or identification that proved that they were descendants. Melvina justified the exclusion of applicants who were poorly behaved, people who had been in jail, known homosexuals, and whites[33] by saying that they did not follow the ways of their ancestors.[34]

Melvina recalled that this was a time when different ethnic associations in Santiago came into being and that their domain was the Caribbean *and* African sectors within Cuban culture. As such, they participated in planning the Festival del Caribe, a week-long celebration of the Caribbean that is sponsored by the Casa del Caribe, where members of the association presented papers, attended meetings, and worked at events such as the Caribbean Expo. All of this gave those who participated access to foreigners in the recently transformed social landscape.

Certainly some have taken advantage of the institution to further their own personal agendas. Several of my interlocutors were dismayed by those in leadership who they believed were allowing the Centre to decline because they were invested in accessing the opportunity to make contacts abroad (through attendance at the Intra-Caribbean Migration seminar in particular) rather than building the institution. In spite of this, when asked about the resurgence of interest, Edward opined that this resurgence was not exclusively materially based. He stated, "There are different motivations. . . . [When it began] remember that this was the Special Period in '93; the people lacked something to fill them spiritually and the Centre was born with an enormous force, with a great quality in its activities and this had an impact on the society. Of course . . . when [the descendants] listened and saw that this had quality, they saw a possibility of participating, that they could join, you would see group after group after group after group of people joining."[35] Edward was joined by other participants in his understanding that the real crisis of the Special Period that led to people coming together was a spiritual one, as this was also one of the explanations that people gave for the rise in religious participation.

However, many of the people in Guantánamo with whom I spoke had decreased their involvement with the Centre because of the tensions around access to resources, as well as the decline in activities organized by the current leadership. My interview with Ruth, who had been active in the Centre as well as All Saints Church and the Sisters of Ruth lodge, was particularly telling. It began with her explaining that her mother was born in St. Ann's, Jamaica, but migrated to Banes with her aunt who raised her. In her early twenties, her mother answered the call of Guantánamo and obtained a job as a domestic in the naval base. When I began to explore her involvement in community institutions, she lamented their decline:

> Now, the young people have left it [the Centre] but before, the older people obligated them to go; now you can't make them. Although the older people, those who went to the church, had the young people go with them, but now they don't: they have an exam, they have this, they have that, . . . and this way it's being lost. Because many, I tell you because I was secretary [at the time], many of the young people who entered [during the revitalization of the 1990s], entered with a different mentality. . . . When there was the boom in the Centre, they began to

think that this was a way that they could travel. . . . The Centre helped
a lot in . . . locating the family and making contact, so people said that
"Oh, I have an aunt, an uncle." . . . So, through the Centre, there were
those [who received] a letter of invitation and could go there, including descendants who have left who worked for the Centre. Before, this
didn't exist. . . .

   It was a beautiful thing . . . because I went there and connected with
the social life, recreational life—because for the most part only older
people go to the church. Upon entering the Centre, I was able to connect again with descendants, those who are truly . . . those who I know.
There are those who were born and went off to school and when they
come and say "I'm the daughter of so and so" and "Oh, you're so and
so's son, she went to school with me." You see? . . . There are those who
have left but their children are here, their children, their grandchildren,
their spouses—it's very beautiful. And also, people from the U.S. had
the opportunity to visit us, people from Barbados came, from Jamaica,
from England. . . . [I go to the Centre], but I don't know, it's not the
same. Something has been lost. This thing of the "boom" has been lost.
I don't know what happened. Now people of my age, we are attending,
but very few of the youth.[36]

The issue of ulterior motives of some members and the related disillusionment with the revitalization was reiterated in a conversation with Eugenia
about her understanding of the resurgence of interest in family origins. "Let
me tell you something," she confided. "The problem is of traveling. In the association, for example, the people [whom the association hosted] came from
Jamaica, from Barbados, [and could] send an invitation.[37] [People seeking
membership] wanted to leave. Everyone's looking for a way to travel. . . .
Look here, never, never have Jamaicans been *tan tan de viajado* [so interested
in traveling]. My grandmother only went to Jamaica once. . . . No one was
thinking about this and what happened is that everyone is looking for their
mother or father now; this I don't understand."[38]

   A revealing exchange might shed light on the way that Cuba's racial and
economic climate may be influencing this motivation to leave. One afternoon during the daily task of separating stones from the rice, Melvina and I
began talking about people who attempt to get the citizenship of their parents or grandparents who immigrated to Cuba. She said that she had actually

begun the application process for Jamaican citizenship but was stalled at a particular point in the bureaucracy. When I asked her why she wanted to get Jamaican citizenship, if it was so that she could travel, she told me that that was not it, that in order to travel, she would need a letter of invitation, money for a ticket, and a place to stay in Jamaica. She doubted that she could get a letter of invitation because she's not close to her family there; moreover, Jamaica, she said, is expensive and there is a lot of violence. "So, why get Jamaican citizenship?" I reiterated. "In case something happens in the midst of things," she said rather cryptically. "Something like what?" I pressed on. At that point, Melvina smiled a smile that indicated "Ah, there's so much for you to understand," and replied, "When he dies, there will be trouble," punctuating this phrase by brushing the second and third finger of her left hand against the forearm of her right.[39] I had quickly learned that this gesture referred to us: the Blacks. It is a way of talking about race in silence and with a drama that is characteristically Cuban. This and other comments that people made as well as my own observations led me to conclude that the new ways in which racism is asserting itself, and the related insecurity that has emerged, were implicated in the effort to revive Anglo-Caribbean-Cubans' origins and reach out to individuals and institutions in the Anglophone Caribbean.

Deunes, the grandson of a Jamaican immigrant then in his thirties whom I quoted at the outset of this chapter, was equally as explicit as Melvina in identifying the problem of racial discrimination. Though a Rasta, an alternative and marginalized identity in Cuba, he conformed to some mainstream social expectations, primarily through maintaining a state job in a produce store and remaining committed to close relationships with neighbors and family. However, he was quite willing to offer a nuanced critique of revolutionary society. One afternoon while we were discussing the problems of the dual economy, he said that Black people are left out of the tourist industry and the dollar economy. Though he didn't have a clear explanation for why that was, when I asked if it was because of racism, he said, as if he were disabusing me of the idea that Cuba is a racial democracy, "Racism does still exist here. It's not that there is any direct rejection or abuse, but indifference. . . . If I go to a store, they say there's nothing there or they don't have what I need. . . . If someone who looks like me, a Black man, but doesn't have dreadlocks, goes into the store, they don't have what he needs, either. But when a white man goes into the store, the clerk says 'Oh, let me see what we have."[40] Thus, his perception is that discrimination is an obstacle to Black people getting their needs met regardless of appearance, that their Blackness itself would deter clerks from attempting to help them.

Several of my interlocutors recounted recent incidents of discrimination and manifestations of racist attitudes. Isabel, who held a supervisory position in a communications firm that is a joint venture with France, observed that it is not only her Blackness but her being a Black *woman* that impacts her work experience. She was one of the heads of her department, and most of her coworkers were women. She said, "You see that they don't like to see a woman as a leader and worse a Black woman; it's not open but you can always tell that it's there. Women always have to defend themselves to move forward and you see this in the overwhelming majority of jobs in Cuba. You always have to fight because they always want to put in the white woman, the little pretty woman, the one whose father is so-and-so. You see how many well-educated young Black women there are and you don't see them in the best jobs."[41]

Melvina concurred. "The discrimination persists, and Blacks have to fight against this. For instance, when a Black woman with the best marks loses a job at the airport to a white woman with a lower mark, the Black woman has to write the Party and fight for the position. The same is true for jobs in the beer and rum factory that pay in dollars. And, when a Black person has such a job, they are harassed so that they leave and a white person can take the job. With the joint ventures, the foreign companies wanted white Cubans and they removed Blacks from the job. This was not Cuba's fault; they were at a disadvantage because the economy was so bad. There are the 'TRD' stores[42] that are Raúl's stores and they hire Blacks there; they think that stores that are Cuban should hire Black workers."[43] Caridad, comparing the presence of Black people in retail across time, reflects, "Before the revolution, in the stores, there weren't people of color working. After the triumph of the revolution, there were more than there are now. The state can't dominate everything so what happens is that friends hire their friends and whites have more personal relationships with each other. . . . White people always think of you as Black regardless of how they treat you; they always think that they're superior. There are neighbors who don't like to see a person hold their head high."[44]

Winton, who was in his seventies and worked on the naval base before the revolution, also had the advantage of offering a perspective informed by his experience of white Cubans and Americans and of racial attitudes before and after the revolution. He recounted working as a busboy at a restaurant on the base: "They [the navy personnel] were from the South. They don't like colored people and when they're drunk it's worse. And when the senior server went to get a tip, they say, 'Get out from here, goonie.' They curse at you and call you bad names. They didn't like to see them earning money. There are bosses who don't like people of color anywhere." Winton then gave his opinion of contemporary race relations, proclaiming that "there is still racism; you always see the difference. White people are with Black people, but it's not from the heart, it's because they have to be. They're waiting for Fidel to fall."[45] Here, Winton expressed a sentiment that others alluded to: namely, that Fidel's charismatic leadership is the only force preventing white racism from being fully unleashed upon Cubans of color.

This is similar to what Melvina expressed about her motivation for seeking Jamaican citizenship: "Fidel is the only thing that keeps the racists in Cuba from coming to the surface; white people here will eat our bones. Fidel is the only thing keeping this from happening but he is going to die, he has to die. White people do not like Black people here. You know, whenever you see on television students who sing or recite something, they always choose a white child. I remember when my daughter was a child and she came home asking why she never gets chosen to recite anything. They say that racism doesn't exist here, but that's a fairy tale. The only reason why things are not worse is because no one can disagree with Fidel."[46]

Diasporic Connections beyond the Special Period

Melvina's comments as well as the investment in intraregional diplomacy indicate the indispensable role of the state in the development of transnational diasporic connections and divergent motivations for such activity. Since the 1960s when Fidel declared Cuba to be an African-Latin nation, the revolutionary government has positioned itself as an ally of anticolonial, anti-imperial, anticapitalist, and antiracist struggles internationally. Indeed, the "Acting on Our Conscience" incident was so remarkable in part because it signaled a departure from the historical relationship between the Cuban government and African American intellectuals and activists, some of whom have considered the revolutionary project to be a beacon in the challenge to U.S. racial politics and economic policy at home and abroad.[47]

From harboring African American political prisoners such as Asata Shakur, to playing a decisive military role in the defeat of apartheid in South Africa, to already having medical personnel on the ground in Haiti when the 2010 earthquake hit, Cuba has been a champion of such struggles in word and deed. However, one of the ironies of contemporary Cuba is the coexistence of its staunch antiracist stance abroad and persistent racial discrimination on the island.

The revitalization of Anglo-Caribbean Cuban connection to the CARI-COM Caribbean is a case in which national and regional agendas overlap with the agendas of those at the local level. It is also one example of how certain types of diasporic relationships are made possible by the state at the same time that conditions in part created by the state (in the form of Special Period reforms) necessitate such connections. As Benson (2013) demonstrates in her analysis of linkages with African Americans in the 1960s, the revolutionary government is invested in certain types of diasporic relationships—for instance, with those who are politically radical rather than with the African American business class. Similarly, at a time of economic crisis and impending ideological isolation, linkages with the CARICOM Caribbean have been expedient for reasons that had nothing to do with race. On the contrary, Cubans of Anglo-Caribbean origin were in part motivated to make similar connections because of the insecurity that decidedly had a racial component.

In an article exploring the fissures between Latin America and the Caribbean, Shona Jackson argues that race is the largest barrier between these overlapping regions, and that the uneven relationship between Blackness and whiteness plays itself out in the region. She reasons that Fidel's declaring Cubans as an African-Latin people in 1966 and pledging support for struggling anticolonial movements "essentially provided a bridge for black (Afro-Creole) nationalism and predominantly 'white' Latin cultural nationalism, with their attendant discourses of créolité and mestizaje, to meet" (2006:29). Though her representation of Latin cultural nationalism is debatable in her exploration of why this bridge has failed to grow over the last forty years, the ways in which national racial ideologies and racial projects might be embedded in the process of regional cooperation is relevant. These aspects are likely worth review when considering Cuba-CARICOM relations as well as the limitations around institutionalized transnational connections initiated by Cubans of English-speaking Caribbean descent.

While there are various obstacles or at least limitations to regional integration,[48] challenges to the development of Anglophone Caribbean organizations in Cuba might shed light upon the nature of these limitations. As of my last field research trip in 2009, I found a lot of internal division at the Centre around donations, the opportunity to travel to conferences, and accusations of mishandling of resources. The association in Santiago had failed to revitalize after its demise in 2001. Some informants reported that this was a result of the discord around dividing the resources that were introduced from abroad while others were under the impression that the government, in an effort to curtail the proliferation of associations and the accompanying contact with foreigners, directed them either to close or to operate under the direction of the Centre in Guantánamo.

The proposal to develop connections between the educational institutions was stalled. According to Edward, there was a lack of interest in the project on the part of the then-president of the university in Guantánamo, who didn't move on this in spite of a letter of invitation to the UWI campuses from Rex Nettleford to pursue this project; apparently, he opted to pursue connections with Peru, Brazil or Spain rather than the Anglophone Caribbean.

Edward's comments illuminate the potential limitations of these connections at both the local and regional levels. In discussing these plans for linking eastern Cuban and CARICOM institutions, Edward explained his perception of the university president's decision to let the relationship with Anglophone Caribbean universities wither. Pointing to the ignorance on the part of many who don't know the high caliber of these universities, that its students have been trained in the British system and that it boasts of internationally renowned faculty-scholars, he suspected that racism and regionalism were responsible. In Edward's appraisal, the president undervalued and dismissed the small Black island nations of the Caribbean.[49]

Whether this was indeed the case or not, Edward's articulation of the situation as emblematic of the assumption of Black inferiority pervasive in Cuban society and of where CARICOM states sit in relation to Cuba in the geopolitical pecking order is quite telling. It indicates a link between the conditions that heightened misrecognition and the emergence of a diasporic subjectivity that enables a shift in identity politics. The Special Period and subsequent transformations in revolutionary Cuban society enabled Anglo-Caribbean Cubans to establish, assert, and affirm a connection to the English-speaking Caribbean, past and present. It provided an opening for reimagining themselves as occupying multiple spaces of belonging and, in so doing, to challenge the resurgence of racial inequality that has come with reform.

This study of the African Anglo-Caribbean diaspora—subject and agent of multiple dislocations—interprets the layers and layering of diasporic space that involves erasure and a rewriting: diaspora as palimpsest. One feature of this layering concerns time. Cubans of Anglo-Caribbean origin are part of the dispersal of people of African descent during both the transatlantic and post-transatlantic slave trades, thus complicating temporal categorizations of diaspora. Palmer (2000) distinguishes between epochs in which dispersals of people from Africa occurred, beginning with the original migration of humans out of the continent and continuing to contemporary movements of Africans to Europe, to the Americas, and beyond. There is also compelling work that questions the emphasis on Atlantic crossings (Zeleza 2005), the lack of differentiation between the African and Black diasporas (Malkalani 2009), and the role of international institutions in producing diaspora (Clarke 2010). My investigation of the African Anglo-Caribbean diaspora in Cuba has led me to interrogate the temporal, ideological, and spatial boundaries of diaspora by considering it as a strategy of existence through connection that extends beyond national space. This strategy was inspired by rising racial inequalities in Cuba after the Soviet period and can be abandoned or augmented.

In this analysis, we see how diaspora—the national and the transnational—operate simultaneously rather than being mutually exclusive, discrete categories of belonging and generators of particular practices. In the case of Anglo-Caribbean Cubans "rescuing their roots" during the Special Period, at the same time that the Young People's Department was involved in developing linkages with CARICOM, these ties were sanctioned and supported by the state. While many were politically engaged in the revolutionary process and embraced their Cubanness, they also engaged in the diasporic practices of remembering ([re]membering), of adopting an idealized view of those who came before them as articulated through the matrix of respectability, of ambivalent belonging, and of voyages of return. In addition, woven through diaspora, the national and the transnational, is connection as strategy, as utilitarian, as a way to navigate the increasingly challenging economic circumstances and precarious political position of contemporary Cuba.

Race continues to be a central issue influencing and informing the trajectory of Cuban national and diasporic politics; the circumstances of Black and mulatto Cubans are a barometer with which to judge the success or failure of the revolution. Those who unilaterally and unequivocally condemn the revolution point to the suffering of Blacks under the current government while those who champion the revolutionary project highlight the strides toward racial equality on the island as well as the role Cuba has played as defender of Black liberation struggles and donor of military and technical assistance to majority Black countries in the Caribbean and Africa. As a highly charged, polarizing subject, race, or perhaps more accurately, persistent racism, has been best avoided.

4

"Somos Negros Finos" (We Are Refined Blacks)

Rescuing Roots as an Assertion of Respectable Blackness

Caridad, a Cuban-born daughter of Jamaican immigrants in her early seventies at the time of my field research, was once a teacher who gave private English classes to middle- and upper-class Cubans before the 1959 revolution. She would often pepper her Spanish with phrases or commentary in English. In one instance, while gazing proudly at the attractive, college-educated daughter of her close friend and my principal interlocutor, Caridad said, "Ella es una negra de salir."[1] Then, turning to me, Caridad remarked in English, "You know, not all niggers are the same."[2]

Aside from being taken aback by her use of the term "nigger," I was struck by the sharpness with which her brief comments reflected an emerging theme in my investigation—namely, the perception that Anglo-Caribbean immigrants and their descendants in Cuba had a way of being Black that was different from those who did not come from the English-speaking Caribbean, and that this difference was an elevating one. As detailed in chapter 1, I was repeatedly told that los jamaicanos were clean, respectful, disciplined, pious, hardworking, invested in education and self-betterment, and proud of being Black. Regardless of a shared racial identity with other people of African origin, they perceived themselves to be distinct from both Haitian immigrants, who they suggested were largely illiterate, confined to agricultural labor, and devoted to *brujería*,[3] and from Black and working-class Cubans,[4] who used foul language and were loud, crude, and prone to disorder.[5]

I propose that the construction and maintenance of a distinct Blackness such as this, one that is rooted in civilizational discourse, is an alternative to ideologies of race mixture and whitening. Its persistence in the contemporary period points to the local impact of globalized inequalities as well as

the ways in which revolutionary society fell short of its objective to eliminate racism. It also illustrates the asymmetries that characterize assertions of
diasporic subjectivity. My interlocutors' narratives of Anglo-Caribbean cultural citizenship and experiences of racism provide a window into how and
under what conditions these asymmetries are reproduced. In this chapter,
I analyze these narratives, provide a view from my own position as a Black
ethnographer in Cuba, and conclude by envisioning more productive ways
of affirming Blackness that do not fall prey to racial and cultural discourses
of mixture, hybridity, or essentialism.

Negotiating Mestizaje

Immigrants from the English-speaking Caribbean to Cuba came from color-
and class-stratified societies in which their efforts at survival and self-improvement were frustrated at every level, and where dark skin was a liability
and African cultural practices were demonized by an aggressive campaign to
infuse middle-class Victorian values into the culture of the colonies (Hoetnick 1967; Bryan 1991; Moore and Johnson 2004). Furthermore, cleavages
within British West Indian social structure were articulated in terms of culture as well as color and, I argue, manifested themselves in the economic and
political lives of immigrants to Cuba.

   As discussed in chapter 1, race was at the epicenter of questions of national
identity in postcolonial Cuba, and the fate of the nation was closely linked to
its racial composition. The fear of a Black numerical and cultural takeover of
the nation, which had lingered on since the triumph of the Haitian Revolution in 1804, fueled the maligning of Blackness and persecution of African
cultural practices as well as the resistance to Caribbean immigration. As in
other Latin American nations, Cuba promoted *blanqueamiento* (whitening)
through interracial sex primarily among the lower classes and between white
men and Black or mixed women, popular and legislative support for European immigration, and protests against Black immigration (Sánchez 1988;
González Suárez 1987; Martinez-Alier 1989; Chomsky 2000; Naranjo Orovio
1997). These measures are a clear indication of the devaluation of Blackness
in spite of, or perhaps as an integral component of, Cuba's national ideology
of racial equality and fraternity.

   One of the flaws in ideologies of racial and cultural mixture is the failure to highlight the hierarchies within and between so-called hybridities. In her discussion of the relationship between hybridity and social inequality, Shalini Puri makes the point that, in spite of the multiple named identities that emerge from the prism of mixture, "an implicit, unacknowledged, and untheorized elevation of one hybrid identity occurs" (2004:23). She argues that the role of what she refers to as "manifestos" of hybridity in the Caribbean and Latin America is precisely to displace the issue of social equality with the rhetoric of cultural equality (2004:50).[6] Thus, the paradox between the reality of racial discrimination and the ubiquitous narrative of racial equality can be eluded. Declarations of the presence and value of cultural mixture obscure the fact that some flavors of the Cuban *ajiaco* (stew)[7] overpower and subordinate others, and that different cultures continue to collide and re-create themselves in the context of systemic inequality.

In Cuba, as in much of Latin America, the celebration of cultural hybridity coexists with a belief in Black inferiority. Resistance to the presence, value, and/or recognition of Black people as equal contributors to the nation has been justified and fomented by characterizations of them as lazy, diseased, sexually available/predatory, brutish, untrustworthy, loud, morally degenerate, prone to criminality, unintelligent, superstitious, and subject to violence and savagery.[8] Along with the notion embedded in ideologies of racial equality that class, not race, is the basis for discrimination against people of African descent, the conflation of such qualities with Blackness and African cultural practices supports a cultural or behavioral explanation for Black people's lower economic status and marginalization within a modern nation.[9] While, in theory, the route to equal inclusion can be achieved through a shift in personal conduct, one that not coincidentally overlaps with middle- and upper-class status, education and the adoption of middle-class culture do not guarantee Cubans of color economic security and social legitimacy.[10]

Los Jamaicanos in Cuba: Creating an Affirmative Blackness

In informal conversations as well as in my more structured interviews, the projection of respectability and a desire to demonstrate that not all Black people are the same was a consistent element of my interlocutor's discourse on race and racism.[11] As I argued in chapter 1, in the prerevolutionary period, an English-speaking Caribbean identity served to both legitimize and assert a respectable Blackness in the context of the Negrophobia of Cuban society. According to my interlocutors, the full roster of attributes and practices that characterize Anglophone Caribbean culture as they live it and observe it in their family members includes being soft spoken, well dressed, respected and respectful, particularly of elders; being honest, trustworthy, and proud; abstaining from habitual alcohol and tobacco use; being invested in education, frugal, independent, religious, unified, and organized (in the sense of community and personal habits); being strict in childrearing practices, responsible, serious, and maintaining a spirit of self-improvement; being observant of mealtime etiquette (saying grace, eating as a family group at table, using a fork and knife, and enforcing children's raising of hands before sitting); being observant of a particular way of speaking and saying "good morning" and "good evening"; knowing natural medicine; being cautious about eating or drinking anything prepared by outsiders; being intolerant of disorder or things done poorly; showing calm and reserve; being educated and cultured; remaining mainly inside the house rather than out in the street; men's being sure to wear shirts in public; being punctual; avoiding profanity; and being proud of being Black.

The single most common umbrella trait that people indicated distinguishes Anglo-Caribbean immigrants and their Cuban born children is *la crianza* or "the upbringing." Both immigrant parents and teachers were notoriously strict, meting out corporal punishment quite liberally. To illustrate the strictness of Jamaicans, Winton recounted the fear he felt when, as a twenty-two-year-old adult, he anticipated his mother's response to his coming home late. He also recalled that, at a much younger age, his aunt would beat him if he even looked at her fruit trees because she thought he was going to steal the fruit. He remembered having to pray six or seven times a day and that he would get hit if he didn't.[12] Melvina was also very vocal about the strictness of her father and grandmother, as well as so many of the adults that peopled her childhood. In her opinion such fierce enforcement of rules caused emotional injury to some members of her generation, though she did feel that there were many benefits to la crianza.

Such benefits overwhelmed any negative assessment of the childrearing practices in other accounts. Carlitos expressed a belief that jamaiquinos taught their children to be honest and respectful, to not rob and disrespect. He said, "The jamaiquinos, the true jamaiquinos and not the improvised ones, raise their children in a very distinct and serious manner that isn't easy because they could punish or instruct you with a look and that's it."[13] Rubén, who was adamant that the revolution had eliminated any differences between Cubans, said he had a very "correct" upbringing, that his family was very cultured.[14] Isabel shared her belief that their upbringing was very good in that it prepared the children for life and how to behave themselves in society. She believed that her upbringing was essential in her success. Though quick to say that Cubans also have a good upbringing, she identified that the "jamaiquino" upbringing, which includes an emphasis on punctuality and a proper way of doing things, prepared her for the responsibility she has in her job. By her account, she is viewed by others at work as a lady, *una negra fina*, as is demonstrated by people apologizing after cursing in her presence.[15]

Rubén explained that the immigrants' manner of raising children with respect is a custom or tradition brought from the English-speaking countries.[16] He was not alone in his articulation of a connection between British colonial culture and the practices common in their community. For instance, Dr. Ruth shared her belief that the insistence on doing things in the right way was a European characteristic and that "the jamaicanos have many European characteristics."[17] Melvina, reflecting about the strength and borderline brutality of Jamaican women, remarked that these are byproducts of being colonized peoples. Perhaps an indication of the change in status, the child-rearing practices of descendants tend to be less strict and less influenced by factors such as the origin of one's spouse and the loss of parental control over children's upbringing through the revolutionary process (as discussed in the preceding chapter). Even now though, some children and grandchildren of British West Indian immigrants resisted having their children—particularly female children—participate in activities that would require them to be away from home in the interest of maintaining tight control over their activities.[18]

Though characterizing Anglophone Caribbean culture in contrast to that which was "typically" Cuban, most of my interlocutors did not explicitly frown upon non-Anglophone Caribbean Cubans. The biggest exception to this was Hortencia, who openly expressed distaste for certain aspects of Cuban culture. In one instance, she remarked, "Cubans eat with a spoon rather than a fork and knife, [and] they don't eat together at the same time. . . . A spoon is for soup and beans but Cubans are like pigs, they do things the easiest way that there is, they don't have culture."[19] She went on to say that she's been to Cuban households and spoke with distaste about Cuban habits such as eating before others, eating in front of guests without a shirt on, or eating in front of the television. She claimed that she was not accustomed to these behaviors, and, indeed, over the several months that I spent living in her home, I did not witness such lax mealtime etiquette.

When I challenged her about her attitudes toward non-Anglophone Caribbean Cubans and her use of negative stereotypes, Hortencia conceded that there may be Cubans who don't behave like this but insisted it was unlikely because people are easily corrupted by bad habits or manners. She explained that she's been to other Anglo-Caribbean Cuban households and noted a consistency among them.[20] Thus, where Cubans were loud, always making some disturbance in the street,[21] jamaicanos were reserved and private; where Cubans lacked manners and formalities, jamaicanos were respectful, neat, and ordered; where Cubans didn't know how to use a fork and knife and sit at the table for meals, jamaicanos were proprietors of mealtime etiquette; where Cubans (and Haitians) were obsessed with *brujería*, jamaicano religiosity was manifested in their primary adherence to Protestantism and other denominations of Christianity.

Interestingly, many who were married to non-Anglo-Caribbean Cubans remarked that their spouses had adopted Anglo-Caribbean traits either because they had grown up around Anglo-Caribbean families, as was the case with Isabel's husband, or they took on these traits as a result of their union. Lester, whose wife is not of Anglo-Caribbean origin, claimed that these differences aren't evident because in unions with Cubans, the Cuban partner "rose to the moral level of the descendant." Every family is different, he said, but this is generally what happened. Reluctant to say that Cubans behave poorly, but insistent that there is always a trait among descendants that is different, such as the habit of greeting people, Lester recalled that his father also indoctrinated his Cuban mother, who, as a result, "had very good morals, stayed home all of the time, and supported this upbringing."[22]

Coming from a culturally mixed Black family and having lived on the U.S. East Coast where there are greater concentrations of people of Anglo-Caribbean immigrant origin, I found this narrative of moral and cultural superiority not only unsettling but also familiar. This tendency to adopt, or at least gravitate toward, negative attitudes about the native population is certainly not unique to Anglo-Caribbean Cubans. As I cited earlier, sociological and anthropological studies of Caribbean immigrants in Central America and the United States indicate this to be the case. Not surprisingly, the distancing from and, in some cases, demonization of a Black American or mestizo Nicaraguan, Belizean, or Honduran population offers economic and social rewards. In the Cuban case, prior to the 1959 revolution, such distinction offered the possibility of legal protection and better employment opportunities. However, what about during the Special Period? What, if any, material basis existed to support this sense of elevated difference evident in my interlocutors' narratives?

Ordering Blackness

As immigrant experiences in other Latin American countries as well as the United States and Britain testify, one of the factors that directs the fashioning of Black subjectivity is the presence of and relationships with other culturally distinct Black groups. In the case of English-speaking immigrants in Cuba, Haitians were one such group. As discussed in chapter 1, Haitian immigrants who entered Cuba in greater numbers, with fewer skills, and with a revolutionary reputation bore the brunt of the anti-immigrant hysteria of the late 1920s and 1930s. Giovanetti (2001) argues convincingly that the fact that Haitians continued to go to Cuba in large numbers after the economic depression and contraction of the labor market explains why they were targeted more than people from the Anglophone Caribbean. While this may be so, when focusing on the rationale provided to legitimize the brutal way in which they were expunged from the country, it becomes clear that they, in comparison with English-speaking Caribbean immigrants, were "Blackened."

As McLeod observes, "Haitians ultimately faced greater discrimination because native Cubans perceived them to be less 'civilized' and more 'barbarous'—indeed, more 'African'—than British West Indians" (2000:15). Within an ideological framework in which "whiteness is the symbol of ideal legal and moral citizenship . . . [and] depends upon the 'Blackening' of less desirable immigrants" (Ong 1996:742), Haitians were situated closer to the racially Black/culturally African pole that lay at the bottom of the social and economic ranking.[23] Anglophone Caribbean immigrants were "whitened" in the sense that they were perceived as more civilized and modern.[24] The employment of a cultural lens through which to evaluate racial categorization, in this case how groups and individuals within the same racial category are ordered, illuminates the process of Black subject-making. The perceived cultural differences between Black people from the Anglophone Caribbean, those from Haiti, and those native to Cuba both constitute and inform Black subjectivities. Subjectivities and the process of subject-making involve not only race, but also culture, gender, class and other facets of self, engendering conflicting evaluations of people within the same racial or class category. The Blackness of Anglo-Caribbean immigrants professes not to be a mark of inferiority, as it is not accompanied by the band of degrading signifiers that plague Cubans both Black and poor. Thus, in theory, it serves to protect them from racialized psychological assault.

Anglo-Caribbean Cubans as Negros Finos

As I discussed in chapter 3, the Special Period provided an opening for a political and economic shift that allowed for and necessitated the reinvigoration of connections with the broader Caribbean. The crisis provoked this assertion of belonging in part because it also provided a wider opening for anti-Black attitudes and racial inequality to impact the lives of Cubans of color more profoundly. The resurgence of Anglo-Caribbean institutions and efforts on the part of Black Cubans of Anglo-Caribbean origin is intertwined with the exacerbation of racial discrimination during the Special Period. An Anglo-Caribbean-Cuban identity offers an alternative way of asserting Blackness, one that is respectable and devoid of folkloricization and the tropes of primitiveness that continue to shackle Blackness in the society's imaginary.

For instance, while acknowledging the progress that has been made as a result of revolutionary policies and the role of external forces in the erosion of racial inequalities, both Edward and Melvina exhibited a keen awareness of such inequalities, both historical and contemporary. It is no coincidence that they were influential presidents of the revitalized English-speaking Caribbean associations in Guantánamo and Santiago. This revitalization occurred at the height of the economic crisis. Their investment in Anglo-Caribbean identity and the revitalization of the institutions of their ancestors was in large part about claiming a space of decency and respectability for Black people who were pushed to desperate and more public measures to compensate for their recent disproportionate decline in standard of living.

Evident in their narratives about the associations, their families and communities, and current struggles is the insistence on demonstrating an alter-

native way of being Black, one that does not conform to degrading stereotypes. For instance, the photographs that Edward showed me illustrated the
presence of a vital Black community that had its own rites and rituals, ceremonies, wealth, and traditions. Emphasizing that West Indians were proud
as Black people, he clearly supports race consciousness. Melvina recounted
meetings and events sponsored by Blue Mountain, emphasizing the orderly,
respectable behavior of descendants. In one instance, they were invited along
with other ethnic associations to an event at ICAP (Instituto Cubano de
Amistad con los Pueblos [Cuban Institute of Friendship of the Peoples]).
She proudly stated that they remained dignified, unlike the Haitians who
behaved subserviently and the Spaniards who got intoxicated. To those who
consider Anglophone Caribbean descendants to act like whites, her response
was "No, I'm Black." This characterization, she felt, is an insult disguised as a
compliment.[25] Thus, she both rejected the racist ideology that asserts Black
homogeneity based on inferiority and refused to be "whitened" based on her
lack of conformity to racist stereotypes.

Such self-representations indicate a move on the part of people of Anglo-
Caribbean origin that situates their experiences at the heart of debates about
Black subjectivity. Blackness and racial politics in the twenty-first century
appear to be in a moment of transition. The late twentieth-century declaration of the social rather than biological basis of race by anthropologists and
other scientists was instrumental in fueling debates about how to understand
and interpret the concept of race and human heterogeneity.[26] Scholars have
been grappling with the basis, usefulness, meaning, and dangers of Blackness and its continued status as an essentialized category of belonging and an
organizing principle in the struggle against racial exclusion.[27] Of particular
interest here is how the presence of immigrants who bring distinct cultural
frameworks for understanding difference might change, challenge, or conform to existing national racial politics.[28]

One proposal for framing what at times is a disjuncture between the ways
in which Black immigrants and native Black populations interpret and experience a Black identity is that Black immigrants might be more inclined to
participate in a politics of deconstruction whereby class, culture, ideology,
and nationality are deployed in the challenge of national racial politics.[29]
Hintzen and Rahier, in their edited volume that examines racial politics
through self-ethnographies of Black immigrants to the United States, assert
that the politics of deconstruction "refers to tactical circumvention of the

status quo through participation in diffuse and alternative politics in other arenas of struggle" (2003:3). They juxtapose this political strategy with a structural politics of race, which also challenges the white supremacist status quo. However, where the politics of deconstruction accomplishes this—by destabilizing notions of a uniform Blackness developed within and circumscribed by the politics of race in the United States—a structural politics of race presumes a more monolithic, rigid interpretation of a particular Black subjectivity that has been located, structurally, at the bottom of the racial order, and that must provide the basis for personal and political alliances.

Some scholars are suspicious of the attention that the multiplicity of Black identities is garnering and are doubtful of its efficacy as a strategy for challenging white racial authority. They insist that disengaging the study of race and understandings of Black cultural production from politics, history, and economics constitutes a denial of the most salient factors that shape Black subjectivity (Noguera 2003; Robotham 2005). Propositions that privilege the diversity of Black subjectivity and disregard or underestimate the significance of a shared racial identity prove worrisome because structural factors such as institutionalized racism continue to impact the life chances of racialized subjects (Brodkin 2000; Harrison 1995; Mukhopadhyay 1997; Mullings 2005).

I am suggesting, however, that this is only an apparent paradox. Illuminating assertions of multiplicity can in fact render a more nuanced analysis of the workings of systemic inequality. Returning for a moment to Caridad's comments, one might argue that, in her declaring that "not all niggers are the same" and that a young, educated Black woman is worthy of occupying a place denied her based on race, she is engaging in a politics of deconstruction and challenging the rhetoric of Black inferiority. Indeed, in representing themselves as well mannered, diligent, and law abiding, people of English-speaking Caribbean origin are challenging the dominant racial ideology that positions Black people outside of the nation based on traits deemed to be a threat to, and thus incompatible with, modernity.[30] At the same time, this self-representation is rooted at least partially in the myth of Anglo superiority and does little to disrupt the civilizational discourse infused in ideologies of racial exclusion. Thus, this case exemplifies how the politics of deconstruction might reinforce the very ideologies of exclusion it is attempting to subvert.

I propose that, in order to understand the meanings and workings of Diaspora, we focus on the ways in which multiple "entanglements" (i.e., culture, status, ideology) function in relation to structurally positioned Black identities and vice versa. Both the diversity of Black subjectivities and structural factors such as racial hierarchy and inequality insert themselves into the manner in which people imagine and perform this diversity. The politics of deconstruction is a critical strategy for confronting racial inequality and for protecting against assaults on Black humanity, but it need not replace, usurp, or submerge structural politics. My research indicates that the structural position of "Black identity" and racialized subjects is itself implicated in the sort of Blackness that subjects reconstruct and perform when engaging in the politics of deconstruction and, as such, must be taken into consideration when evaluating its deployment.

Rasta: An Alternative Discourse to Respectability

Although I argue that the resurgence of Anglo-Caribbean Cuban associations was evidently a strategic move in a changing economic and social climate, this process did provide a forum in which Black people could, as a group, publicly assert an affirmative Blackness. For those who were not involved in the associations, there are signs that this need to contest the predominant views of Blackness manifests itself in other ways, the most striking of these being Rastafari. Katrin Hansing (2006) finds that Rastafari in Cuba, across the three different ways that mostly Afro-Cuban youth have adopted it (as religion, philosophy, or style), share a commitment to affirm African-inspired aesthetics and values. Furthermore, they share the social experience of the consequences of such a stance, which are persistent police harassment and general social condemnation. Stemming from these experiences, they share a belief that, in socialist Cuba, the myth that Cuba is a multiracial democracy and egalitarian society is tantamount to Babylon. Hansing reasons that, "By embracing Rastafari's anti-hegemonic, anti-racist, egalitarian, freedom-embracing and overall humanistic message, they are identifying with a philosophy they view as truer and more just than the one they see, hear and live in" (2006:742).[31]

Both David and Deunes, two of my interlocutors who came of age during the Special Period, identified themselves as African. Their connection to Jamaica, the origin of their great-grandparents, was alive to them as the birthplace of the Rastafari movement and as a closer link to Africa. Though both viewed themselves as playing active roles in their communities, being sought out by others for support and guidance through difficult times, they recognized that their decision to follow the path of Rastafari placed them outside of Cuban social norms. It also made them a target for police harassment—David had been arrested and jailed for a year during which time his locks were shaved, and Deunes avoided public places such as the central park and locations frequented by tourists for fear of encounters with the police that would end similarly. They both struggled with being Rasta in a society that misunderstands them and perceives their path as subversive. With an understanding of politics that does not include individual refusal to conform to hegemonic aesthetics, values, and beliefs, they insisted that they are not at all political, that Rastafari is expressly outside of politics.

Though by no means "counterrevolutionary" or dissident, the principles and lifestyle that they are affirming in being Rasta contradict a very critical hegemonic value in Cuban society, namely that of conformity[32]—in particular, conformity to the devaluation of Blackness. With implications illustrated by but far beyond the aesthetic, the wearing of dreadlocks (an affront to those who take offense to being confronted with so much *pelo malo* [bad hair]), the identification as African in a nationalistic society that adheres to racelessness as one of its dominant narratives, and the commitment to a philosophy that professes Black divinity in the form of Haile Selassie—all present a challenge to dominant assumptions about racial and cultural ordering. While the African cultural presence in Cuba is certainly recognized and celebrated, it is also relegated to the folkloric past.

With the turn to tourism, along with the Black and brown bodies that dance, drum, and "perform" religion, African cultural traditions are used to sell the island as an exotic tourist destination (Hagedorn 2001; Cornebise 2003; Argyriadis 2008). Furthermore, nonstereotypical media representations of Cubans of African descent are glaringly few and far between (Pérez-Sarduy and Stubbs 2000; Morales Domínguez 2013). I would argue that, in such a climate, committing to Rastafari, just as devoting oneself to invigorating a particular version of Anglophone Caribbean culture, is a means of asserting an affirmative Blackness.

Of note, however, is the contrast between the kind of Blackness asserted by Rastafari and that projected by those linked to the ethnic associations. While the former emphasize a connection with Africa and reject Eurocentrism as mental slavery, the latter derive their sense of cultural elevation from practices more closely aligned with late nineteenth-century British colonial indoctrination. While Rasta is blatantly nonconformist in its opposition to the dominant view of Blackness, the discourse of Black respectability deployed by many Anglo-Caribbean descendants simultaneously legitimizes and subverts the racial and cultural hierarchy in which Blackness is equated with inferiority.

An example of how such a contrast might be lived occurred one afternoon when Deunes sat down to a meal at Melvina's house and asked for a spoon in place of the culturally loaded knife and fork. Melvina turned to me, the foreigner, and explained how she had taught her husband, a Cuban of Haitian descent, to use a knife and fork, implying that this is one of those backward yet correctable Cubanisms. Deunes responded that he knows how to use a knife and fork but prefers to use a spoon because it is all that is needed. He later explained to me that his preference reflected his path, one in which simplicity is valued and the trappings of class division that complicate the activity of nourishing oneself are cast off. Perhaps indicative of Melvina's resistance to this, she suggested that he use a knife and fork on at least one other occasion and, in spite of his high regard for and deference to his tía (aunt), Deunes held his ground (and his spoon).[33]

Another incident emblematic of this intergenerational conflict occurred in Leticia and Isabel's family home, a wooden structure built by their grandfather, a successful tailor, in the 1940s. The house was in serious disrepair but was graced by beautiful antique wooden furniture acquired before the revolution. It sheltered and was frequented by Isabel, her husband, two adolescent children, David and Leticia, and two cousins.[34] I went to the house with the intention of meeting informally with David. Arriving at a house where I could hear reggae music playing from the backyard and still sleepy from the siesta, I was delighted that what began as a recruitment effort ended up in a lively intergenerational interchange about race, education, and the rewards and constraints of revolutionary society.

Requesting not to be vocally recorded as we sat on the patio of his family house, under huge trees and with the tunes of Junior Kelly in the background, David began our informal interview by telling me that his Jamaican ancestry heavily influences his beliefs and that Jamaicans are Africans. Lamenting Black people's lack of knowledge about their African identity, he deployed a familiar rhetoric of racial uplift: Black people don't know that they come from kings and queens, that the first people were Black, that Blacks had kingdoms and were founders of civilizations, that God is Black as was Jesus, and that white people have hidden this knowledge from us so that Blacks are mentally enslaved. He brought out a document that referred to the Lynch laws, which described in detail the methodology of keeping Black people enslaved.

When I asked where he learned this, he said that he began studying the scripture after finishing high school. His father is a Seventh Day Adventist and exposed him to the Bible and religion. He still has this Bible and said that his consciousness came during this time, at around age seventeen, when a Rasta began talking to him about Black consciousness and Rastafari. He began studying his Bible and had a revelation about the origin of Black people and the fact that we've been taught that Africa is a bad place and that Black history begins with slavery.[35]

Quite talkative and animated, David appeared completely comfortable expounding upon his truth without interruption. At the point when I interjected into his monologue the question about where and how he came to this understanding, he added that these things are not taught in school, that all they teach you is the history of Black people since slavery, since their arrival in Cuba, and not the history of Africa and its role as the cradle of civilization.[36] In David's estimation, they only teach you what they want you to know and cultivate in students a hatred for the United States by drilling into them the history of the relationship between Cuba and the United States.

At this point, Leticia, his mother, came and joined the conversation, clarifying that they don't teach students to hate the people of the United States, but that a distinction is made between the actions of the government and the population. Isabel, his aunt, seemed to be in agreement with David in terms of the extent of race-based oppression that has existed and the general lack of knowledge about Africa, that Africa is always represented as the dark continent. Though David recognized that Cuba is a society that has maintained African cultural traditions, he emphasized that there is a concerted effort on the part of whites to keep knowledge of Africa from Black people. When I asked whether they thought that their white neighbors actually had this knowledge and were keeping this from them, David conceded that they are ignorant as well.

Generational tensions were revealed through the course of this discussion, which quickly evolved into a heated exchange with its fair share of raised, overlapping voices and points punctuated by *freir huevos* (literally meaning to fry eggs but colloquially meaning to suck your teeth), indicating an emotional investment in the opposing positions about education and, by association, the revolution. There appeared to be a generational division in the perspective on education, with those who came of age in the Special Period having witnessed material deprivations in spite of education as well as diminished educational opportunities.[37] In contrast, many who had experienced the revolutionary process in the early years or who had seen the constraints that their parents faced in prerevolutionary Cuba were critical of young people's lack of enthusiasm for or outright unwillingness to pursue education and legitimate, though poorly remunerated, forms of employment.

When I returned to Cuba in 2008, David was enrolled in university and pursuing a degree in sociology. However, at the time of the initial conversation, he was not in school, something that Leticia and Isabel did not support. He argued that he didn't need a degree to have knowledge, that he pursues this knowledge on his own through meditation and through reading the Bible and whatever other texts he can get his hands on.[38] In order to study what he'd like to study, he reasoned, he'd have to travel and this is impossible to do under the current system. Clearly frustrated by his mother, who wants him to get an education, he argued that she has a degree and isn't interested in opening her mind, that her education hasn't freed her from her ignorance. In turn, Leticia expressed her belief that David and those of his generation are frustrated and that the desire to leave Cuba is due to their own ignorance of what Cuba was like before the revolution and what life is like in other places.

David attributed his departure from the path of his mother and her generation to living in a different time and place. As evident from the excerpts above, he found his family members who don't understand his path to be ignorant. They, along with other Black people, have benefited from the revolution in that they have a better life than before and thus the system has worked for them. However, their advancement was within ideological confines that he has moved beyond. He professed that he is not against the revolution or the system and actually spoke at length and with respect about Castro's ability to use the United States' own laws against it, that Castro was able to liberate Cuba from the United States. But his exposure to Rastafari teachings and decision to follow this spiritual path has had a tremendous influence on the way that he views the rest of Cuban society.

Unlike so many other youth I encountered who did not raise the option of social or political involvement as a solution to their frustration about the

limitations of the society, David articulated his view of what his role in contemporary society was to be. Based on his understanding of Rastafari as providing counsel and acting as a sort of moral compass, he envisioned his contribution to revolutionary society to be as a healer and guide, providing his
fellows with an alternate perspective on daily problems, many of which stem
from materialism and dysfunctional gender relations. Thus, while he was not
involved in the structures erected by and within the revolution to serve as
vehicles through which Cubans demonstrate a certain social commitment,
and indeed was somewhat marginal as he had recently been released from a
year-long period of imprisonment for questionable charges, he nonetheless
was articulating an investment in addressing social concerns.

Deunes identified himself as a revolutionary but reinterpreted the meaning of the term such that it conflicted with the way in which it is most often
used and understood in Cuban society. Commonly, someone who is said
to be *muy revolucionario* deeply believes in the Cuban revolution and its
ideals, often participates actively in the mass organizations, is Communist
and staunchly anti-imperialist. This revolutionary views the Cuban revolution as the best route to realize the goal of a national sovereignty and a just
society. In Deunes' contrasting view, revolution is defined as and through
change. Because change is something he has believed in strongly and has
enacted in his life, he viewed himself as a revolutionary.[39]

What is most interesting about this perspective is that Deunes rooted it in
his identity as a Rasta; in his estimation, Rastafarians reject the ills of society
in pursuit of transforming it into a more peaceful, spiritual human existence.
Rastas do seek and support social justice and thus must not have allegiance
to a system that condones, perpetuates, or fosters injustice.[40]

Conclusion

In *Black Skin, White Masks*, Fanon (2008) critiques the use of colonialist
discourse by the colonized Black seeking subject status because this discourse can only allow the Black to speak of himself as Other. In Fanon's
estimation, it is only through concrete, revolutionary action to overthrow
oppressive forces and achieve freedom that Black people can achieve subject
status. A key element of the Cuban case as compared to other American
locations in which African culture and Blackness are devalued and Black
people themselves mobilize culture to ameliorate conditions of inequality

is the Cuban revolution. The revolutionary mandate of equality resulted in the reduction of racial disparities in education, health, income, and many spheres of employment. Blackness came to be less of a liability for institutional advancement and accessing resources, though it continued to be associated with negative traits and behaviors, affecting Black Cubans across the class/education/status spectrum. However, although the revolution undermined the structural basis of racial inequality, the comments and stories of my interlocutors indicate that anti-Black racial attitudes have had an impact on their professional and personal lives. The revolution's denial of difference and silence about racism allowed discrimination to persist and fester.

The collapse of Soviet socialism and tightening of the U.S. embargo led to a resurgence of institutional racial stratification in Cuba that has been ongoing since the 1990s. This, I argue, has been met with a call to once again create, project, and embody a Blackness that is an alternative to popular conceptions that have increasingly detrimental consequences. To continue to be lodged in popular consciousness as the subservient, ignorant, illogical, and primitive element of the nation is to compromise equality. The employment of the language of civilization to differentiate some Blacks, in this case people of Anglo-Caribbean origin, illustrates the asymmetries evident in episodes of diasporic belonging.

The Rastafari movement offered my interlocutors who came of age during the Special Period yet another alternative Blackness. For them, Africa is the link to redemption and respectability; Rasta and others who do not conform to "Babylon" are the true revolutionaries. However, for my interlocutors who drew upon the matrix of respectability to demarcate difference, the connection to the Anglo-Caribbean hinged on distance from other African diasporic populations; it is in this way that they engage in a making, remaking, and *unmaking* of diaspora.[41]

5

"¿Gracias a la Revolución?"

Narratives of Social Mobility as Spaces of Subject Formation

Those people who have studied and gotten advanced degrees can't save money and take a trip or save money and buy a television or stereo because of the exchange rate. The way to overcome this is to work in tourism and those jobs are mostly for whites, which leaves [Blacks] [he makes the characteristic forefinger's brush on the forearm to signal the group] in a worse situation. "Los negros estamos embarcados" (We Blacks are left hanging).

Deunes, grocery store clerk, great-grandson of Jamaican immigrant, June 15, 2005, interview with author, Santiago

One of the most notable aspects of the revitalization of Anglo-Caribbean institutions was that the people who were sought out and who joined, at least initially, were professionals and technicians. In the case of Blue Mountain, the few resources that they were able to gather in order to organize celebrations and other events came through the access to goods that members had and services that they could provide. For the British West Indian Welfare Centre, their goals of creating educational programs and medical support clearly required professional leadership. As Edward explained, "We established [a] series of lectures for the general membership. . . . Now, [we have] more advantages because we are using the force of the Centre's own membership who are qualified. . . . There are doctors, engineers, professors, etcetera, etcetera, all of course trained by the revolution, and we use this to improve the membership in different areas, in particular in the question of health and disease."[1]

This emphasis on the professional identity of the associations reared its head in discussions about the recruitment and acceptance process. Initially, people who were known members of the community formed the association.

But after the call was put out more broadly through the media—a radio program in the case of Blue Mountain—the process of selection ensued. Those who were not known had to present a membership application, two photos, dues of ten pesos, and documents providing proof of their Anglo-Caribbean origin, which could be the passport or birth certificate of their immigrant parents or grandparents. As I discussed in the preceding chapters, Anglo-Caribbean-Cuban identity as defined by the professional leadership was the source of a certain amount of cultural capital. I argue that it became a way of being Black that challenged pervasive notions of inferiority and offered a possible route to overcoming the situation in which they were "left hanging."

In this chapter, I shine a light upon the recurrent theme of achieving professional status, interrogating the purpose that this narrative of social mobility serves in processes of Black Cuban subject-making. Rather than being a simple respouting of rhetoric about the successes of the revolution and about Blacks as beneficiaries of the revolution or being an illustration of the *doble moral* (literally "double moral," the term refers to disingenuously adhering to official rhetoric in public), these narratives are a means to critique the current crisis. Here, I consider this critique in relation to the emergence of a "new" Cuban subject in the post-Soviet era (a diasporic subject), as well as to the old manifestations of anti-Black racism that were perhaps aggravated by the opportunities for social mobility that the revolution provided.

"¿Gracias a la Revolución?": Subjectivity, Narrativity, and Anglo-Caribbean-Cuban Social Mobility

> The subject is at once a product and agent of history; the site of experience, memory, storytelling and aesthetic judgment; an agent of knowing as much as of action; and the conflicted site for moral acts and gestures amid impossibly immoral societies and institutions. . . . Yet subjectivity is not just the outcome of social control or the unconscious; it also provides the ground for subjects to think through their circumstances and to feel through their contradictions, and in so doing, to inwardly endure experiences that would otherwise be outwardly unbearable. . . . [Subjectivity] is fear and optimism, anger and forgiveness, lamentation and pragmatism, chaos and order.
>
> *João Biehl, Bryon Good, and Arthur Kleinman, "Rethinking Subjectivity," 2007*

As discussed, narratives of social mobility made possible through the opportunity to obtain a free education were recurrent in reflections on the impact of the revolution on Anglo-Caribbean communities. In what follows, I focus on the voices of my interlocutors as they relay their occupational and educational experiences, which are reflected through the lens of present-day Cuba. Given the resurgence of racial inequality and the way in which this calls into question the government's rhetoric of raceless nationalism, these narratives of social mobility are presented by some as testimony to the merits of the revolution. However, at the same time that they are a defense against critics of the Cuban government, they are also a means of critiquing the current state of affairs. They are a way that these subjects are "thinking through their circumstances" and "feeling through their contradictions."

"I Am Ignorant, but All My Children Are Professionals"

Jorge Smith was seventy-six years old when I first met him on a bench in Santiago's central park where he was holding court with other retirees nearly every morning between 8:00 a.m. and 11:00 a.m. He was a vibrant, active husband, father, grandfather and great-grandfather. Pointing to a bicycle painted a faded ballerina pink, he told me, "That is my car," and laughed; indeed, it was not unusual for me to see him riding his "car" through the hilly streets of Santiago.

Smith, "el Viejo," as he is called, is the Cuban-born son of Jamaican immigrants who is quick to smile and joke, particularly about his amorous pursuits past and present. As explained in chapter 1, Smith's mother died shortly after being hospitalized for mental illness, and he was raised by English teachers until age twelve when his father remarried. He was hired to work on the Guantánamo Naval Base at age seventeen through his father, who held a job in the canteen. He worked on the base from 1943 to 1949 as a dishwasher and then as an orderly in the hospital, and he looked upon this time of partying and gambling with great fondness. He explained that he left this job, where he made twenty-seven pesos a week—a healthy salary at that time—because, after World War II, there were a lot of people who needed jobs on the base. So, rather than stay in Guantánamo, he opted to return to Santiago to live full time. There, he apprenticed with a Jamaican as a bricklayer and worked in a factory at this trade until 1959 when he joined the military. At the time of the research, he was receiving a modest pension that was supplemented by remittances from one of his children who was working as a Spanish teacher in Jamaica.

Contrasting the past with the present, Smith held the memory of how the city of Santiago used to be, showing me the locations of shops that sold modern consumer goods long vanished from Cuba while talking about his weekend job as a "tour guide" for sailors. He made a commission from steering sailors to shops and hotels. He remembered the names of the brothels and the conversations he had (in English) with the sailors and the conversations he had (in Spanish) with the sex workers who paid him a 20 percent commission. He recalled that they charged five dollars "for a short time" and twenty dollars for the whole night, when "the woman belongs to you." Of prostitution in today's Cuba, he says:

> Life for the women was more difficult because they had to stay in the red light district. . . . Now they all are mixed in with the entire population, which is worse because you don't know who is la Buena [good] and who is la Mala [bad]. Now they do it because the dollar is here and you need dollars and the only way to get dollars is to associate with those who bring them and they keep opening dollar stores. That's why there's so much.
>
> When there was the socialist camp, these countries had a relationship with Cuba. After it fell, things got worse, the blockade worsened as well. We're not afraid that it's going to get worse from the time just after the socialist camp fell. The lack of fear has to do with the fact that people have the morale of the movement. A beautiful thing is that all of my children have professions. . . . I'm ignorant but my children, they are educated.[2]

The fondness with which Smith recalled his days on the naval base and life in Cuba during the days of Batista when there was a strong U.S. presence contradicts the official discourse that represents this era as the epitome of misery, suffering, and subjugation.[3] Though his memory of the period is no doubt influenced by the tendency to glorify youth, the advantageous position he occupied relative to other Black working-class people who did not speak English or have access to employment on the naval base was also certainly a factor. It is quite telling that Smith compared the pre-1959 period with the post-1989 era through an evaluation of prostitution then and now, as the rise in sex work has been a topic of scholarly interest and public debate (Davidson 1996; Kempadoo 1999, 2004; Hodge 2001; Cabezas 2004; Allen 2007). Rather than charging sex work with deteriorating the moral fiber of revolutionary society, Smith is pointing to the way in which the dual economy has made relationships with foreigners a necessity for all Cubans. Whereas official discourse claims that Cubans who engage in prostitution do so in order to consume luxury goods rather than meet basic needs, Smith recognizes that jineterismo is an inevitable outcome of the dual economy and reliance on tourism. Thus, this is a means by which to critique the reforms rather than the women themselves.

Two facets of Smith's story illustrate an unfolding political logic that indicates an ambiguous positioning in relation to revolutionary society. The first is his articulation of the blurring of boundaries between who or what is "good" and who or what is "bad." Through his observation concerning the clandestine yet ubiquitous presence of sex workers in public space, he perhaps unintentionally evoked the limitations of applying binary categories to everyday realities. The good and the bad, as with the socialist and the capitalist, are comingling and becoming difficult to differentiate, appearing increasingly interdependent (Brotherton 2008).

The second is the way in which he punctuated his discussion of contemporary hardships and transformations with an affirmation of the revolution's strengths and successes as evidenced by the opportunities it provided his children. He did not simply give lip service to official discourse but incorporated the fullness of his own experience into his analysis. He enjoyed Batista-era Cuba, in which he occupied a privileged position relative to other non-English-speaking Black people; he incorporated into revolutionary society through the military and supported the revolution in part because it gave his children the opportunity to receive an education, an opportunity he did not have; and at the time of the interview he was critical of market-driven government reforms. Like others, he has been engaged in a process of weighing past and present, victories and failures, in an attempt to understand and represent their realities.

"¿Gracias a la Revolución?": The Anglo-Caribbean Cultural Matrix

At the time of my interview with him, Pablo was a sixty-five-year-old Guantanamero whose father was born in 1897 and came from Jamaica to Cuba in 1920, where he married the daughter of antillanos. As Pablo showed me his father's passport and other documents, he said, "My father worked on the railroad. . . . He was very social, a member of the lodge, and had six children: the eldest was a doctor, two are nurses, one is a housewife, one is a professor, and the other a skilled technician. My father was very respected; so were the other jamaicanos when they came to Cuba."[4]

While he acknowledged that some jamaicanos left Cuba after the revolution, he praised the revolution for providing those immigrants with the opportunity to be educated. However, as he continued to talk, it became clear that his older siblings were actually educated prior to the revolution. He recounted:

> There were a lot of Jamaicans here and when they were all going back to Jamaica, my father wouldn't go because his children went to the university here. The older ones went to university before the revolution. My brother began studying before the revolution, left to fight, then began again. Many people of color weren't able to go to school because they didn't have the money.
>
> My brother was able to begin his education through a lot of sacrifice. They were jamaiquino, they didn't smoke, they didn't drink and dedicated their salary to take care of their children. My father only drank a beer at the beginning of the year. He wanted all of his children to be educated. All money went to clothe, feed, and educate the children. . . . My brother studied to be a doctor and my sister was sent to the Normal School to study to be a nurse. It was rare to see a family send their children to school to achieve an advanced degree; first, because they were Black and second because of their class.[5]

These remarks suggest that Pablo believed his own family to be exceptional and is proud of their achievements. He is invested in constructing jamaicanos as strict, disciplined, patriarchal, Christian,[6] upstanding community members who value education and are capable of obtaining it on their own. At the same time, he repeatedly expressed gratitude to the revolution for his family's success. He shared that his eldest brother, the doctor, completed three missions abroad in Angola and Ethiopia. The younger sister, who is a nurse, went on a mission to Haiti, and the other sister, who works in Havana, also as a nurse, has been recognized for excellence in her field. For Pablo, the revolution gave his family an invaluable boost in life chances that were already elevated due to their being situated within an Anglo-Caribbean cultural matrix.

Similar to others whose families were upwardly mobile prior to the revolution, Pablo's narrative contests the notion that Blacks owe any position or prestige they have to the revolution, which is intricately linked to the paternalistic stance that Cubans of color must be grateful and loyal to the revolution. At the same time that he acknowledges that education was out of reach for many, he submits that with hard work, clean living, dedication, and sacrifice, upward mobility was possible for Blacks prior to the revolution. Thus, his narrative reveals a certain ambiguity regarding one of the cornerstones of revolutionary success, demonstrating how the particularities of prerevolutionary social location combine with experiences in the revolution to produce more complex and unexpected outcomes.

"Pero Todos No Somos Iguales" (But We're Not All Equal)

"Todos somos iguales" (We are all equal) is a popular refrain rooted in the ideas of José Martí that reinforces the notion that the 1959 revolution eliminated social hierarchy and all forms of discrimination. In practical terms, however, acceptance of and adherence to this ideal have been less than perfect.

Born in 1950 to the son of Jamaicans and the daughter of Haitians living in Santiago, Leticia came of age during the revolution and her family history exemplifies the ascent of Black immigrant families through the revolution. A very energetic divorced mother of two young Black men, Leticia attended an Olympic training school as an adolescent and eventually went to the university to become a professor of physical education. She was extremely active in her position at the university and was constantly participating in *trabajo voluntario* (volunteer work). At the time of this field research, she was awarded a new apartment as recognition of her dedication to the revolution—as she said, simulating wiping sweat from her brow, that apartment was not given to her, she earned it.

In narrating her own and her family's experience in Cuba, Leticia emphasized the unprecedented opportunities in the early years of the revolution. However, much like Jorge Smith and Pablo, interwoven within her narrative were observations that offer a more nuanced, complicated evaluation of revolutionary society. She explained,

> My grandfather died believing in the revolution because . . . they struggled a lot, emigrating from Jamaica because of the difficulties there,

and they saw that the revolution was to help and support the people. When the revolution was making progress, it made everyone literate, they gave free education when before my grandfather had to pay for my father and my aunt to go to the nuns' school to study. My aunt studied in the nuns' school with money my grandfather made as a tailor. With the revolution, this was abolished. . . . At that time, to go to medical school, you had to pay and you had to associate with certain people and for poor people or Black people to get in, they had to make a big deal. . . . It was for people with money; you had to pay money and that's who had money. So, my grandfather saw . . . that with the revolutionaries you could study and they saw a great difference. And what happened was that they liked the revolution a lot.

Up to today, though, we have our problems of racism. . . . Fidel said that everyone is equal but this isn't yet the reality. People still have hidden things and can't be open. . . . You don't see it openly because this doesn't exist in Cuba but what I'm saying is that there are persons who still have their beliefs, some little things like "a white woman shouldn't marry a Black man," and these things they pass on to their children.[7]

Thus, as an exemplary worker, one who highlighted the opportunities that the revolution offered her in her youth and who continued to believe that young people in Cuba must pursue education, Leticia did not subscribe to the notion that race is of no consequence in Cuba. Furthermore, she was willing to admit this to a foreigner, and one from the United States no less.[8]

However, there are limits to Leticia's critique, as she attributes enduring racism to individual prejudice rather than to any systemic discrimination against Black and mulatto/mestizo Cubans: this, in spite of the fact that the year before this interview her son had been in jail for over a year, something we discussed at length, as she believed he was innocent and was quite preoccupied with his well-being.[9] Although the details of his incarceration were difficult to verify, her son, David, the Rasta whom we met in the previous chapter, might have been a victim of the systematic harassment and incarceration of young Black men, with those with dreadlocks being particularly subjected to such treatment.[10] That Leticia was willing to contradict Fidel and, as evidence of racial prejudice, acknowledge the discrimination against people of African descent when it came to choosing marriage partners—but not with regard to her son's experience—underscores the need to move toward a more nuanced understanding of the ways in which Cubans discern, interact with, and evaluate the evolving, dynamic sociopolitical environment.

Ambivalent Revolutionary

Melvina was in elementary school when the revolution triumphed in 1959. Her mother was a seamstress from a poor family—her maternal grandmother was a laundress. Her father, a carpenter who worked on the Guantánamo Naval Base during the week and spent weekends at the home he himself built in Santiago, returned to Jamaica in the mid-1960s. He had plans of bringing Melvina's brother Percy with him and educating him in Jamaica, but Percy, a young teenager at the time who was caught up in the revolutionary fervor of the early years, refused to leave Cuba. All of the children remained in Cuba, with Melvina becoming an English professor, Percy an aeronautical engineer, and their sister a cardiologist who spent much of her career on missions in Africa. An advocate of Black pride and respectability, her narrative of social mobility and nostalgia for early revolutionary *cubanía* (Cubanness) is not only a means by which to critique the present, but also demonstrates how the contradictions that emerge from such readings are one way in which these particular subjects challenge binary formulations of social relations.

Interspersed within Melvina's narrative of social mobility and the early revolutionary period were recollections of the excitement and adventure that characterized this time. One afternoon after lunch, she and her husband reminisced about a youth that was both theirs and the revolution's. They recalled that everyone from all of the different disciplines at the university had to go out to work in the fields "por la patria" (for the Fatherland). It was 1970 and they were a part of La Zafra de los Diez Milliones (Ten Million Tons Harvest) when ordinary Cubans went out to the countryside to help ensure that the country reached its goal of harvesting ten million tons of sugar cane for the revolution. The men cut cane while the women gathered it, and Melvina laughed as she recounted trying to get out of whatever agricultural work she was assigned because she hated being under the hot sun: "There was more *cubanía* then," Melvina said, "not like now."[11]

Melvina was among the most vocal critics *and* defenders of the Cuban government and of contemporary revolutionary society. Always ready to offer her opinion, she swayed between declaring that "this place is a jail," due to her claim that one out of every three persons is a member of the security force, to enumerating the ways in which Fidel[12] provides opportunities for the youth, to admonishing racially discriminatory hiring practices in all industries that gave Cubans access to dollars. Unlike Leticia, Melvina pointed to the many manifestations of systemic racism that have emerged with the post-Soviet economic reforms as well as suggesting some of the ways that discrimination persisted prior to the Special Period. However, with the depenalization of the dollar in 1993, investment in tourism, and initiation of joint ventures, such discrimination has intensified. In the current economic landscape, in which taxi drivers earn more than physicians, education, the historic route to securing a relatively well-remunerated position in the labor hierarchy, no longer ensures access to economic or social capital. Melvina insisted that such access is racialized, providing examples of Blacks either being denied opportunities or having to fight for opportunities in industries that paid in CUCs.

Given her insistence upon the disadvantages that darker skinned Cubans face, the following story she relayed to me after returning from the center of town one morning places the ambiguities of the subject in stark relief. While we were preparing the *almuerzo* (lunch, large midday meal), Melvina mentioned that while out, she came across a group of Jamaican tourists who were attempting to purchase something from one of the stores next to the central park. Noting that they were having difficulty communicating with the store clerk, she stepped in to translate for them. In the meantime, she recounted, a group of *negros* (said with disdain) with dreadlocks crowded around the tourist shop, pressing up against the glass storefront. When one of the Jamaicans asked why these people were sticking to them like that, Melvina told them it was because they wanted money. Melvina said that she felt ashamed "to see all of those *negros* acting that way with all the jobs there are in Cuba. . . . They don't want to work," she concluded in disgust.[13] At the time, I noted that Melvina's response to the Jamaicans and her comments about the *negros* contradicted other observations she had shared about the systemic lack of opportunities and the ways in which Black and mulatto Cubans are at a particular disadvantage.

Such incongruities are part of the way in which people narrate and live their lives, illuminating and contributing to processes of subject formation. The reconceptualization of narrativity of the 1980s and 1990s asserted that social identities are constituted through narratives, through the stories that individuals tell about themselves (Somers 1994:606). As a "strategy of existence" (Biehl, Good, and Kleinman 2007:5), individual subjectivity is produced through human lived experience and fundamentally contradicts much of the rational actor worldview (Ellis and Flaherty 1992). Processes of subject formation, with modern subjectivity understood to be "a synonym for inner life processes and affective states" that "intertwine with particular configurations of political, economic, and medical institutions" (Biehl, Good, and Kleinman 2007:6–8), inform identities and refer to modes of belonging. The experience of social mobility that was so ubiquitous in my interlocutors' accounts of their family and personal histories contributed to constituting their social identities, which were informed by processes of subject formation and drove the revitalization of Anglo-Caribbean institutions.

The explanation for why this particular group of Black Cubans moved to "rescue their roots" at a moment of extreme economic crisis lay partially in who they understood themselves to be in relationship to revolutionary society. As Somers argues in advocating a narrative identity approach, "Social action can only be intelligible if we recognize that people are guided to act by the structural and cultural relationships in which they are embedded and by the stories through which they constitute their identities" (1994:624). In the course of this research, the underlying significance of the actions of these individuals and this collectivity emerged in part through the narratives of social mobility themselves as well as through the ways in which these narratives were a springboard for social critique.

Anne M. Lovell, in an anthropological study of schizophrenics' constructions of self, suggests that anthropologists, in our own role as interlocutors and storymakers, "juxtapose perspectives grasped from similar narratives ... to shade some of the blank spaces left in the narrative process" (1997:356). I maintain that this shading rendered an image in which these particular Cubans complicate the boundary between official ideology and private critique, illustrating the multiplicity of emergent political subjectivities. If memory and narrative are building blocks of identity and subjectivity (Rivkin-Fish 2009:90), these narratives are practices of social memory that construct particular kinds of subjectivities. Only when this practice is looked at alongside contradictory conditions, such as the experience of racial discrimination and rising social inequality, do we see how narratives are a means through which Black Cubans critique current economic and social conditions and articulate a more nuanced relationship to revolutionary society.

Recent research on the radical changes in Cuban society indicates that contradictions between the socialist values of collectivity, self-sacrifice, and antiracism and the economic imperatives of market relations have produced a new(er) Cuban subject. Laurie Frederik (2005) identifies this subject as Hombre Novísimo, an even newer man forged in the fires of the Special Period, bending but not breaking under the pressures of the new social order. This urban Hombre Novísimo retains the Hombre Nuevo's moral stance against capitalist greed but must contend with the society's ambivalence toward "global culture," which is "essentially understood in this socialist society as anything motivated by money or individual gain" (2005:402).[14]

Also attesting to the transformation of Cubans' political subjectivities, Sean Brotherton finds that the interdependence of capitalism and socialism as illustrated in Cuba's health sector has given life to a hybrid, fragmented subject who *willingly and begrudgingly* incorporates an incipient form of capitalism into the fabric of his daily life (2008:267). Others insist that this new political subject, more than the old, is pressed into deep duplicity as economic imperatives motivate Communist Party members to bribe doctors for medical excuses that exempt their children from participating in revolutionary consciousness-building schools in the countryside (Blum 2008) and to bribe *Santeros* to sell sacred secrets to cash-rich foreigners (Wirtz 2004; Delgado 2009).[15]

The African Anglo-Caribbean diaspora complicates articulations of subject formation in Cuban society and encourages us to consider the political subjectivity of diaspora. The move on the part of Black Cubans of Anglo-Caribbean origins to "rescue their roots" during the worst years of the Special Period can be read as yet another example of economic imperatives pushing Cubans into strategic alliances that contradict their more authentic beliefs and moral principles. When we take into consideration the experience of Cubans of color who might be grappling with the contradictions between the rhetoric of antiracism and the reality of rising discrimination, we see that their conflicting evaluations of revolutionary society are an expression of a particular ethics. Anglo-Caribbean Cubans are contesting their misrecognition as unhyphenated Black Cubans, an identity that subjects them to assumptions of inferiority and immorality. I suggest that, in the case of this diasporic formation, there is an imagining and assertion of an ethical subjectivity and a "strategy of existence." As I will explain, this imagining and assertion is enabled not only by multiple modes of mobility, but also by the imposition of immobility.

Mobility, Immobility, and Diasporic Subjectivity in the Era of Transitioning Socialism

One July evening after instructing me on how to make *pru oriental*,[16] Humberto, a fifty-two-year-old, brown-skinned Cuban veterinarian, began asking me questions about being Black in the United States. He wanted to know if I had ever read the *Autobiography of Malcolm X* and if I knew that Antonio Maceo's legacy was intellectual as well as military.[17] At one point, he looked at me and said in an almost conspiratorial tone as if he were exposing a well-kept secret, "Todos somos iguales . . . pero todos no somos iguales" (We're all equal . . . but we're not all equal). Recounting the ways in which Cubans of color still experience social discrimination and inquiring further about U.S. race relations, he ended by saying, "I don't have a problem with the United States. I just want to live the rest of my life in peace. I'm tired of all of this war war *war*!"[18] Humberto made this declaration in the wake of escalating tensions between Cuba and the United States triggered by the fall of European socialism.[19] The tentative market reforms that the Cuban government began implementing in the early 1990s to avert economic collapse but maintain socialism inadvertently heightened racialized inequality, revealing that Cuba is not only not-quite-postsocialist, but also not-quite-post-racist.

This particular moment with Humberto was one of many that evoked connections and cross-fertilizations made possible by migrations forced, voluntary, and derailed. Socially, Humberto is a Black descendant of Haitian immigrants and married to the daughter of Jamaicans. In a conversation with a Black anthropologist of Montserratian descent from the United States who enters and exits Cuba at will (sort of),[20] Humberto drew upon his knowledge of a Black nationalist leader from the United States (whose mother was a mixed-race Grenadian and whose father was a Black Georgian Garveyite)[21] and a Cuban general (the son of a Black Venezuelan farmer and mulata Cuban mother), who exiled in Haiti, Jamaica, and Costa Rica in the long struggle for Cuban independence. Evoking two leaders who are in many ways the prime symbols of Black masculine strength, dignity, and self-respect, Humberto illustrated the centrality of the struggle against mis-recognition and abjection.

Embedded in the exchange between Humberto is one of this book's principal nodes of inquiry: that concerning the tensions within and uses of diaspora[22] revealed through intersecting physical, social, and symbolic (im)mobilities. I insert "(im)" to signal that diaspora is as much produced through and emerges from immobility as mobility. Humberto engaged me around these interconnections in Black experience in the context of expressing his frustration with the reality that "todos no somos iguales" from the position of one whose social mobility was derailed and professional status diminished. Humberto's interest in and evocation of diaspora exists in a context of not only an economic crisis that wreaked havoc on the existing system of social reward, but also the significant logistical obstacles facing those wishing to migrate.

Indeed, I later learned from Melvina, Humberto's wife and one of my principal interlocutors, that at one point during the worst years of the Special Period, he had intended to leave Cuba as a *balsero*.[23] Unbeknownst to Melvina, he had planned to join colleagues from work who were making the perilous journey. However, when it was time to leave and his boss came to collect him, he was nowhere to be found; thus, the opportunity to pursue this desperate measure was lost to him. It was only when he returned home and became distraught upon discovering that he had literally missed the boat that he revealed his intentions. His thwarted mobility, both in the social and geographic sense, lay in stark contrast to my relative mobility. Thus, that moment of creating diaspora was enabled as much by fixity as by trajectories of displacement.

Humberto's statement that "todos somos iguales . . . pero todos no somos iguales" also speaks to the coexistence of contradictory realities: Cubans are all equal but Cubans are also not all equal. Perhaps one of Jafari Allen's interlocutors articulated this seemingly counterintuitive subject position when he said, "You want to understand our culture? Study slavery . . . the rumba, literature, but look at all the contradictions too. . . . We are freer than most but cannot leave the island. We are richer and poorer. African and Spanish. We are Caribbean and Latin American. We are Revolutionary but [also] traditional" (Allen 2011:10). These contradictions were evident in my interlocutors' narratives of social mobility. Following, woven within, or otherwise revealed to be integral to these narratives were experiences that complicated this mobility, in particular those of discrimination and inequality that are particular to professionals of color.

Predicament of the Professional

> When a black man succeeds in any activity, he suffers
> even more humiliation and racial discrimination.
>
> *Juan R. Betancourt,* Doctrina Negra, *1955*

> It could be that jamaicanos were proud of their race, why not? They were
> Black people who weren't crude, uneducated, who didn't swear or steal, so
> they may have thought that, "We're Black, but at least we're Black people who
> study, think and do things in life." . . . It's a tradition here [in Cuba] to think
> that Black people have all of these negative traits. They always expect a Black
> person to be crude and ignorant and so when you're not like that, they say you're
> pretending. . . . You have to be poorly dressed, ignorant, dirty, ugly and speak
> poorly and it bothers people when you're a Black woman who isn't like that.
>
> *Hortencia, interview with author, August 4, 2004, Santiago*

While it is tempting to believe that the problem of racial discrimination was not solved *in spite* of the social mobility that Cubans of color experienced as a result of educational opportunities during the revolution, I argue that persistent racism is evident in part *because of* this mobility and the increasing professionalization of Black and mulatto Cubans. Hortencia was not alone in her perception that there is a certain hostility against Cubans of African descent who do not conform to racist assumptions about Blackness. This points to a remarkably intractable and often overlooked manifestation of racism; namely, the particular forms of discrimination that educated professionals and/or those in positions of authority face. My interlocutors, the majority of whom were professionals,[24] repeatedly pointed to the challenges that they and others like them faced as a result of a deeply entrenched belief in Black inferiority regardless of class and education.

Cuba's history from the colonial through the republican period provides an abundance of examples of the resistance to the equitable treatment of Black people who achieve a higher level of education and/or are in positions of authority (see Helg 1995; Ferrer 1999; de la Fuente 2001b; Bronfman

2004; Guridy 2003, 2010; Pappademos 2011). From the imposition of the caste laws in colonial America, which expressly limited the social mobility of free people of color, to the deep fear of Black political power evident in the international responses to the Haitian Revolution, to the true motivation behind many lynchings that occurred in the U.S. South, the history of people of African descent in the Americas is bursting with examples of hostility toward the upwardly mobile. In the case of Cuba, we can look to the Wars for Independence, in particular the dilemma of Antonio Maceo, and the Massacre of 1912 as well as pre-1959 exclusionary practices in order to establish that there has been a pattern of containing successful Cubans of color, particularly those Black elites who did not collude with white mainstream party politics, as Pappademos (2011) convincingly argues.

While Maceo is celebrated and pointed to as proof of Cuba's commitment to racial equality, the obstacles that he faced as the leader of the anticolonial war provide tremendous insight into challenges that Blacks in positions of power confront as well as what such challenges reveal about Cuban racial politics. At the same time that a man of color was able to rise to one of the highest positions in the land, commanding white and Black officers alike, he was consistently called upon to allay fears that he was masterminding a Black rebellion. This included promoting white officers instead of their more deserving Black counterparts and at times diminishing his role and the role of men of color in the liberation effort (Ferrer 1999; de la Fuente 2001b).

Maceo's career and events following his death evidence the contradictions of race at the founding moment of the Cuban nation, contradictions that persist to the current day. Sometime between 1896, when Maceo fell in battle, and 1900, when the pamphlet "El craneo de Maceo: Estudio antropológico" was published, the body of Antonio Maceo, the Bronze Titan, was exhumed and examined by scientists obsessed with racial classification. Conveniently, they concluded that Maceo had the body proportions of an African but the brain of a European, thus making him a superior man (Bronfman 2004:1). In this assessment, they are both affirming and subverting contemporary discourse. On the one hand, they find that a man of color can be superior, a notion that certainly challenges the basic tenet of white supremacist ideology, but on the other, they reinscribe the notion that intellectual ability is only bestowed upon the European.

The second moment in the early history of the republic that we can consider is the 1912 Massacre, also known as the "Race War," touched upon in chapter 1. During this dark period of Cuban history, white militia, under the auspices of putting down a Black rebellion and preventing another U.S. military occupation, murdered anywhere between 3,000 and 6,000 Cubans of color in Oriente (Tomás Fernandez Robaina estimates 12,000).[25] The episode that ostensibly triggered this brutal repression was the armed protest of members of the Independent Party of Color, a group of Afro-Cuban veterans and activists who were resisting their subjugation within the nascent republic. They formed a political party whose agenda was to advocate for the equal inclusion of people of color and the poor.

At the time of the massacre, the Party itself had been outlawed based on legislation that banned race-based political parties; its members were asserting their right to organize against the racialized injustice that was on the rise in part as a result of the U.S. presence in "independent" Cuba. This incident was unique in the scale of brutality used to repress Cubans of color, but not in its expression of hostility towards those Blacks and mulattoes who posed a challenge to white authority, paternalism, and ultimately, white supremacist ideology.

While there is some debate about the consequences of the 1912 Massacre on Black/mulatto political activism, the persistent patterns of exclusion against which Cubans of African descent struggled are fairly well documented. There were obstacles to higher education and a range of occupations, exclusion from private social clubs, which were critical to business networks, and restricted access to public spaces such as parks and beaches. Poor Cubans regardless of their racial identity were certainly excluded from some of these same circles. However, I am more concerned here with how Cubans of color were specifically targeted for exclusions that not only placed limitations on their social mobility, but also were in response to the level of mobility that Cubans of color had achieved in spite of the challenges to this ascendance.

In the revolutionary period, some of the barriers that had previously prevented those talented and motivated individuals from reaching their potential were removed. However, the revolution did not address, or perhaps even anticipate, the resistance to and consequences of having Black people assume positions of status and/or authority in spite of this history.[26] For instance, in 1970 sociologist Geoffrey Fox observed that "some white workers found it hard to adjust to [the] changes and resented what they perceived as an official bias toward Afro-Cubans. Particularly difficult was the social and physical closeness that integrated schools, recreational facilities, and mass organizations imposed on blacks and whites . . . [the] perception that blacks felt as if they were 'better' than whites or were 'better off' than whites in the island was shared by several white workers . . . who resented the dismantling of traditional racial hierarchies" (quoted in de la Fuente 2001b:279). The silence around race and discrimination that was officially imposed after Fidel Castro declared racism to have been eradicated meant that there was no means to directly combat what would have been a subtle yet pernicious form of racism.[27]

The repression of Black intellectuals and closure of race-based organizations compromised the ability of Cubans of color to contest racial discrimination. Without independent organizations, most notably a press, that ensured the collective voices of Black and mulatto Cubans were projected into the national space, no platform was available from which to acknowledge and challenge inequality, which existed in both private and public affairs.[28] Those Cubans of color who contested the shutting down of dialogue about race, such as Carlos Moore, Walterio Carbonell, and Juan Betancourt Bencomo, were silenced through censure, isolation, incarceration, and exile.[29]

The state's prohibition on racial discrimination, while guaranteeing equal access to employment, education, housing, public space, and health care, does not regulate sentiments and behaviors within the private and intimate spheres.[30] In Cuba, where connections are critical to anything, from easing the daily acquisition of certain goods, to being chosen to study a particular major, to getting an air-conditioned office, racial attitudes that link Blackness with criminality, superstition, intellectual inferiority, and aesthetic undesirability result in systematic discrimination. Although the consequences of such beliefs have been more severe since the economic crisis of the 1990s, the accounts of my interlocutors indicate some continuity between the early revolutionary period and the period following the collapse of Soviet support.

While some expressed the belief that racial discrimination had been eliminated, the majority of Cubans of color that I encountered (including those not of English-speaking Caribbean origin) thought that anti-Black attitudes and discrimination persisted in Cuban society. The most frequent examples of this involved references to white Cubans not wanting their daughters to be involved with Black men, not wanting their children to consider Black friends as equals, and situations in the workplace. One recurrent theme was precisely this question of white resentment toward the presence and/or authority of Blacks. The experiences that my interlocutors recounted indicate that some whites were ambivalent at best and contemptuous at worst toward professionals of color.

One example of this recurrent narrative of workplace discrimination was that of Tomás. Trained in veterinary medicine and pathology in the '60s, he began to excel in his field, which earned him promotions as well as the wrath of his white coworkers—who began to undermine him. Tomás recalled that his response to their malice was to continue to work harder and become more successful, which he suspects ultimately backfired. His coworkers eventually sabotaged his lab work, accusing him of counterrevolutionary activity for which he was imprisoned for four years in the late 1970s.[31]

Others told stories of racial bias in the selection of some colleagues for promotions and more comfortable working conditions, which could of course have less to do with naked discrimination and more with social networks. However, what I found remarkable were the comments people made about *attitudes* toward them or those they knew. As described earlier, both Winton and Caridad shared their belief that whites don't like to see Blacks get ahead; Hortencia said that her boss accused her of pretending to be "refined"; and Edward attributed university officials' dismissal of the proposal to formalize connections with the University of the West Indies to their racist perception that these were inferior institutions. While I read my interlocutors' comments as perceptions rather than commonly held beliefs or social facts, I maintain that this potentially significant manifestation of racial bias calls for further investigation and should be considered in any proposal to address the problem of inequality.

Conclusion

Dreams Multiplied . . . A Final Entrée to Cuba

On a humid Wednesday morning, June 10, 2005, my hour-long flight from Miami to the Antonio Maceo Airport in Santiago de Cuba touched down. I was returning for my fourth field research trip to Cuba. Upon disembarking, I was struck by a new or else previously undetected sign that greeted travelers as they ambled toward Customs. The sign read:

> Cubanacan, Agencia de Viajes. Ofertamos Alojamiento, Renta de Autos, Taxis, Excursiones, Asistencia en Aeropuerto, Boletos Aéreos, Charteo de Aviones y Helicopteros. Multiplicamos Sueños. We Multiply Dreams (Cubanancan, Travel Agency. We Offer Accommodation, Car Rental, Taxis, Excursions, Airport Assistance, Airline Tickets, Airplane and Helicopter Charters. We Multiply Dreams.)

It was a relatively simple sign in blue, red, and white: the colors of the Cuban flag morphed into a promise of pleasure through meeting needs that were wildly extravagant in the Cuba that I had come to know.

Conspicuously punctuated by the English translation of "Multiplicamos Sueños," this ad promised not only to *realize* but to *multiply* dreams. I was taken aback by this adoption of the capitalist strategy to magnify, increase, and create, rather than to simply meet, consumer needs. How different were the dreams and destinies of the targeted market of foreign tourists and Cubans living abroad from those of the English-speaking Caribbean immigrant laborers who began pouring into eastern Cuba nearly a century ago, I thought. I also could not help noting the contrast between the bold claim to multiply dreams and the actual plaque, modest in terms of size and presentation, lacking in the grandeur and glamour of similar offers in other tourist destinations. Its awkward insertion into the airport's austere surroundings betrayed not only the disjuncture between foreign fantasies and Cuban realities, but also the profound tensions that dominate social discourse in contemporary Cuba.

Cubans across spectrums of race and origin are struggling to navigate the multiple chasms that characterize the twenty-first-century landscape. The focus of this book has been the course that Black Cubans who have distinguished themselves based upon their Anglo-Caribbean background have charted. I sought to understand why, decades after the majority of immigrants settled in Cuba, there has been a revitalization of Anglo-Caribbean institutions and community.

Getting the story of the revitalization required following my interlocutors through their narratives of a collective past. This past began in Jamaica, Barbados, St. Lucia, Montserrat, St. Kitts, Grenada, and other former British colonies; it followed them through Panama's canal zone, United Fruit Company, the Cuban American Sugar Company, Banes, Baraguá, Santiago, Caimanera, Guantánamo, and the U.S. Naval Base; it continued among rebels in the Sierra and in Santiago, family members on opposite sides of the Cold War, and a society that became more equal for some and less free for others. My interlocutors needed to dig through all of this in order to rescue their roots and tell their stories.

In my analysis, I have positioned people of Anglo-Caribbean origin in Cuba at the interstices of colonialism and sovereignty, capitalism and socialism, foreign and native, marginalization and inclusion, diaspora and nationalism. I have asked what kinds of subjectivities are forged at these various crossroads and how the claim to multiple spaces of belonging in the midst of economic crisis and uncertainty sheds light on processes of subject-formation.

I suggest that in late twentieth-century Cuba, Black and diasporic subjectivities, constituted through a different set of circumstances and events triggered by the collapse of the Soviet Union, allowed for the emergence of an African Anglo-Caribbean Cuban diasporic identity. By the same token, African Anglo-Caribbean Cuban subjectivity makes possible a particular Black identity that challenges the narrative of Black inferiority, the consequences of which were markedly exacerbated during the Special Period. I argue that the economic crisis and social transformations taking place prompted this particular group of Black Cubans to reinvigorate their Anglo-Caribbean origins as a means to assert a respectable Blackness. I have described this articulation of diaspora as palimpsest, where social narratives of belonging were elaborated upon, effaced, and rewritten.

Los Jamaicanos as (Post)Colonial Diasporic Subject

As I have mentioned, the African Anglo-Caribbean diaspora in Cuba requires investigation of the temporal, ideological, and spatial boundaries of diaspora. I have considered diaspora as a strategy of existence through connection that extends beyond the national space—a strategy inspired by rising racial inequalities in Cuba after the Soviet period. This strategy can be abandoned or augmented, depending on political, economic, and social developments.

As discussed in chapter 1, British West Indian immigrants, attracted to Cuba by employment created in large part through neocolonial relations with the United States, established and maintained distinct and vibrant communities. Their status as English-speaking British subjects differentiated them from both Haitian immigrants and working-class Cubans of color. At the outset of the Cuban Revolution, members of this community were still culturally and politically linked to the British Empire,[1] economically dependent upon the U.S. presence, and yet invested in the future of their adopted country. During Cuba's transition from a neocolonial state to a socialist one highly dependent upon the Soviet Union, immigrants from the English-speaking Caribbean and their children occupied an ambiguous position within the Cuban nation. Foreigner and citizen, English- and Spanish-speaking, of empires and nations, they have for some time embodied the in-betweenness recently attributed to the contemporary Cuban subject.

As such, the ways in which Anglo-Caribbean Cubans have negotiated and are negotiating the transformations precipitated by the disintegration of the socialist bloc offer insights into the lived reality "between the posts," the phrase that Chari and Verdery (2009) introduce. Specifically, we can gain some sense of how this multilayered, ambiguous postcoloniality is being lived through the postsocialist era. The paradoxical character of post-1989 Cuban society is no doubt both shaping and reflected in the emergent political subjectivities of these Black Cubans of Anglo-Caribbean origin. Their narratives of social mobility destabilize notions of coherent self-making, revealing the tensions generated by subject formation between and within the "posts." They illustrate that certain subjectivities are informed not only by the dialogical relationship between their economic and social marginalization in the wake of market reforms but also by pre- and post-1959 processes of racial inclusion and exclusion.

A Peculiar Challenge for Antiracist Activism

In chapter 4, I problematized claims to a respectable Blackness in a climate of increasing racialized inequality; then, in chapter 5, I went on to argue that the related narratives of social mobility are both affirmation and critique of official ideology and contemporary social relations. One of the social dynamics to emerge from using Anglo-Caribbean Cubans as a lens through which to observe contemporary Cuba is that Black social mobility experienced through the revolution has led to unique manifestations of racism. The historical pattern of discrimination directed toward people of African descent who have broken through racial barriers in the areas of education, employment, and even political office complicates claims to a raceless society. It also has implications for the direction of transformative visions and antiracist activism in Cuba and beyond. Although some antiracist organizations have set forth proposals to address inequality in Cuba, these proposals do not directly engage the unique challenge faced by professionals of African descent.[2]

This dilemma of achieving professional status and continuing to confront the belief in Black inferiority in a society professing to be antiracist has implications beyond Cuba's borders. Indeed, it is particularly relevant for other Latin American countries that hold onto the ideology of racial democracy, race-blind nationalism, or racelessness as well as for the United States, where claims of a post-racial society spurred by the election of Barack Obama suggest that it is moving closer to the Latin American model. One incident that reinvigorated this question of the perception of Black professionals occurred in 2013 when the Cuban government sent 400 doctors to Brazil to address extreme racial and regional disparities in health care provision. Brazilians protested their presence, and while their objections had much to do with the perceived negative impact these cheaper Cuban doctors would have on

Brazilian doctors, there were also racist overtones as depicted in a cartoon in an article entitled "Racism Greets Imported Cuban Doctors in Brazil."[3] The cartoon features a dark-skinned male physician, distinguished as Cuban by an airport sign behind him and a Cuban flag in his pocket, examining a blond Brazilian female physician (she is also wearing a lab coat and tie), who shouts "Escravos!" (Slaves!) in spite of the tongue depressor positioned in her mouth. The words "Xenofobia" and "Racismo" appear above the Cuban physician's head to indicate his thoughts in response to her exclamation. The Brazilian doctor is referring to the Black doctor's relationship with the Cuban state—the state pockets the lion's share of the money that Brazil pays for this service. But the predicament of the Black professional leads us to question whether the cartoon's artist, via the Brazilian doctor, is also evoking slavery and postemancipation servitude, signaling that the physician's Blackness negates any authority that his professional position would otherwise grant him. This also opens interesting questions about how the racialized experiences of the thousands of Black Cuban professionals on missions abroad might be shaping analyses of race within the borders of *la patria*.

"Taking Back What Is Rightfully Ours"

In the midst of writing this book, I had an unanticipated encounter that left me questioning claims of belonging and the ongoing usefulness of strategies to combat misrecognition, such as those employed by Anglo-Caribbean Cubans. It occurred while I was taking a break from work and treating myself to a massage. When the therapist began asking me about what I did, rather than reinvent myself as an author of children's stories or a flight attendant, I told him a bit about my research. Unfortunately for me at that moment, he was quite inquisitive because, as he said, "My grandfather was Cuban . . . or really Spanish. He came to Cuba in the early twentieth century." I responded by saying that I study the descendants of people who migrated to Cuba from the English-speaking Caribbean during that same time period. I thought, but did not say, that his grandfather might have been among those Spaniards encouraged to migrate to Cuba in order to right the racial imbalance exacerbated by Black Caribbean migration.

The therapist then shared that his grandfather had been a successful landowner who had a plantation in Cuba but left for the United States after the revolution. Then, taking on an authoritative tone, he pronounced, "My brother and I are waiting for things to change, for Castro to die, so that we can go back and claim what is *rightfully ours.*" After his pronouncement he filled in my stunned silence with ramblings about the questionable feasibility of a plan to take over the land that his grandfather had owned; however, his belief in his right to this land was unwavering.

I was immediately reminded of remarks that Ariel Fernández Díaz, a Cuban hip-hop artist who migrated to New York in the early 2000s, made at a talk about Black Cubans and hip-hop in Cuba (Fernández Díaz 2007). When asked about the future of Blacks in Cuba, he predicted that what will occur in Cuba will be reminiscent of what occurred at the conclusion of the Independence Wars. Fernández Díaz was referring to the fate of Antonio Maceo and his famous protest at Baraguá. At the conclusion of the Ten Years' War, Maceo refused the terms of the treaty offered by the Spanish as it did not declare Cuba a free nation. While his fellow generals acquiesced to a continuation of colonial rule, he protested. This, as well as his brilliance as a military strategist, later earned him status as a national hero.

Fernández Díaz forecasted that when relations with the United States normalize, today's Cuban leaders, similar to Maceo's nineteenth-century peers, will eventually make deals with the Americans, selling out Black Cubans and, indeed, all Cubans who desire equality and social justice (Fernández Díaz 2007). For Fernández Díaz and other young people—such as Deunes and David, who envision themselves as the real revolutionaries within the revolution—Cuba is actually rightfully *theirs.* Regardless of the frustration and bitterness that perhaps fueled Fernández Díaz's remark, the question of the restructuring of allegiances, particularly as it pertains to race, is one to attend to as Cuba moves ever forward into the twenty-first century.

Notes

Preface

1. I am here referring to the period beginning in 1989 when the Soviet Union and the Council for Mutual Economic Assistance (CMEA) collapsed, withdrawing economic support from Cuba and marking the formal dissolution of Eastern European socialism.

2. For an engaging discussion of this film, see Giovannetti 2002.

3. With full recognition of the flexibility and instability of racial terminology across time, space, and place, I use the terms Black, mulatto or mestizo, and Cubans of color interchangeably and in a way that most closely approximates the use of these terms as social and racial categories in Cuba.

4. In his seminal 1893 essay entitled "My Race," José Martí argues for the equality of all men and proposes that it is character rather than color that separates them. Rather than proclaim that race is a fiction or that Cuba is a raceless society, he insists that race is essentially irrelevant and denounces those who behave otherwise, both Blacks and whites, as racist. This is a foundational concept in Cuba's racial ideology.

5. See de la Fuente 2001a. "The Resurgence of Racism in Cuba" is one of the first analyses of this growing racial disparity.

6. See http://www.afrocubaweb.com/actingonourconscience.htm for the text of this essay.

Introduction: Nested Diasporas, Multiple Mobilities, and the Politics of Black Belonging

1. This phrase comes from Audrey Charlton's dissertation on Jamaicans and Barbadians in Cuba through 1959. She quotes one of her Jamaican informants who remarked that "Now Kasia [a neighbor whom she liked] proud to know she fadah [West Indian]. She outlooking. It now dey feel proud again" (2005:4).

2. For genealogies of diaspora, see Clifford 1994; Palmer 2000; Edwards 2003; Thomas and Campt 2006; Cohen 2008; and Banerjee 2012.

3. For extensive discussion of these concepts and the distinction between them, see Biehl, Good, and Kleinman 2007; Butler 1993; S. Hall 1981, 1987; Brady and Shirato 2010; and Weedon 2004.

4. Field note, August 3, 2004, Guantánamo.

5. The constitution of 1940 classified anyone born in Cuba as Cuban, whereas prior to this, the children of foreigners had to apply for Cuban citizenship upon reaching adulthood. See Cervantes-Rodríguez 2010, 140.

6. I am thinking here of Purcell's (1993) transactional processes, Edmund Gordon's (1998) Anglo-superiority, Moberg's (1996) Marxist class segmentation model, and Bourgois' (1989) conjugated oppression.

7. The scholars mentioned in the preceding note focus on Central America. For work on immigrants in the U.S., see Bryce-Laporte 1972; Foner 2001; Hintzen 2001; Waters 2001a, 2001b; Kasinitz 1992; Rogers 2006; Pierre 2004; and Vickerman 1999.

8. The fact that Cuba (not to mention China) remains a socialist country, in which the single-party state controls the means of production, disrupts the narrative that we live in a postsocialist world. However, the term *postsocialism* here refers to a global landscape in which the European socialist bloc no longer exists.

9. The Jamaican population (in Jamaica) was 831,383 in 1911 and was only around 850,000 ten years later, suggesting a significant drain of the population through migration (to Cuba as well as the United States and other Latin American locations) (Wynter 2001:263).

10. McLeod's figures from 1912 and 1931 indicate that around 116,000 British West Indians traveled to Cuba (2000:55).

11. Chailloux and Whitney estimate 170,000 people British West Indians entered Cuba by 1931 (2005:62).

12. Between 1913 and 1923, about 75 percent of the immigrants came from Jamaica and the majority of the 25 percent remaining came from Barbados (Charlton 2005:33). However, immigrants hailed from throughout the colonies, and depending on time period and specific location, those from the smaller islands could be a dominant numerical presence. For discussion of the non-Jamaican presence of British West Indians in Cuba, see Giovannetti 2001:50.

13. See Pérez de la Riva 1975; D. Marshall 1985; Richardson 1989; Scott 1997; Chomsky 2000; Putnam 2002, 2013; Cooper, Holt, and Scott 2000; de la Fuente 1997; and Naranjo Orovio 1997.

14. Coined by Gayatri Spivak (1988), *strategic essentialism* refers to a political strategy adopted by subordinated people in which they highlight commonalities and forge a common identity in an effort to challenge various forms of domination.

15. Guridy makes a similar argument in his analysis of early twentieth-century Afro-Cuban and African American relations. He states, "Diaspora did not conflict with Black aspirations for national citizenship," finding that these relationships "were motivated by material incentives as much as a desire for belonging" (2010:4).

16. Roque Cabello and Sáchez Herrero (1998) and other scholars indicate that the economic crisis actually began in the 1980s as the growth of 1980–1985 was due to previous investments and subsidies and was followed by poor economic performance.

17. Both the Torticelli and Helms-Burton bills further restricted Cuba's access to essential resources, consumer goods, and credit.

18. This was initiated by the legalization of the U.S. dollar in 1993, which resulted in both U.S. dollars and pesos being in circulation simultaneously. In 2004, the CUC or peso

convertible, a currency pegged to the U.S. dollar, became the primary currency accepted in what had become known as "dollar" stores. While many, if not most, essential and nonessential goods and services are sold in pesos convertibles, colloquially referred to as *CUC*, *chavito*, or *divisa*, most Cubans are officially paid in Cuban pesos (CUP). The most notable exception to this is those Cubans who work in the tourist industry where they receive tips and (for some) a part of their salary in CUC.

19. It was announced in 2013 that the country would be gradually abolishing the dual economy. See http://www.bbc.com/news/world-latin-america-24627620. To date, there has been no discernible movement toward making this a reality. See http://www.nytimes.com/2014/12/15/opinion/cubas-economy-at-a-crossroads.html?_r=0.

20. For more on dollarization and remittances, see Blue 2007 and Eckstein 2004.

21. *Buena presencia* refers to the practice of discriminating against people who have physical features (color, hair, facial features) associated with African origins because such features are perceived to be incompatible with a "good appearance."

22. Light or white Cubans too are engaged in jineterismo but it may be in a less public arena. Indeed, their whiteness makes their activities less visible or subject to such stigmatization. See Roland 2010.

23. Due to the revolution's failure to improve in the area of housing, people of African descent are more concentrated on the outskirts of the cities in *barrios marginales* where there are fewer services and worse housing stock (de la Fuente 2001b). Also see Nadine Fernández's (2010) ethnography on interracial couples in Havana for insights into the reproduction of racist attitudes in revolutionary society.

24. Since the early 1990s, there has been a marked increase in work engaging race relations on the island. This includes work produced within and outside of Cuba. See Alvarado Ramos 2006; Sawyer 2005; Fernández 2010; Núñez González et al. 2011; Clealand 2012; de la Fuente 2001a; de la Fuente and Glasco 1997; Pérez Sarduy and Stubbs 2000; N. Fernandes 2006; Allen 2011; Roland 2010; Hansing 2006; Hernandez-Reguant 2009; McGarrity 1992; Morales Domínguez 2013; Aranda Covarrubias 2011; Espino Prieto and Rodriguez Ruiz 2006; and Martínez 2007.

25. I explore this extensively in my chapter "The Passing of a Black Yankee: Fieldnotes/Cliff Notes of a Wannabe Santiaguera" (Queeley 2009).

26. Although I was not a tourist per se, there is considerable slippage between "tourist" and "foreigner." In order to avoid association with the former in the hopes of establishing myself as an ethnographer, I tended to steer clear of establishments patronized by tourists.

27. See Michalowski 1996 for elaboration on the relationship between macro-social geopolitical forces and the micro-social ethnographic encounter and on the social scientific representation of that encounter.

28. In March 2008, Raúl Castro, who had become Cuba's president in February, instituted several reforms. Along with removing the restrictions on Cubans owning cell phones, personal computers, DVD players, and other electronic equipment, the reforms allowed Cubans to patronize tourist establishments that were formerly off limits.

29. The term *rasta modas* refers to young men of color presumed to grow dreadlocks as a style to attract foreigners interested in a more exotic aesthetic. They are not Rastafari per

se. See Hansing's (2006) ethnography on Rasta in Cuba as well as Furé Davis (2011) for an overview of Rasta in Cuba.

30. Only people living in Guantánamo were able to pick up the satellite signal from the U.S. Naval Base, however.

31. Publications based on ethnographic research conducted on revolutionary society prior to the collapse of the Soviet Union (between 1959 and 1989) include Zeitlin 1967; Fagen 1969; Lewis, Lewis, and Rigdon 1977a, 1977b, 1978 (three volumes published as part of Oscar Lewis's Project Cuba [1969–70] and terminated by Cuban authorities who confiscated much of their ethnographic data); Butterworth 1980; Arguelles and Rich 1984; Rosendahl 1997; Daniel 1995; Bengelsdorf 1994; and Leiner 1994.

32. For an excellent assessment of Ortiz's work, see Font and Quiroz 2005. Cabrera, who died in 1991, explored and valorized Afro-Cuban culture through ethnographically informed creative writing. For recent analysis of anthropological research, ethnographic writing, and literature in Cuba before and after the revolution, see Rodriguez-Mangual 2004 and Maguire 2011.

33. Several social scientists conducting ethnographic work have noted such challenges: Hansing 2006; Fernández 2010; Fernandes 2006; Hay 2009; Roland 2010; Sawyer 2005; and Brotherton 2008.

34. Field note, June 10, 2005, Santiago.

35. Literally, *los métodos de Bush* means "Bush's methods" and refers to the new legislation that tightened the U.S. embargo the summer prior to the 2004 election.

36. Notable exceptions to this tendency in the anthropological literature include Rosendahl 1997; Frederik 2012; and Pertierra 2011.

37. For an anthropological study of racial and ethnic identity that focuses on the historical experience of Jamaican and Barbadian immigrants throughout the island, see Charlton 2005.

38. *Centrales* refers to the agricultural complex that dominated postcolonial Cuban sugar production. Given the instability in the price of sugar, investors in the sugar industry, primarily from the United States, developed and expanded the *central* system, so that it was large, modernized, heavily mechanized, and more efficient, thus making the investment more profitable. See Dye 1998; Ayala 1999.

39. Roughly translating as "guest houses," *casas particulares* are typically rooms in people's homes that have been fixed up to accommodate foreigners who pay in foreign currency or, as of 2005, pesos convertibles.

40. I used snowball sampling to recruit these participants. During my initial research trip, through the contacts I was making in academic circles, I was given the number of the former president of the now-defunct Anglo-Caribbean Descendant Association in Santiago. After I had met and spent time with her, she then mentioned other people that I could talk to both in Santiago and Guantánamo, many of whom in turn introduced me to additional participants. I also followed up on referrals given to me by one of the Jamaican Cuban immigrants I interviewed informally while in New York.

41. With the advent of the Special Period, Cuba instituted a special measure that prohibited the owners of certain livestock, cattle for instance, from slaughtering their animals

either for their own consumption or for the purpose of selling the meat. This livestock is regarded as property of the state.

42. In one of Hay's informants' group discussions, one woman makes the point that *negra* is different coming from a Black person than a white Cuban, supporting this argument (Hay 2009:68). It is also important to note that *negro/a* and *negrito/a* are used as terms of endearment by and toward people of all racialized phenotypes, further demonstrating the multiple meanings of racial terminology.

43. Giovannetti (2002), in his analysis of the documentary *Los Hijos de Baraguá*, notes that not only did some interviewees protest being referred to as jamaicanos, insisting that their island identity be recognized, but they also viewed the term jamaiquino as pejorative.

44. I also encountered the term *negros ingleses* in Sánchez Guerra's brief history of British West Indian immigrants in Guantánamo (2004) but have not encountered it outside of this work.

45. Graciela Chailloux writes, "What was important for those who remained was the fact that they now constituted families of 'pichones'—children of immigrants. These families were usually large and known as the Caribbean Cubans" (Chailloux and Whitney 2001:51). Here is yet another term. Although I did infrequently hear them referred to as *los caribeños*, I don't recall ever hearing them referred to as *cubanos caribeños*.

46. Initially employed systematically in the work of Cuban anthropologist Fernando Ortiz, the term *Afro-Cuban* has most often been used by Cubans to describe cultural practices rather than people themselves. There has been some debate about the use of this term as it implies a division between Cuban and Afro-Cuban that many reject. By this logic, separating out the "Afro" is a way to deny the centrality of African cultural practices and those of African descendants to national culture. However, some Cuban activists and cultural workers routinely use this term in their work (e.g., Pérez Sarduy and Stubbs 2000; Rubiera Castillo and Martiatu Terry 2011).

47. *Motos* are one of the more expensive forms of transportation, charging ten pesos a ride as compared to the *guaguas* (buses), *camionetas*, *camiones*, and *coches* that charge one peso and under.

48. As explained on p. 15, *jinetera/jinetero* means "rider" and is used to describe those who make money off of foreigners, most often as sex workers or street hustlers.

49. See n29, p. 187. The various motivations for growing locks include trying to attract foreign tourists interested in a more exotic appearance and asserting a nonconformist Black identity.

50. The *carnet* is the identity card that all Cubans receive at the age of twelve and generally carry around with them all of the time.

51. Field note, June 7, 2005, Santiago.

52. In Cuba, there is a system whereby visitors buy stamps for different denominations that are affixed to their visa and signify authorization for different lengths of stay. For instance, if one has a thirty-day tourist visa, it can be renewed for another thirty days, but one has to buy a twenty-five-dollar stamp to do so.

53. *Pru oriental* is a drink particular to the eastern side of the country, made from boiling various roots.

54. In the course of the research, the contemporary transnational character of partici-pants' family and social networks led me to explore the option of expanding the study to include Cubans of Anglo-Caribbean descent living in the United States. Though I ultimately decided against this, I did contact and interview six individuals living in Florida and New York. Although the Anglo-Caribbean Cuban immigrants to the U.S. with whom I spoke in depth are not formally part of the study, I consider these informal and semiformal inter-views to have contributed to my knowledge of this population.

55. *Militante* refers to Party members who can occupy various positions in government.

56. *Barrios marginales* is a term used for neighborhoods on the outskirts of the city that are disproportionately affected by water and electricity shortages and populated by people of more African descent.

57. People who dance *danzon*, a style of dance primarily performed by older Cubans.

58. Guerra (2012) also acknowledges the role of the Special Period in bringing about ten-sions that her history of the early revolutionary period addresses.

Chapter 1. British West Indian Migration to Cuba: The Roots and Routes of Respectability

1. Quoted in S. Marshall 2006:131 (emphasis mine), the epigraph is taken from a paper presented by Croos Valiente and Lewis at the British West Indian Welfare Centre's first in-ternational symposium on the British West Indian presence in Cuba, March 1996.

2. The Nationality Act of 1948 declared that British subjects could also be citizens of the United Kingdom or Commonwealth citizens. The Nationality Act of 1982 abolished the category of British subject.

3. Analyzing these claims, Putnam (2014) argues that they constitute a "vernacular politi-cal philosophy" that Caribbean British subjects/citizens developed in their efforts to contest racial subjugation in the context of empire.

4. Other investigators who have interviewed Caribbean immigrants and their descen-dants in Cuba and combed through archival material concerning this population reproduce this particular narrative (Giovannetti 2001; Chailloux, Whitney, and Claxton 2006; S. Mar-shall 2006). Historians Chailloux and Whitney (2005) make the claim that "At the heart of the family not only was the religiosity that characterizes Anglo-Antilleans maintained. The respect for elders, attachment to work and education, attention to manners, [and] the train-ing of women for industriousness [*sic*] in the home, music and handicrafts distinguished [Anglo-Antillean] homes." They add that "a veneration of self-betterment and good man-ners has been a badge of the family upbringing among Anglophone Caribbeans" (2005:78). Indeed, Chailloux refers to them as a "labor aristocracy" due to their knowledge of English and ability to use it as symbolic capital (Chailloux and Whitney 2005:3).

Information concerning the question of political involvement is more contradictory. While the notion that the immigrants did not meddle in the affairs of their host country predominated, both their documented involvement in labor activism (Carr 1998b) and Gar-veyism (McLeod 2003; Muñiz and Giovannetti 2003; Guridy 2003; Estévez Rivera 2003) and the evidence I uncovered through field research reveals a more complicated picture. I explore this conflict between their self-representations as apolitical and the reality of activism extensively in chapter 2.

5. Only three participants expressed the belief that there were no differences. It is noteworthy that two of these individuals sought to impress upon me that all Cubans are equal, thanks to the revolution. For one interlocutor, the privilege that was accorded to immigrants from the Anglophone Caribbean was due solely to language. This is in contrast to characterizations of other participants, some of whom specifically emphasized the difference between jamaicano and cubano "culture," which I will explore in depth.

6. Similar to that of other Anglophone Caribbean diasporic communities, this self-making practice includes its deployment against other abjected populations. For West Indian Cubans, this includes Haitians as well as working-class Cubans of color, while for West Indians in other parts of the Americas, this might include indigenous groups and mestizos as well as native Black populations. For U.S. examples, see Rogers 2001; Hintzen 2004, 2010; and Waters 2001a, 2001b. For Central American examples, see Gordon 1998; Purcell 1993; Harpelle 2001; Bourgois 1989; and O'Reggio 2006. McLeod, 1998, 2010, treats the forced repatriations of the 1930s and '40s; Giovannetti, 2001, 2006a, 2006b and Charlton, 2005, explore migrants' British subject identity; and Gómez, 2005, looks at the Haitian presence in Cuba: all four mention the perception of English-speaking Caribbean respectability relative to Haitians. Muñiz and Giovannetti (2003) in their work on British West Indian immigrants, or cocolos, of the Dominican Republic also describe them as respectful, disciplined, well mannered, and having good hygiene, "attribut[ing] this to the higher level of economic and social development of British colonies in comparison to Haiti and their identity as British subjects" (2003:147). They go on to explain that this perception is rooted in the association between Britain and civilization in comparison to Haiti's association with Africa and primitiveness.

7. As Giovannetti (2006a) points out, migrants were familiar with the racism and discrimination of the plantation system as this is what they confronted at home and in other Latin American labor destinations. Given the ubiquity of race and class hierarchies in the Americas, it is likely that they had similar strategies for navigating this reality.

8. For treatment of the postemancipation period, see Moreno Fraginals, Moya Pons, and Engerman 1985; Beckles and Shepherd 1996; D. Hall 1978; Bolland 1981, 1992; Cooper, Holt, and Scott 2000; Besson 1992; Holt 1992; Austin Broos 1992; Brodber 2004; D. Marshall 1985; Knight 1970, 1978, 1985; Chomsky 1996; and Scott 1985, 2008.

9. This was known as the "free village movement" in Jamaica. See Mintz 1958 and Mintz and Price 1985.

10. Much of the earlier research is the work of labor historians who focus on the use of British Caribbean immigrants in Latin America, and Central America in particular, within the burgeoning U.S.-controlled enterprises (see Ayala 1999 for treatment of the post-1898 transformations in the sugar industry in the Spanish-speaking Caribbean). These provide insight into the Panama Canal and United Fruit Company plantations as racialized spaces where differences of color and culture were both used by managers to divide the labor force and asserted by Black immigrants and their descendants to claim a more privileged position within the labor hierarchy (Conniff 1985; Petras 1988; Bourgois 1989; Echeverri-Gent 1992;

Newton 1984; Chomsky 1996). Other studies focus on cultural production (Bryce-Laporte 1998; Purcell 1993; Aceto 2002), the shifting relationship to the state and nation (Harpelle 2001), and the politics of identity (E. Gordon 1998) in this compelling and contradictory environment of simultaneous racial subordination and ethnic superiority.

Scholarly research on British West Indian immigrants to Cuba in particular mirrors these themes. Franklin Knight (1985) was among the pioneers of those who looked at the use of Jamaican workers in Cuba as a step in the transition from slave to free labor. Indeed, earlier work by Cuban historians focused on the role that they played in early twentieth-century imperialist machinations, characterizing the importation of Caribbean workers as a form of slavery and characterizing the immigrants as a homogeneous mass of exploited laborers (González Suárez 1987; Álvarez Estévez 1988; Pérez de la Riva 1975). More recent work by Cuban scholars has provided a lens into these peoples' lives as social beings, with Espronceda Amor's (1999) comparison of Haitian and Anglophone Caribbean family formation and Estévez Rivero's (2003) treatment of the UNIA in Santiago being exemplary of this trend. Historians such as Cadence Wynter (2001), Sharon Marshall (2006), and Tracy Graham (2013) have taken pains to trace the connections that immigrants maintained with Jamaica and Barbados. Of these, Graham's work stands out as following Lara Putnam's (2002) lead by focusing on the experience of female migrants in their challenge of elite patriarchal notions that would restrict their quest for the greater opportunities that existed abroad. Chailloux and Whitney (2001, 2005) and Whitney and Chailloux Laffita (2013), through archival research and oral history interviews, have also made significant contributions to our understanding of the immigrants' associational life and the process of "becoming Cuban (or not)" (2013:39). Claxton (Chailloux, Whitney, and Claxton, 2006), Derrick (2001), S. Marshall (2006), and C. Moore (2008) are among those Cuban descendants of Anglophone Caribbean immigrants who have published accounts of the communities to which they and/or their forbears belonged.

Subsequent work has also attempted to provide a textured representation of immigrants' lives and their relationship to the new Cuban nation. For instance, Carr's (1998a, 1998b) work reconstructs their participation in the labor unrest of the 1930s, challenging representations of them as a docile, conciliatory labor force ready to do the bidding of foreign capital. Charlton's unpublished dissertation (2005), which is in part based on interviews of immigrants and their descendants, explores the question of their identification as British subjects and use of the British Consulate to advocate for better treatment and funding for repatriation. Giovannetti (2001, 2006a, 2006b) also concerns himself with these themes, paying particular attention to the abuses that prompted immigrants to appeal to the Consulate, processes of identification, and the heterogeneity of the "British subject" as was evident in, among other things, the salience of island identities. Not only were British West Indians at times differentiated from each other and at times regarded as all "English," but they also were both distinguished from and lumped together with Haitian immigrants. McLeod (2000), Casey (2012), and Gómez Navia (2005) examine the Haitian experience in Cuba and include some comparison of Haitians' experiences to that of the British West Indians, the other Black immigrant group in Cuba at the time.

11. Indeed, Pérez de la Riva makes the point that, due to U.S. dominance, the U.S. model

of immigration and settlement was inappropriately applied to this Caribbean population whose migrations were often followed by returns (1975:75).

12. They were a part of a larger migration of Europeans to the region. From 1880 to 1930, between 10 and 11 million Europeans migrated to Latin America, with most going to Brazil, Argentina, and Uruguay, as part of this explosive period of transatlantic commerce and migration (Andrews 1997:12).

13. According to the Cuban Census of 1919, "Jamaicans" and "Other West Indians" numbered 41,159, with 39,137 classified as "colored." Also see Giovannetti 2001:43. Just as with the outbreak of the Haitian Revolution that shifted the burden of world sugar production onto Cuba, the suspension of European beet sugar production due to World War I led to a sugar boom and thus an increased demand for labor. While they certainly never superseded the Spanish immigrant population, the concentrated influx of laborers during this time period certainly had a bearing on the social climate and experiences of the migrants. As Giovannetti explains, "any understanding of the reaction to the presence of thousands of Black migrants within Cuban society has to take into account such a short period of mass migration" (2006b:104).

14. According to *Cuba Económica y Financiera* (1944:29), in 1919, 27.8 percent of the population of Oriente was "colored." In 1931, 454,469 people (42.4 percent) in Oriente province were classified as "colored" out of a total population of 1,072,757. While there is no distinction between foreign and native people of color here, one might surmise that this increase is in part due to the influx of Caribbean immigrants. For instance, the 1931 and 1943 censuses do provide data categorizing the foreign born population according to "whites" and "color," but there is no further breakdown based on origin of those foreigners classified as "color," nor is there an explanation for the basis of this categorization. McLeod notes that between 1912 and 1931, 183,000 Haitians entered Cuba compared to 116,000 British West Indians (2000:57).

15. For instance, Whitney and Chailloux Laffita find that both "Haitian and British Caribbean workers had been blamed for supposedly rising crime rates and the introduction of 'primitive' practices such as witchcraft and voodoo" (2013:11). British Caribbean immigrants were even lumped in with Chinese workers as both were viewed as a menace to the nation and spurred requests for Spanish immigrants (Cervantes-Rodríguez 2010:133)

16. With regard to skill, there is considerable uncertainty regarding the capabilities of British Caribbean immigrants, and thus it is difficult to compare them with Haitians or even within their own group. Though the lion's share identified themselves as unskilled laborers, there were skilled laborers among them who might have begun on better footing than their fellow sojourners (see Carr 1998b; McLeod 2000; S. Marshall 2006; Chailloux and Whitney 2005). The issue of immigration was extremely political, which calls into question the reliability of reported migrant occupations. For instance, someone who was contracted by a sugar company but perhaps had knowledge of a trade might declare himself to be an agricultural laborer rather than a blacksmith because it was their experience in cane fields that was relevant to their employer. Another consideration that complicates ascertaining the particular resources of British West Indian immigrants is that the laws and regulations regarding immigration differed throughout the British colonies (Whitney and

Chailloux Laffita 2013:61; Wynter 2001:263; Giovannetti 2001). The issue of literacy appears to be clearer. The literacy rate of British West Indian migrants is reported to have been high relative to their Haitian counterparts as well as to native Black and mulatto Cubans, placing them in a superior position among the laboring class. Carr 1998b, McLeod 1998, Chailloux and Whitney 2005, Gómez Navia 2005, McGillivray 2009, Casey 2012, and Putnam 2013 all make note of this. Between 1912 and 1929, the illiteracy rate for Haitian immigrants arriving in Cuba was 84.4 percent as compared to 9.3 percent of British West Indians. According to the census of 1899, 24 percent of Afro-Cubans could read and write compared to 44 percent of white Cubans—by 1907, the rate increased to 45 percent for Blacks and 58 percent for whites (Helg 1995:129). By 1919, the rate of Blacks and native whites seemed to have stabilized as 44.8 percent of the "colored" population of Oriente, 76.6 percent of foreign whites, and 57.6 percent of native whites could read and write (Director General of the Census 1922:370). There are no reliable comparable statistical data on the literacy rates of foreign Blacks after their arrival and settlement in Cuba. Given the defunding of public education in the British West Indies described by Shirley Gordon (1963), the reportedly high percentage of immigrants who entered Cuba legally between 1912 and 1929 and claimed to be literate is puzzling (also see Campbell 2002). Chailloux and Whitney contend that British West Indians were educated in the Protestant churches, each of which had a primary school attached to it (2005:57). It is possible that those who migrated legally were disproportionately from that middle stratum that was able to obtain some primary education, however inadequate, as Putnam asserts that "British West Indians abroad may have been the most highly literate group of colonial subjects anywhere in the interwar world" (2013:128). A stark contrast in literacy with their "native" and foreign racial counterparts, even if it is somewhat exaggerated, might explain the enduring perception of people from the English-speaking Caribbean as being educated and better able to move out of agricultural work. In addition, their ability to understand English, the language of the foreign power dominant in Cuba, might have been conflated with literacy and education. Thus, how literacy was defined and what these relatively high literacy rates reveal about the segments of the population from which the immigrants emerged remains in question. Regardless, perceived differences in literacy along with language, skills, and religion constituted the imagined border that created distinct group identities. As I will argue extensively in chapter 4, this distinction was an elevating one.

17. Until World War II, this base was used primarily as a coaling station.

18. Americans went about building roads, bridges, highways, a trolley system, parks, pavilions, sports stadiums, power and plumbing systems, and railroads, all of which involved builders, contractors, architects, engineers, lawyers, bankers, materials, and capital—all provided by the U.S. Pérez argues that this transformation of public space and daily living had a greater impact than the U.S.'s political relationship with Cuba at the turn of the century: "The larger significance of the North American intervention, and certainly the enduring consequences of this presence, had less to do with political relationships than with social realignments. It was embedded in the ways in which U.S. normative systems and moral hierarchies worked their way into everyday life, primarily in the form of a vast cultural transfer, one that was facilitated by the great material impoverishment of Cubans in 1898" (1999:115).

19. For instance, Jatar-Hausmann writes of her grandfather's process of social mobility, "Don Cruz had left poverty in the Canary Islands almost a half century ago. At fifteen years of age he arrived in Cuba looking for a land of opportunities, and he had found it. Without a university degree, he saw his four children graduate at the University of Havana. He had worked his way up from delivering groceries in a small town, to owning and managing a nice hotel in Havana" (1999:2).

20. As Helg details, "Except as musicians, Spaniards exceeded the number of Afro-Cubans in all professional occupations. . . . Even in the distribution of public jobs, with salaries paid by the Cuban state, Spaniards were in a good position compared with Blacks; in 1907 there were 20 Spanish government officials (compared with 9 Afro-Cubans), and 377 Spanish male teachers (compared with 113 Afro-Cubans); Spaniards were on a par with Afro-Cubans as firemen, and only as policemen and soldiers were they less numerous than Afro-Cubans (13 percent [of the force] were Spanish compared to 21 percent Afro-Cuban). . . . Because of the received preference in some trades, Spaniards strengthened the colonial Spanish–controlled guilds, which included few white Cubans and often turned away Afro-Cubans" (1995:110).

21. Although this has been the subject of some debate in Cuban historiography, as is evident from the contrasting way in which Ferrer (1999) and Helg (1995) frame Cuban racial politics, the events of the nineteenth and twentieth centuries do not support the notion that the U.S. somehow corrupted a people wholly committed to racial equality and justice. Also see Knight (1970), who challenges the argument that racial slavery in Cuba was relatively benign.

22. In 1907, 7 percent of government administrative jobs went to Afro-Cubans and all of these were lesser-skilled jobs such as janitor, messenger, and clerical worker. Out of 8,238 policemen and soldiers enlisted, 21 percent were Afro-Cuban, all in lower ranks. Afro-Cubans represented 439 of 5,964 teachers, 9 out of 205 government officials, 9 out of 1,240 physicians and surgeons, and 4 out of 1,347 lawyers (Helg 1995:100).

23. Among these demands were an increase in compulsory free education from 8 to 14 years old; free technical, secondary, and university education; state control of private schools; abolition of the death penalty; reform of the judicial and penitentiary systems; establishment of an eight-hour work day and a system that gave Cubans priority in employment; and the distribution of national lands to Cubans (Helg 1995:147).

24. *Adelantar de raza* means "to advance or improve the race." It is a term and process that has both phenotypic and cultural/behavioral connotations and one that is obscured most of the time by less pernicious, euphemistic labels such as "miscegenation" and "intermarriage."

25. Cuba was of course not alone in this. The British Caribbean had a pigmentocracy, and rejection of African cultures and Blackness were embedded within notions of racial self-improvement. However, given the demographic differences between Cuba and the British Caribbean, the latter by and large did not adopt policies aimed at whitening the population.

26. This was particularly notable in the tobacco industry, where Spaniards were "favored for more highly paid positions as cigar rollers," driving Cubans to the cigar industry in Tampa and Key West (Andrews 1997:14).

27. Around a million immigrants entered Cuba between 1902 and 1925; 600,000 stayed and 60 percent were from Spain. The other 40 percent were Jews from central and eastern Europe, Syrians, Lebanese, Palestinians, Chinese, North Americans, Mexicans, Puerto Ricans, and other Antilleans. Spanish immigrants, with the possible exception of those from the Canary Islands, did not go to Cuba to perform agricultural labor (Álvarez Estévez 1988:4).

28. Although according to Tracy Graham there were some voices sympathetic to the plight of British West Indian workers, these came from Oriente, not Havana (2013:140, 161).

29. As Giovannetti outlines, British support was inconsistent over time as it went from defending their West Indian subjects to the point of serious diplomatic conflict between 1917 and 1921, to reducing the diplomatic staff and closing consulates in areas with large migrant populations in the mid-1920s (2006b:112).

30. Bryan (2001:70), citing Franklin Knight's 1985 article as well as the *Jamaica Gazette*, makes the point that folklore about working for a dollar a day in the Spanish Caribbean versus for 1.5 shillings a day in Jamaica was misleading because (1) it was often more than a dollar a day (consular reports in Santiago indicate that Jamaican cane cutters earned $2.00, $2.50, and $3.00 a day prior to the 1921 depression, an amount that later declined to $1.50 a day, still above the $1.00); (2) wages fluctuated from 1900 through 1938, and this irregularity meant that immigrants had no guarantee of sustained earnings; and (3) the 1.5 shillings per day is artificially low because it was the average for field laborers and did not take the higher wages of artisans into account.

31. In her comparative study of Haitian and Jamaican families in Cuba, Espronceda Amor finds high rates of endogamy among the Jamaican population and argues that this obstructed integration into Cuban society. She also finds that for Jamaicans who tended to marry within their group, the group often came to include immigrants from other English-speaking islands; furthermore, as with Haitians, it was common for immigrants to marry the Cuban-born offspring of earlier waves of immigrants (1999:62). .

32. After 1940, the year in which the new constitution dictated that everyone born in Cuba had Cuban nationality regardless of the origin of their parents, it is difficult to ascertain whether or not those people categorized as "Cuban" are the children of Anglophone Caribbean immigrants born in Cuba and raised in the immigrant enclave. Indeed, this was the case in many of the families with whom I came into contact. Furthermore, in the Census of 1931, the category "foreigner" included those born in Cuba to foreign-born parents. Cervantes-Rodriguez (2010:140) adjusts for this, calculating that 407,216 of the 443,197 foreigners in Cuban in 1931 were actually born outside of the island.

33. Other indications that there was indeed a mixture of legal and consensual unions emerged in informal interviews.

34. These schools existed both independently of other English-speaking Caribbean organizations and within them, such as was the case with the British West Indian Cultural Centre's school. Espronceda Amor (1999) found that these schools existed within various institutions such as the Catalina lodge and the All Saints' Episcopal Church in Guantánamo. Also see Chailloux and Whitney (2005:75) for their discussion of the establishment of English schools. For instance, they found that schools had teachers from Jamaica and that the British government supplied the materials in the 1940s.

35. Field note, July 12, 2004, Guantánamo.

36. Author interview with Winton, July 11, 2004, Guantánamo.

37. Author interview with Jorge Smith, June 29, 2004, Santiago de Cuba.

38. British West Indians accounted for 80 percent (825) of the baptisms performed at All Saints' Episcopal Church between 1906 and 1929. Of the 42 Episcopal congregations in Cuba in 1924, more than half had British West Indian congregations. There was also church activity in the rural areas among *braceros* (day laborers), though there was more reliance on lay preachers due to the greater instability of the population (McLeod 2000:179).

39. For more on the religious landscape of immigrant communities, see Giovannetti 2001 and Espronceda Amor 1999.

40. Author interview with Edward, August 12, 2004, Guantánamo.

41. In addition to their various positions on sugar plantations, migrants headed to the coffee plantations situated in the mountains of Oriente in order to participate in that harvest from September to November, the month that the 145-day sugar harvest began. They often didn't return to their islands of origin during the remaining months because there was no work for them there (Chailloux and Whitney 2005:60).

42. Of the legal immigrants who arrived in Cuba between 1916 and 1927, 16.7 percent—and including more than half of all female British West Indian arrivals—had worked as seamstresses or domestic servants before sailing to Cuba (McLeod 2000:84). By 1930, of the immigrants from the English-speaking Caribbean living in Cuba, 38.5 percent were identified as domestic laborers: "The ability to speak English led many British Caribbean islanders into the service sector—as chauffeurs, cooks, gardeners, and school teachers—especially for families from the U.S. and upper- and middle-class Cubans who prized such language skills. . . . British West Indian immigrants proved particularly adept at finding employment outside of the sugar sector and in urban areas which not only promised to be less arduous than cutting cane, but also provided a steady income during the *tiempo muerto*" (Chailloux and Whitney 2005:94). As the majority of the domestic jobs were considered to be women's work and English-speakers were preferred laborers, the growth in this sector that accompanied the influx of U.S. capital and personnel encouraged Anglophone Caribbean women to migrate, thus accounting for the greater gender parity relative to other immigrant laborers.

43. McLeod (2003) notes that the perception that Garveyism fell on deaf ears in Cuba is largely based on a 1921 article in the *Heraldo de Cuba* that reported Garvey's visit to Club Atenas (a club of elite Cubans of color) to be met with disinterest because Cubans of color had already achieved tremendous equality. This was based on an exchange with the club's president Miguel Angel Céspedes and doesn't account for nonelite or upwardly mobile Cubans outside of Havana. Indeed, in her memoir, Castillo Bueno ("Reyita") discusses becoming involved in the Garvey movement, emphasizing that the promise to go back to Africa was what drew her to it (2000:26–29). The pull of Africa is also the subject of Garnes's 2009 analysis of the UNIA in Cuba based upon the recollections of West Indian residents. In addition, Pappademos (2011) argues that members of Africanist societies, unlike elite Afro-Cubans who were driven by self-interest rather than race consciousness and distanced themselves from African cultures, advocated for an alternative vision of the Cuban nation

in which the African presence was not incompatible with modern nationhood. This challenges the notion that Cubans of color would have been disinterested in Garvey's message.

44. See Hill 2011 for invaluable primary source documents that demonstrate the movement's genesis in diaspora as well as its global reach.

45. Historians have found that there was some regional variation in the content and compromises of the organization's Cuban chapters (see Guridy 2003 on the UNIA in Santa Clara, and McLeod 2003 for differences in chapters in Havana and Santiago). In her work on Garveyism in Santiago, Estévez Rivero (2003) found that there were 150 founding members of the city's UNIA chapter. Its mission was to "promote the spirit of pride in the black race and love amongst members of the race, to help those in need, to promote Christian feelings, found universities, institutions, and secondary schools in order to improve the culture and education of black people, to create businesses and industries with the intention of carrying out commercial exchange between Africa and America" (2003:71–72).

46. See Stoler 1989 on sexual morality and middle-class respectability in the colonial context.

47. This specific example was in the case of the Santa Clara UNIA where people had some means of subsisting on their own; however, there were migrants throughout the island who began their own businesses and found other employment that decreased their dependence upon plantation agriculture.

48. Author interview with Teresa, June 10, 2005, Santiago.

49. See Lipman for discussion of naval base expansion and hiring practices (2009:31–44).

50. There is some debate regarding the distinction between diaspora and transnational. Here, I am drawing from the concept of a "transnational social field" described by Levitt and Glick Schiller (2004) and engaging scholarly conceptualizations of diaspora that have emerged since the 1990s.

51. Benson (2013) highlights the revolutionary government's attempt to attract African Americans to Cuba by proclaiming that they had eliminated racism and demonstrating this through providing visiting African Americans with first-class treatment while Afro-Cubans continued to be treated as second-class citizens.

52. Author interview with Lester, August 2, 2004, Guantánamo.

53. Author interview with Elton, August 23, 2004, Santiago.

54. Author interview with Jorge Smith, June 27, 2004, Santiago.

55. Author interview with Winton, July 11, 2004, Guantánamo.

56. Author interview with Edward, August 11, 2004, Guantánamo.

57. See Lipman 2009 for a demographic description of the base in the mid-twentieth century.

58. El Centre was the epicenter of social activities, hosting wedding receptions and celebrations ranging from Christmas and Easter to Emancipation to Queen Elizabeth's Coronation to Cuban orchestra performances, such as those by Beny Moré—this last being an indication of members' engagement with the local as well as the global.

59. For instance, minutes from meetings in the 1950s reflect that they had the resources to pay $550.00 for the installation of a sanitary pipe, toilets, and tile floor and to pay $1000 (by installment) for property they were acquiring, in addition to $22.00 in lawyer fees.

60. British West Indian Welfare Centre, meeting minutes, April 25, 1954.

61. British West Indian Welfare Centre, meeting minutes, October 23, 1955.

62. British West Indian Welfare Centre, meeting minutes, February 27, 1955. At this meeting they discussed convening another meeting to choose "a fund scheme to make a donation to the building of a hospital for the Jamaica University where all British West Indians are concerned."

63. Indeed, one of the greatest contributions of Gilroy's *Black Atlantic* (1993) is its intervention upon this tendency toward ahistoricity.

64. See Duany 2002 for discussion of the Puerto Rican case, in which he argues that Puerto Ricans are indeed transnational subjects in spite of their island's status as a U.S. territory.

65. For work that looks specifically at remittances, see Levitt 1998; E. Taylor 1999; Guarnizo 2003; and Eckstein 2004.

66. I am not suggesting that those who work for U.S. transnational corporations are automatically part of a transnational social field that includes the U.S. The legal status and the isolated and all-encompassing character of the military bases and certain companies are critical to this dynamic.

67. Author interviews with Isabel, July 30, 2004, Santiago, and Lester, August 2, 2004, Guantánamo.

68. Author interview with Winton, July 11, 2004, Guantánamo.

69. Author interview with Jorge Smith, June 23, 2004, Santiago.

70. Author interview with Lester, August 2, 2004, Guantánamo.

71. Author interview with Elton, August 23, 2004, Santiago.

72. "Exiling on the base" refers to the situation from 1964 onward in which Guantánamo Naval Base officials gave workers the choice of quitting their jobs or remaining on the base "in exile" from Cuba.

73. Author interview with Edward, August 13, 2004, Guantánamo.

74. Author interview with Melvina, July 1, 2004, and July 7, 2004, Santiago.

75. Ibid.

76. Author interviews with Ricardo, Pablo, Deunes, Caridad, and Jorge Smith, summer 2004, Santiago and Guantánamo.

77. Author interview with Carlitos, July 30, 2004, Santiago.

78. Author interview with Eugenia, June 16, 2005, Santiago.

Chapter 2. Get Out or Get Involved: Revolutionary Change and Conflicting Visions of Freedom

1. "Tengo," Poemas de Nicolás Guillén, Poemas del Alma, http://www.poemas-del-alma.com/nicolas-guillen-tengo.htm (accessed September 6, 2014).

2. For work on various analyses of and Afro-Cuban responses to the revolution and position in Cuban society, see Mesa-Lago and Masferrer 1974; Casal 1979; Serviat 1986; C. Moore 1988; McGarrity 1992; de la Fuente and Glasco 1997; Pérez-Sarduy and Stubbs 2000; de la Fuente 2001b; Sawyer 2005; Martínez 2007; Morales Domínguez 2013; Morejón et al. 2009; and Benson 2013.

3. Of this number, approximately 640,237 came to the U.S. These figures are based on U.S. immigration statistics (Clark 1975:74).

4. West Indian immigrants participated in nationally based labor organizations closely linked to the Communist Parties and organized labor unions themselves. Immigrants often found themselves constitutive of a highly vulnerable laboring class as foreigners, as Blacks, and as part of a broader class of workers who were actively engaged in a struggle for improved conditions. According to Latin American labor historian Barry Carr, Caribbean *braceros* were touched by the heightened class conflict that asserted itself through the political agitation and union organizing in the sugar industry during the 1930s, in spite of the divisive impact of language differences as well as regional and local cultural variation (1998b:89). In the Cuban protests of 1933, which consisted of strikes and occupations throughout the sugar industry, there was significant Antillean participation. The courageousness of such actions must not be overlooked, as immigrants to Cuba were in a particularly precarious position. Indeed, their British passports were stamped with a warning that they had to comply with the laws of the country and refrain from interfering in domestic affairs (R. Lewis 1988:109). In spite of this, they formed their own labor union in Cuba called the *Unión de Obreros Antillanos de Santiago de Cuba* and participated in national labor congresses. In Costa Rica, Anglophone Caribbean immigrants created the Artisans and Laborers Union of Costa Rica, which was active 1909–1914 and was a means to form organized resistance against the economic and social abuses of the United Fruit Company. For instance, in 1910, they organized workers to resist a 12 percent wage reduction that amounted to workers' financing a new tax on bananas (Harpelle 2001:26).

5. Winston James (1998), in his examination of Caribbean radicalism in the United States, finds that people of English-speaking Caribbean origin, such as C.L.R. James and Claudia Jones of Trinidad, Hubert Harrison of St. Croix, and Ferdinand Smith of Jamaica, were instrumental in advocating for a Marxist analysis of the Black condition. Others such as Cyril Briggs, W. A. Domingo, Claude McKay, and Richard B. Moore formed and were leaders of the African Blood Brotherhood in 1919 in Harlem, an organization that combined radical Black nationalism with revolutionary socialism (James 1998:156). Lara Putnam (2013) focuses on the Black press and popular culture as sites of West Indian/American radicalism.

6. In the case of the British West Indian Cultural Centre, Cuban-born children were initially excluded from full membership. They were expected to be participants without any decision-making power, a dynamic that contributed to some tensions between the "Old Centre" and "New Centre" during the period of revitalization. In Costa Rica, a dynamic evolved in which Costa Rica–born West Indians became invested in the future of the country during the civil unrest of the late '40s. Finding that people of African descent were excluded from mainstream political parties and that the West Indian (turned Afro–Costa Rican) community remained without representation at a crucial time in Costa Rican history, these people formed an exclusively West Indian political group called the Comité Dimitriou. This radical group was affiliated with the Communist Party and spoke in the name of working-class members of the community, but it disintegrated in the wake of the 1948 civil war (Harpelle 2001:170). Thus, in the transition from being an embattled immigrant group

to a national minority subjected to systemic racism, political activism shifted in a more radical direction, however short lived.

7. Batista's first presidency coincided with the World War II years of economic boom. The beet- and cane-sugar economies of Europe and Asia, respectively, were devastated, and thus Cuba was once again in an advantageous position in the world sugar market. It was also during the war years that the U.S. expanded the Guantánamo Naval Base, providing the opportunity for stable, better paying employment for thousands of English-speaking Caribbean immigrants and their children. However, inflation, corruption, and mismanagement restricted the improvement of the economic lives of most Cubans and thus the extent of the period of prosperity was limited. When the inevitable stagnation followed in the '50s, the Cuban population, including the middle class, was by and large living in precarious economic circumstances and descended into political turmoil (Pérez 1995:296).

8. Though the people I worked with referred to the movement as El Clandestino, the proper word is *clandestinaje*.

9. According to Cannon, after the triumph of the revolution, "mass graves of victims of Batista's army were being uncovered the length of the island. Centres of torture were found, full of instruments. Whole families had been beaten to death, homes burned, towns destroyed. It is estimated that during his seven-year reign, Batista's armed forces, police, military intelligence, Bureau to Repress Communist Activities, and hired thugs had killed some twenty thousand Cubans" (1981:108).

10. Author interview with Josefina, June 24, 2005, Santiago.

11. Some participants used this name to refer to the rebels. It is a reference to the Kikuyu anticolonial fighters of Kenya where "those people who participated in the forest fight and those people who helped the forest fighters of their own free will, without taking to the forest themselves, can be considered as belonging to the Mau movement" (Buijtenhuijs 1973:4).

12. Author interview with Melvina, June 24, 2005, Santiago.

13. Author interview with Tío Richard, June 16, 2005, Santiago.

14. "¡Hasta Mis Sabanas Tuve Que Vender!" (I Had to Sell Everything [Down] to My Sheets!), *Granma*, December 26, 1986.

15. The term "brown" refers to her grandmother's phenotype as she was very light-skinned with wavy hair. Indeed, Eugenia referred to her as "white," while my own reading of her photographs as well as Melvina's perception indicate that she did not appear to be and was most likely not considered a white woman by fellow Jamaicans. Eugenia was virtually the only research participant whose phenotype places her in the mulata category.

16. Author interview with Eugenia, June 16, 2005, Santiago.

17. "¡Hasta Mis Sabanas Tuve Que Vender!" (I Had to Sell Everything [Down] to My Sheets!), *Granma*, December 26, 1986.

18. Concrete changes in the areas of literacy and education, agrarian and urban reform, desegregation of public space, and income redistribution contributed to the new government enjoying widespread popular support and falling out of favor with middle- and upper-class white Cubans who did not support these early policies (Clark 1975; Casal 1979; Pérez 1995; Pérez-Stable 1999; Pérez Sarduy and Stubbs 2000; de la Fuente 2001b; Kapcia 2008; Benson 2012). During the first year of the revolution, the government cut rents and tele-

phone rates, increased wages, created new jobs, made home ownership a reality for many, recovered $400 million worth of valuable property and goods illegally acquired by the Batista regime, nationalized almost two billion dollars' worth of U.S. industries, turned old military garrisons into schools, began cleaning up trade unions, outlawed prostitution, and opened schools to retrain thousands of women.

19. Author interview with Leticia, July 4, 2005, Santiago.

20. Author interview with Elton, August 23, 2004, Santiago.

21. Author interview with Carlitos, July 30, 2004, Santiago.

22. For a succinct chronology of events, see Stubbs 1989, xi–xii.

23. For additional sources on Guantánamo's role in U.S.-Cuba relations, see Ricardo 1993; Schwab 2009; Hansen 2011.

24. Entire sectors of the old economy, such as insurance services, real estate agencies, law firms, rent collectors, travel agencies, and gambling casinos were superfluous and disappeared. Broker and middleman positions of all types were abolished, thus thousands of middle-class Cubans were without jobs (Pérez 1995).

25. For an excellent first-hand testimony concerning this predicament, see Sporn's (2000) documentary *Cuban Roots/Bronx Stories* featuring Carlos Foster, the Cuban-born son of Jamaicans, who was well on his way to becoming a popular night club singer in Havana at the time of the revolution.

26. For a comprehensive and accessible overview of the revolution through the 1990s, see Kapcia 2008.

27. See Nelson 1970 on the complications of Cuban population statistics during this period.

28. Author interview with Winton, July 11, 2004, Guantánamo.

29. Author interview with Pamela, July 16, 2004, Guantánamo.

30. Some informants had family members who left in search of opportunities to study in other Caribbean islands, such as Jamaica and Puerto Rico. Other family members who migrated had traveled to the U.S. with family or spouses who left for reasons often not directly related to the political climate of the country.

31. Author interview with Edward, June 5, 2005, Guantánamo.

32. Ibid.

33. Author interviews with Eugenia, June 16, 2005, Santiago; Melvina, June 24, 2005, Santiago; and Carmen, June 29, 2005, Guantánamo.

34. The Batista government's crackdown was not a ubiquitous practice. As Pappademos (2011) notes, there is evidence that Batista worked with and supported some of the race-based clubs. Also see de la Fuente 2001b for discussion of Afro-Cuban clubs.For instance, Club Caribe documents from 1954 and 1959 contain government letters notifying the organization of its dissolution; Club Polar in Caimanera requested official recognition in 1955, providing its mission statement, but then subsequent documents include a letter from the revolutionary government notifying the organization of its closure in 1961; the file for Logia La Estrella Naciente de Cuba, formed in 1918 in Santiago, contained letters dated 1952 warning of noncompliance, including one from the head of secret police notifying the organization of its dissolution. Other organizations that were dissolved in the 1950s include British

Early Rose, Santiago; Brillante Estrella de Cuba, 1957 dissolution; Loyal Pearl of Cuba Lodge no. 18, 1952 dissolution; Asociacion Juvenil de "Reina Ester," 1965 dissolution due to youth moving to adult lodges.

35. Author interview with Edward, August 13, 2004, Guantánamo.

36. Author interview with Leonarda, June 29, 2005, Guantánamo.

37. Author interview with Purcival, June 30, 2005, Santiago.

38. Author interview with Carmen, June 29, 2005, Guantánamo.

39. Batista lead a revolt in 1933 that toppled Manuel de Céspedes, and he wielded tremendous power through the rest of the decade but was not elected to the office of president until 1940. He remained in office for four years and returned to power in 1952 after staging a coup. He later ran for and "won" the presidential elections of '54 and '58, which were widely considered to be a far cry from free and fair (Pérez-Stable 1999).

40. For instance, in 1953, 70 percent of the Cuban population of nearly 6 million was engaged in small-scale subsistence farming as owners, renters, and squatters. Most of these individuals lived in desperate conditions, without access to minimum education, health, and housing facilities. The 500,000 Cubans who comprised the urban working class were employed in manufacturing and various service sectors, including domestics, street vendors, waiters, and entertainers (Pérez 1999:296). The depressed conditions in both urban and rural settings were compounded by the crisis among a middle class that was threatened by the mounting political instability and growing economic uncertainty. According to Pérez, the appearance of economic development and a high standard of living based on prevailing measurements concealed the tensions that resulted from fluctuations of the export economy that continued to create conditions of apprehension affecting all classes. The middle class "found little comfort in statistical tallies that touted their high level of material consumption and placed the island near the top of the scale of per capita income in Latin America. The social reality was quite different" (1999:296).

41. It is important to note, however, that Cubans across the color spectrum did not begin on a level playing field, something that Morales Domínguez (2013) identifies as responsible for ongoing inequality.

42. Named after the mother of Antonio Maceo.

43. Thirty percent of the teachers were Black and mulatto, and Afro-Cuban women were well represented among the domestics educated through the literacy campaign (de la Fuente 2001b:275).

44. Author interview with Beth, June 29, 2005, Guantánamo

45. Author interview with Esperanza, June 8, 2005, Guantánamo.

46. Author interview with Caridad, June 2, 2004, Santiago.

47. Author interview with Leticia, July 4, 2005, Santiago.

48. Author interview with Melvina, June 24, 2005, Santiago.

49. *Soul Train* was an iconic weekly variety show in the U.S. that debuted the music and dance of Black America during its long run from 1971 through 2006.

50. Author interview with Lester, August 2, 2004, Guantánamo.

51. Field note, August 29, 2005, Guantánamo.

Chapter 3. Special Identities in Cuba's Special Period: Race, Region, and Revitalization

1. Adams et al. 2009. Entitled "Acting on Our Conscience: A Declaration of African American Support for the Civil Rights Struggle in Cuba, 11/30/09," this statement called for the immediate release of Dr. Darsi Ferrer, an alleged Afro-Cuban "civil rights activist" imprisoned by the Cuban government under false charges. It professed that "[We] cannot be silent in the face of increased violations of civil and human rights for those black activists in Cuba who dare raise their voices against the island's racial system" and goes on to state, "We support Cuba's right to enjoy national sovereignty, and unhesitatingly repudiate any attempt at curtailing such a right. However, at this historic juncture, we also do believe that we cannot sit idly by . . . and allow for . . . the black population as a whole to be treated with callous disregard for their rights as citizens and as the most marginalized people on the island."

2. Zurbano was subsequently demoted on the basis of the *Times'* distortion. See West-Durán 2013.

3. The 1986 Congress marked a departure from the silence on racial inequality as leaders acknowledged this to be an issue in revolutionary society; however, the collapse of the Soviet Union and ensuing economic crisis once again deprioritized this social reality.

4. An abbreviation of Caribbean Community, CARICOM is a regional organization of former British West Indian colonies (in addition to Haiti, which was admitted in 2002, and Surinam, admitted in 1995) that includes Antigua and Barbuda, the Bahamas, Belize, Dominica, Grenada, Guyana, Jamaica, Montserrat (not independent), St. Lucia, St. Kitts and Nevis, St. Vincent and the Grenadines, and Trinidad and Tobago.

5. Fidel declared the Special Period in 1990; however, precisely when the Special Period ended is up for debate. Jorge Pérez López (2002) argued that there is no end in sight for Cuba's Special Period. He explained that Cuba's economy was in a free fall until 1994, the first year that it experienced growth, but that this growth was interrupted in 2001 principally due to the global economic slowdown following the September 11th attack and Hurricane Michelle. In an assessment of the economy from 2005 to 2006, he concluded that there is no definitive answer for whether or not the Special Period is over (Pérez López 2006). See also Benzing 2005; Brundenius 2002; and Mesa-Lago 2001.

6. Field note, June 9, 2004, Santiago.

7. Field note, August 6, 2004, Santiago.

8. Field note, May 30, 2003, Santiago.

9. Field note, July 15, 2004, Santiago.

10. *Orisha* is the Yoruba name for a deity; *orishas* are also referred to as *santos* or saints.

11. Field note, July 16, 2004, Guantánamo.

12. Author interview with Melvina, June 24, 2005, Santiago.

13. Author interview with Eugenia, June 16, 2005, Santiago.

14. Author interview with Purcival, June 30, 2005, Santiago.

15. Author interview with Carmen, June 29, 2005, Guantánamo.

16. *Extranjero* can signify "foreigner" when used as a noun, "foreign" when used as an adjective. *Ir al extranjero* signifies to go abroad, *del extranjero* means from abroad, and *lo*

extranjero means foreignness or that which comes from abroad. Here I use it to refer to the rise of that which is foreign, the foreigner, and going abroad.

17. In addition to the scholars who are working directly on tourism in Cuba (Goodrich 1993; Davidson 1996; N. Fernández 1999; Hodge 2001; Facio, Toro-Morn, and Roschelle 2004; Cabezas 2009; Roland 2010), the presence of foreign tourists and the growth of the industry is necessarily incorporated into ethnographic work that explores other facets of life in post–Soviet era Cuba (Hansing 2006; Hernandez-Reguant 2009; N. Fernández 2010; Allen 2011)

18. In 1994, Baloyra forecast the inevitability of further reform. He observed that "the contrast between foreign capitalist opulence and domestic socialist mediocrity is just too strong at all levels. For example, concerning tourism, criticism has emerged from within the party itself over the system of apartheid created by the increasing number of foreign tourists visiting the island, which has resulted in the virtual exclusion of *criollos* (natives) from the choice spots in the littoral and has put extra pressure on the supply of food in the country. Cubans are practically excluded from the 'dollar area,' and ordinary citizens cannot make purchases in well-supplied stores reserved for foreign tourists, entrepreneurs, and diplomats" (1994:35).

Indeed, shortly after coming to power in 2008, Raúl lifted the ban on Cubans' use of tourist accommodations and services. Although this is little more than a gesture, given that the overwhelming majority of Cubans do not have the means to afford these facilities, its significance is twofold. First, it exemplifies a dynamic that some argue has allowed the Cuban government to survive, namely, accommodating certain demands in order to diffuse unrest while not ceding control. Second, open access to hotels renders more dramatically the divide between those Cubans who have access to foreign currency and those who do not.

19. As stated earlier, the dollar ceased to be accepted in stores as a unit of exchange in 2008 when the government introduced pesos convertibles, also known as CUCs.

20. In 2013, it was announced that the ration book would be phased out of use in Cuba.

21. I encountered this with academics who, for instance, gave language classes to foreign students. Brotherton (2012) discusses the recent expansion of black market health services in which physicians charge CUC for pilfered medicines as well as their services. In addition, some of my informants worked in jobs where they were paid part of their salary in CUCs.

22. While I know of people who worked in or were preparing to be sent to Jamaica, Haiti, Angola, Botswana, South Africa, Zambia, and China, the most common destination during this period was Venezuela. Emblematic of the relationship between Cuba and Venezuela as well as the growing anti-neoliberal movement of the region, Cuba has sent thousands of professionals to the country in addition to hosting thousands of Venezuelan patients and students. I found that Cubans range in their opinions about this exchange from believing it to be an important strategic and moral move on Cuba's part to resenting the government's willingness to remove badly needed professionals from the island for *la política*. Regardless, being sent on a mission is perceived to be an opportunity to improve one's standard of living because those skilled workers who leave earn more than they would in Cuba and have access to consumer goods abroad.

23. *Soca* is a genre of Caribbean music that originated in Trinidad in the 1960s.

24. In 1996, the countries represented in the membership were "Jamaica 288, St. Kitts and Nevis 76, Barbados 26, Antigua-Barbuda 30, St. Thomas 30, St. Lucia 21, Grenada 15, the British Virgin Islands 6, Guyana 6, Martinica [*sic*] [possibly Dominica or Martinique] 2, Trinidad/Tobago, Turcos/Caicos and USA 1 each, the rest are spouses." See Jones 2005.

25. Marlene MacPherson, "Norma Ming connects with her roots," *Gleaner Outlook Magazine* (Jamaica), May 27, 2007, http://jamaica-gleaner.com/gleaner/20070527/out/out2.html. (See McGarrity 1996 for discussion of the Cuban diaspora in Jamaica.)

26. Cotman quotes Deputy Foreign Minister for American Affairs Ramón Sánchez Parodi as saying in a 1989 interview printed in *Granma*, "The priority now is to place Caribbean integration in the Latin American context, given the growing economic and political polarization of the present world" (2006:146).

27. For example, establishing the CARICOM-Cuba Free Trade Agreement, including Cuba in the Caribbean Regional Negotiating Machinery (body that develops regional positions in international economic negotiations), including Cuba in the Caribbean Tourism Organization, and protesting Cuba's exclusion from the Free Trade Agreement of the Americas (Basdeo 2005).

28. See "Region Observes CARICOM/Cuba Day," Jamaica Information Service, December 8, 2007, http://jis.gov.jm/region-observes-caricomcuba-day/.

29. See CARICOM press release, December 9, 2011, http://www.caricom.org/jsp/press-releases/press_releases_2011/pres475_11.jsp.

30. Susan Greenbaum argues convincingly that mutual aid societies of Black Cuban immigrants to Florida were an instrumental aspect of their transnational strategy, illustrate the limitations of rational choice theory, and serve as a site upon which the links between cultural and economic capital are clearly visible (2002:16–21).

31. Author interview with Melvina, August 10, 2004, Santiago.

32. Ibid.

33. While the majority of immigrants were classified as Black (*negro*), there were white British Caribbeans who migrated to Cuba (as evidenced by the formation of the Anglo-Caribbean Inter-Association Committee in Havana, which was predominantly white according to Whitney and Chailloux Laffita [2013:155]). There were also brown (light-skinned) immigrants, one of whom participated in this study, and those who married or had children with white or light-skinned Cubans and had white or light-skinned offspring.

34. Author interview with Melvina, August 10, 2004, Santiago.

35. Author interview with Edward, August 4, 2004 Guantánamo.

36. Author interview with Ruth, June 5, 2005, Guantánamo.

37. One of the requirements for Cubans to receive authorization to travel is a letter of invitation from the country (institution or individual) where they would like to go.

38. Author interview with Eugenia, June 19, 2004, Santiago.

39. Field note, June 24, 2004, Santiago.

40. Field note, June 16, 2005, Santiago.

41. Author interview with Isabel, July 30, 2004, Santiago.

42. At this time, there were three different companies that managed dollar stores in Cuba: TRD, Pan-America, and Cubalse.

43. Author interview with Melvina, June 30, 2004, Santiago.

44. Author interview with Caridad, July 2, 2004, in Santiago.

45. Author interview with Winton, July 12, 2004, Guantánamo.

46. Author interview with Melvina, June 24, 2004, Santiago.

47. Concerning the relationship between African Americans and Cubans, see Brock 1998; Greenbaum 2002; Guridy 2010; and Benson 2013.

48. The majority of Cuba-CARICOM trade is with Belize, Jamaica, Barbados, and Trinidad and Tobago, and it lags behind trade liberalization arrangements that each has with other economic groupings and individual countries (Venezuela, the Dominican Republic, Costa Rica, and Colombia with CARICOM; Cuba with MERCOSUR states Brazil, Uruguay, and Paraguay [Grant 2005]). Furthermore, intraregional trade is far from self-sufficient; however, Nuñéz and Verba note that "even if the volume of trade is not significant on the macroeconomic level, it could still have a great impact at more concrete levels of society as a supplier of particular needed resources" (1997:93). Another major issue around regional integration concerns migration as illustrated in Annalee Davis's documentary *On the Map* (2007), which takes as its subject contemporary intra-Caribbean immigration through the portrayal of the undocumented immigrant experience in Barbados, Guyana, and Trinidad.

49. Author interview with Edward, August 4, 2004, Guantánamo.

Chapter 4. "Somos Negros Finos" (We Are Refined Blacks): Rescuing Roots as an Assertion of Respectable Blackness

1. This phrase is translated as either "She is a Black woman to go out with" or "She is a Black woman who is advancing." The first interpretation signifies that, in spite of her Blackness, she is good enough to be taken out in public. The second indicates that she is a Black woman who is leaving Blackness. (For discussions of this term, see N. Fernández 1996 and Roland 2010:154.) Both interpretations reference a phenomenon within white supremacist racial ideology in which a person might attempt to "treat" the stain of his or her African ancestry with other qualities such as education, occupation, religion, and behavior. Having "treated" his/her Blackness, the individual Black subject is perceived to be more deserving of inclusion into the nation (see Martinez-Alier 1989; Do Nascimento 1977; R. Graham 1990; Wade 1993; Hasenbalg 1996; Duharte and Santos 1997; Martinez-Echazabal 1998; Twine 1998; Belliard 2001; and Andrews 2004 for discussions of Blackness and racial ideology in Latin America).

2. Field note, July 16, 2004, Santiago.

3. Literally meaning witchcraft, *brujería* is a somewhat derogatory way to refer to African religious practices and can also be used to describe human manipulation of the spiritual world, frequently but not necessarily with malicious intent.

4. In comparing people of Anglophone Caribbean origin to Cubans, there was often some slippage between race and class. At times, respondents would refer to Cubans as a group, and when I asked specifically about the race of these Cubans, they would say "all Cubans," but other cues would indicate that they were referring to Cubans of color. This

might be related to the privileging of national identity over racial identity or the historically rooted tendency for the importance of racial distinctions to wane the lower one is on the class hierarchy. See Martinez-Alier 1989 on this point.

5. The distinction made between British West Indians, Haitians, and Cubans and its political, economic, and social underpinnings are explored in historical literature on race and Black immigration to Cuba (McLeod 2000; Giovannetti 2001; Álvarez Estévez 1988; de la Fuente 1997). (See chapter 3 for a description of the relationship between the labor market and ethnic distinctions. These distinctions are by no means consistent in Cuban racial discourse.) As Helg (1995) documents in the case of the campaign against the Independent Party of Color, Haitians and Jamaicans (both those in Cuba and abroad) were said to be instigating and supporting Black Cuban resistance, thus race and rebelliousness linked these groups (see Helg 1995, chapters 7 and 8).

6. See Hale 1996; Moreiras 1999; De Grandis and Bernd 1999; Mabardi 2000; Tanikella 2003; Kraidy 2005; and Hutnyk 2005 for other critiques of hybridity in the Americas.

7. *Ajiaco* is a Cuban stew containing meat, root vegetables, and various seasonings. Together they create a flavor distinct from these individual ingredients. As a result, Fernando Ortiz used this stew as a metaphor for Cuban society in which people from disparate geographic and cultural locations have come together to create a distinct culture. Shannon (2008) uses this metaphor to explore the exclusion of Haitians and their descendants from Cuba's national imaginary.

8. See Fernández Robaina 1990; Ferrer 1999; Helg 1995; Martinez-Alier 1989; and de la Fuente 1995, 2001b on historical characterizations of Afro-Cubans.

9. It is important to note that elite Cubans of color who were embedded within the clientelist networks that constituted the political system were full participants in this marginalization. Indeed, Pappademos (2011) argues that analyses of racial politics during the republican period mistakenly assume that all Cubans of color, including the elite, had a race consciousness, when evidence indicates that they had no such sense of collective identity. Rather, they distanced themselves from African origins, promoted the notion that African identities were antithetical to the civilized, modern nation that Cuba was to become, and adhered to a politics of respectability. With the dominant discourse professing that class and character, rather than color, are the measures by which society judges and orders its citizens, Black subjects not surprisingly have attempted to prove themselves to be in possession of a character and culture deemed worthy of modernity.

10. As de la Fuente found in his historical analysis of racial equality in Cuba, "[T]he social situation of black professionals [prior to 1959] was in fact precarious. . . . Although education and 'culture' made this group eligible for middle-class status, their skin color, social origin, and financial situation, as well as white racism, kept them dangerously close to the world of poverty and manual labor that they were trying to escape" (de la Fuente 2001b:153).

11. This research did not include non-Anglophone Caribbean Cubans and does not claim that such a strategy is unique to this group.

12. Author interview with Winton, July 11, 2004, Guantánamo.

13. Author interview with Carlitos, July 31, 2004, Santiago. Carlitos was not alone in implicating that some of those now claiming English-speaking Caribbean ethnicity are

inauthentic due to the potential benefits from affiliating with ethnic associations (as discussed in chapter 3).

14. Author interview with Rubén, August 4, 2004, Santiago. The Cuban word used to describe this is *educado*, which translates literally as "educated."

15. Author interview with Isabel, July 30, 2004, Santiago. *Fino/fina* translates literally as "refined." When preceded by *negra*, there is an implication that a woman is refined considering she is a Black woman.

16. Author interview with Rubén, August 4, 2004, Santiago.

17. Author interview with Dr. Ruth, July 12, 2004, Guantánamo.

18. Field note, June 8, 2004, Santiago. For instance, Melvina would not allow her daughter to go on overnight trips while in junior high school. She commented on the freeness of Cuban parents who have their daughters' boyfriends in their house, eating their food, sleeping with the girl in the house, and then when they break up, another boyfriend appears and the same thing happens. She is strictly against this practice and the only other person that she knows who is like that is a descendiente.

19. Author interview with Hortencia, August 4, 2004, Santiago.

20. Ibid.

21. Given the emphasis placed on the quiet, reserved demeanor of jamaicanos, I found this excerpt from *Gleaner* (Jamaica) in 1884 particularly amusing: "Now a love of noise is a sign of the savage. It is also an indication of vulgarity. It suggests that those who make it find a sheer delight in barbarous cacophony, or desire to annoy others, or wish to attract attention to themselves" (quoted in Moore and Johnson 2004:154).

22. Author interview with Lester, August 2, 2004, Guantánamo.

23. Aihwa Ong's work on immigrants and social stratification, although based upon Asian immigrants to the United States, is useful in illuminating the racialized social framework within which other immigrant groups place themselves and are placed in societies dominated by white supremacy. Entering into the debate about European objection to immigration based on the culture rather than the race of the immigrants, Ong argues that "racial hierarchies and polarities continue to inform Western notions of cultural difference and are therefore inseparable from the cultural features attributed to different groups." She maintains that "the white-black polarities emerging out of the history of European-American imperialism continue to shape attitudes and encode discourses directed at immigrants from the rest of the world that are associated with racial and cultural inferiority. . . . This dynamic of racial othering emerges in a range of mechanisms that variously subject nonwhite immigrants to whitening or blackening processes that indicate the degree of their closeness to or distance from ideal white standards" (1996:751).

24. Indeed, Ong asserts that "attaining success through self-reliant struggle, while not inherently limited to any cultural group, is a process of self-development that in Western democracies becomes inseparable from the process of 'whitening'" (1996:739), and thus the narrative of social mobility that emphasizes individual achievement and sacrifice can be viewed as an inherently whitening process.

25. Field note, July 3, 2004, Santiago.

26. Early twentieth-century scholars such as W.E.B. Du Bois, Franz Boas, and Melville

Herskovits were pioneers in challenging the predominant belief that race was a biological phenomenon. With advances in genetic science that occurred in the late twentieth century, this challenge to the biologizing of race gained more traction, inspiring a renewed interest in engaging race. The anthropological literature on the subject of race and racism is extensive. See the following articles that have appeared in the *Annual Review of Anthropology:* Williams 1989; Harrison 1995; Wodak and Reisigl 1999; Mullings 2005; and Abu El-Haj 2007. Also see Baker 1998 for an excellent history of anthropology and the race concept.

27. For instance, see Dickerson 2004; Gilroy 2000; Wright 2004; D. Thomas 2004; Hintzen and Rahier 2003, 2010; Clarke and Thomas 2006; Fox 2006.

28. Though the issue of Black immigrants is of most concern here, Ong's 1996 work on Asian immigrants to the United States reinforces my argument. Also, while I will not be examining the emergence of a "biracial movement" in the United States, activism on the part of people of "mixed" racial parentage to claim distinct categorization has no doubt contributed to these debates about racial politics and Black subjectivity.

29. This is not to say that native Black populations do not also employ a politics of deconstruction, strategically asserting their diversity in order to challenge racist notions of monolithic Blackness used to justify exclusionary practices.

30. Hintzen makes this argument in his discussion of West Indians in the San Francisco Bay Area. He asserts that they use constructions of "home" and representations of their personal achievement to establish their difference from Black Americans and to contest their exclusion from the modern American space based on the alleged link between Blackness and inferiority (2004:298).

31. It is noteworthy that Rastafari is a predominantly male movement in Cuba and thus the interpretation of it as liberatory and egalitarian is through a male lens. Furthermore, most of the Rastas in Hansing's study adhered to dominant Cuban gender norms (2001:738).

32. While I address the implications of this challenge to conformity only as it relates to Blackness, Rastafari locates power in the individual and opposes systems that attempt to control individual will. As Chivallon (2002) explains, "Even while deploying a powerfully mobilizatory rhetoric of particularizing symbols of identity (Africa vs. Babylon, Blackness vs. Whiteness), Rastafarianism operates in a space that is open and without constraining norms. . . . Still more astonishing is the fact that this resistance against order arises not from the difficulties any group might encounter in the effort to create 'structured organization' but, instead from a genuinely ethical posture expressed through the philosophy of 'I-an-I' ('I an I' in Jamaican Creole, an affirmation of 'We' as the meeting of two individualities). That posture undergirds the movement ideologically" (2002:371). Indeed, Deunes and David definitely expressed this resistance to constraints, whether imposed by capitalism or socialism and enforced by the state, family members, or the community. David treated anything that ended in "ismo" with suspicion, insisting that the term "Rastafarianism" not be used, precisely because of this resistance to the programmatic, ideological, oppressive codification of the philosophy that the suffix "ism" enacts.

33. Field note, July 8, 2004, Santiago. It is important to take a moment to emphasize the distinction that exists for some people between Rastas and *rasta modas*. I found there to be

a general distaste for the latter, while perceptions of the former were less disapproving and not perceived to be one of the ills brought about by tourism.

34. Indeed, emblematic of the tremendous contradictions in Cuba, one afternoon, one of these cousins who lives from illegal activity was playing video games on a laptop computer, which had been set on a beautiful antique wooden table. That table is always covered in plastic because the holes in the roof are so severe that when it rains outside, it rains inside.

35. Author interview with David, August 10, 2004, Santiago.

36. Morales Domínguez (2013) cites the Western education and Eurocentric curriculum in Cuba as responsible for the ignorance of so many Cubans who hold racist beliefs.

37. See Azicri 2000 for an analysis of changes in higher education in the 1990s.

38. Interestingly, at this point in the conversation, he brought out his grandmother's 1883 copy of a religious book called *Prophets* and said that there was a lot of knowledge in it that he can't access because it's in English.

39. Author interview with Deunes, July 8, 2004, Santiago.

40. Ariel Fernández Díaz, one of the pioneers of Cuban hip-hop, pointed to generational conflicts and racism as being responsible for the popularity and content of Cuban hip-hop: "We were trying to take back the spirit of the early years of the revolution. . . . We need to say the truth, we have people talking to you all day and telling lies. . . . I am a revolutionary, a true revolutionary. . . . Any politician knows that if you bring everything to somebody, he's free and doesn't need you anymore so at some point you need these people to depend on you. . . . Like they say, you give a man a fish he eats for a day, you teach a man to fish, he always has something to eat. The revolution didn't teach people how to fish" (Fernández Díaz [lecture] 2007).

41. Gordon and Anderson (1999:284) identify the making and remaking of diaspora and I am here highlighting that part of this process involves the distancing or disentanglement from extra-national connections. Patterson and Kelley (2000) also argue that diaspora, as practice and process, is made and unmade.

Chapter 5. "¿Gracias a la Revolución?" Narratives of Social Mobility as Spaces of Subject Formation

1. Author interview with Edward, August 4, 2004, Guantánamo.

2. Author interview with Jorge Smith, July 28, 2004, Santiago.

3. Even Carlos Moore, one of Fidel Castro's and the Cuban government's staunchest critics, declares that he would prefer a failed revolution to the prerevolutionary society in which he was raised (2008).

4. Author interview with Pablo, July 11, 2004, Guantánamo.

5. Ibid.

6. Pablo denied English-speaking Caribbeans' involvement in African-based religious practices.

7. Author interview with Leticia, July 4, 2005, Santiago.

8. Gropas also notes that Cubans have a tendency to "defend the Revolution against

foreigners, who [are] seen as criticizing it without having lived it or understood the changes that it brought about" (2007:534).

9. Field note, June 10, 2004, Santiago.

10. Another research participant who was also Rasta and consistently harassed by his supervisors at work due to his dreadlocks confided that he limits his movements around the city for fear that he will be arrested and the police will cut off his locks as has happened to other brethren. The treatment that Rastas in Cuba receive is in part due to the high value placed on conformity, the rejection of a Black aesthetic (i.e., *pelo malo*, bad hair), and the association between dreadlocks, marijuana, and jineterismo (see Hansing 2006; F. Davis 2011).

11. Field note, June 15, 2004, Santiago.

12. In Cuba, "Fidel" is the name used to refer to Fidel Castro the individual as well as to the state apparatus.

13. Field note, June 14, 2004, Santiago. It is notable that this exchange occurred prior to the 2010 announcement by the unions that there would be massive layoffs that would release anywhere from 500,000 to 1 million workers from state employment (http://www.nytimes.com/2010/09/14/world/americas/14cuba.html?_r=0, http://www.bbc.com/news/world-latin-america-11291267).

14. Conceptualized by Che Guevara, the *Hombre Nuevo* or "New Man" is the citizen and worker born out of the transition from capitalism to socialism and characterized by a new consciousness of self-sacrifice. The self-sacrificing New Man is a consummate worker motivated by the moral imperative to contribute to collective rather than individual gain. This idealized revolutionary figure betrays revolutionary ideology's gender and sexual biases, prompting Jafari S. Allen to write, "There is not enough newness here" given the "fidelity to narrow bourgeois structures of heterosexual coupling and nuclear families" (2011:111).

15. Economic imperatives have indeed enacted social transformations in Cuba and elsewhere in the post-Soviet world; however, ethnographic inquiries have illustrated that declarations professing the global triumph of capitalism, the wholesale liberation of former "captives of communism," and the much-anticipated embrace of the market were grossly misguided (for examples see Burroway and Verdery 1999). Much of this work challenges the so-called backwardness of post-Soviet subjects who fail to summarily denounce the former social order. It explores the presumed intransigence of particular socialist practices such as bartering and collective ownership, nostalgia and the politics of memory, and the marginalization of former socialist subjects based upon their association with a pathologized past (Burroway and Verdery 1999; Rivkin-Fish 2009; Hörschelmann 2002; Bloch 2005; Buyandelgeriyn 2008; Truitt 2008). These scholarly debates about the true origins of and impetus for currently common practices associated with a socialist "past" call into question this notion of rupture and its inevitability while demonstrating how experiences of the past and, perhaps more importantly, perceptions of those experiences come to bear on interpretations of the present.

16. As noted in the introduction, *pru oriental* is a home-brewed fermented drink containing plant roots, sugar, and a variety of spices that originated on the eastern side of Cuba.

17. Known as "The Bronze Titan," Antonio Maceo was the celebrated general of the late

nineteenth-century Cuban wars for independence. Often referred to as mulatto, he was a brilliant military strategist and is recognized as a founding father of the Cuban nation.

18. Field note, July 27, 2004, Santiago. Indeed, as a result of this and other discussions about race *aquí y allá*, I gave him a copy of W.E.B. Du Bois's *The Souls of Black Folk* after finding, much to my delight, a Spanish translation at one of the book stores on Calle Enramadas the following year (field note, July 15, 2005, Santiago).

19. For instance, when the Soviet Union collapsed, sending Cuba into an economic tailspin, the U.S. passed the Torricelli Bill in 1992 and the Helms-Burton Act in 1996, legislation that strengthened the embargo against Cuba. The Cuban government interpreted and framed this as an act of aggression.

20. As a United States citizen, I am required by the U.S. government to have a license to travel to Cuba. I was denied an individual license and therefore traveled on the institutional licenses held by the universities with which I have been affiliated. Through taxation and currency conversion fees, the Cuban government takes approximately 18 percent of U.S. dollars brought into the country. Apart from these legal and financial impediments, acquiring the appropriate visa can also be a challenge due to the sensitive and somewhat volatile nature of U.S.-Cuba relations (see Michalowski 1996 on the influence of U.S.-Cuba relations on conducting ethnographic research in Cuba). At the time of this writing, these relations are in a period of transition following the 2014 announcement that President Obama and President Castro have met and are moving toward restoring diplomatic relations, which could involve eventually lifting travel restrictions.

21. Lara Putnam weaves Malcolm X's family history throughout *Radical Moves* (2013) in order to illustrate the circuits of Black nationalism and Black internationalism during the interwar period.

22. Here I am referencing Brent Hayes Edwards's work in which he interrogates both the uses of diaspora by scholars, a line of inquiry that he refers to as the "politics of nominalization" (2001:46), and diaspora as a set of practices (2003).

23. The term *balsero* refers to those people who left Cuba bound for the United States on makeshift rafts.

24. Of the twenty-two in their fifties and sixties who were the first generation to be educated in revolutionary society, seventeen received post-secondary education and twelve held higher status positions such as physician, university professor, and engineer.

25. See "El Doce—1912: The 1912 Massacre of AfroCubans," http://www.afrocubaweb. com/history/eldoce.htm.

26. Historian Devyn Spence Benson (2013) makes a similar argument based upon documents from the early revolutionary period.

27. While Carlos Moore (1988) makes a similar argument, he concludes that Black people are worse off due to the revolution, a position that all indicators on Black Cubans—indeed all Cubans—do not support.

28. It is noteworthy that explorations of racial politics of the island tend to gloss over distinctions within racialized groups, particularly along ethnic, gender, class, and color lines, a notable exception being Pappademos' (2011) treatment of the republican period. Even Carlos Moore, himself a Jamaican Cuban who went into exile after being punished for

challenging the silence on racism and who has had a particularly and publicly contentious relationship with the government, does not explicitly address how his indictment of Fidel Castro and the government's policies on race might be colored, so to speak, by his Anglo-Caribbean origins. This is particularly true of *Castro, the Blacks, and Africa* (1988). *Pichón* (2008), his memoir published twenty years later, does provide a window into how Blackness is experienced through Anglo-Caribbeanness as well as masculinity; however, the question of how the legacy of Garveyism in Anglo-Caribbean communities, for instance, interjected itself into the rhetoric of racial pride and insistence on addressing the Black condition is not fully engaged. I am not suggesting that this is a position exclusively taken by Anglo-Caribbean Cubans, particularly given that the 1960s was a time period of Black pride and empowerment. Rather, I contend that their unique historical relationship to this particular ideology might have bearing upon the ways in which they have inserted themselves into the revolutionary project at different points from the 1950s onward.

29. See Guerra 2012 for analysis of Black *fidelistas*' platform.

30. For an excellent ethnography on racial attitudes and practices as evidenced through the experiences of interracial couples, see N. Fernandez 2010.

31. Author interview with Tomás, May 3, 2003, Guantánamo.

Conclusion

1. In 1962, Jamaica and Trinidad became the first of the British Caribbean colonies to become independent states. However, this did not necessarily change immigrants' perception of themselves as belonging to Empire. As one of the women interviewed by Gloria Rolando in *Los Hijos de Baraguá* proclaimed, "I'm a British subject" (Rolando 1996). Interestingly, Brereton (1989) argues that, in the case of Trinidad, the claim to a British cultural identity was that much more important for upwardly mobile Blacks and coloreds because they occupied such a precarious position in the social order. Without wealth or membership in the political ruling class, they had little more than their Britishness to buoy their social worth.

2. As of this writing, there are seven antiracist organizations and collectives in Cuba. Among them are the Cofradía de la Negritud (Fraternity of Blackness), founded in 1998; the Cuban chapter of Articulación Regional Afrodescendiente de América Latina y el Caribe (ARAAC) (Regional Articulation of Afrodescendents in Latin America and the Caribbean), which held its first meeting in 2012 and was officially established in 2013; La Comisión José Aponte, which is the Cuban government's antiracist organization; Fundación Guillén, also founded in 2013, which focuses its intervention on arts and culture; and Red Barrial Afrodescendiente (Afrodescendant Neighborhood Network), which was founded in 2013 and directs education and inquiry about racism in neighborhoods and at work centers (http://www.afrocubaweb.com/afrocuban-blogs.html). Also see de la Fuente 2009.

3. The cartoon by Carlos Latuff is reproduced on *GlobalVoices*, http://globalvoicesonline.org/2013/09/11/racism-greets-imported-cuban-doctors-in-brazil/. A postscript to the original article beneath the cartoon reads, "Since the publishing of the original version of this post in Portuguese on 6 Sept. 2013, an antiracism wave has spread across Brazilian cyberspace with banners and messages of support for the Cuban doctors, such as the one above."

Bibliography

Primary Sources

Ango-American Antilleans Association
1944–50   Papers. Subject, Foreign Companies: File 2568, Dossiers 3, 7. Municipal Archive, Santiago, Cuba.
Asociación Progresista de las Indias Occidentales Inglesas del Central Delicias, Puerto Padre (West Indian Progressive Association of Central Delicias)
1943   Papers. Subject, Foreign Companies: File 2568, Dossiers 3, 7. Municipal Archive, Santiago, Cuba.
Asociación Sucursal de la Liga de Jamaica en Santiago de Cuba (Branch Association of the Jamaica League in Santiago de Cuba)
1919–52   Papers, including Report on the Proceedings of the Annual Convention. Subject, Patriotic Societies: File 2623, Dossiers 1, 2. Municipal Archive, Santiago, Cuba.
Braga, George Atkinson
1980   "A Bundle of Relations." Braga Brothers Collection. University of Florida Latin American and Caribbean Collection, George Smathers Libraries, Gainesville, Fla.
British West Indian Welfare Centre
1946–1956 Meeting minutes of the British West Indian Welfare Centre. Guantánamo, Cuba.
Caribbean Community Secretariat
2011   "Declaration of Port of Spain on the Occasion of the Fourth Summit of Heads of State and Government of the Caribbean Community," December 9. http://www.caricom.org/jsp/pressreleases/press_releases_2011/pres475_11.jsp (accessed March 2012).
Club de Adelanto de Antillanos Britanicos (Club of Advancement of British Antilleans)
1946   Papers. Subject, Mutual Societies: File 2583, Dossiers 4, 6. Municipal Archive, Santiago, Cuba.
Club Caribe: Sociedad de Instrucción y Recreo (Club Caribbean: Society for Instruction and Recreation)
N.d.   Papers. Subject, Caimanera: File 197, Dossier 12. Municipal Archive, Santiago, Cuba.
Club Polar
1955–61   Papers. Subject, Caimanera: File 197, Dossier 16. Municipal Archive, Santiago, Cuba.

Cuba Económica y Financiera
1944   Vol. 19(221).
Cuban Trading Company
1924   Paper no. 7. Ed. D. Polledo. Braga Collection. Record Group 2, Box 58, Series 109-C, 1911–1943. University of Florida Latin American and Caribbean Collection, George Smathers Libraries, Gainesville, Fla.
Director General of the Census
1922   Census of the Republic of Cuba, 1919. Havana: Maza, Arroyo y Caso. https://archive.org/details/ajb5563.0001.001.umich.edu (accessed August 14, 2014).
1945   Census of the Republic of Cuba, 1943. Havana: P. Fernández. University of Florida Latin American and Caribbean Collection, George Smathers Libraries, Gainesville, Fla.
Guantánamo Cricket Club
1956   Papers. Subject, Sports Societies: File 2485, Dossier 4. Municipal Archive, Santiago, Cuba.
Logia La Estrella Naciente De Cuba (Rising Star Lodge of Cuba); British Early Rose Lodge; Logia "Brillante Estrella de Cuba" (Bright Star of Cuba Lodge); Loyal Pearl of Cuba Lodge no. 18.
N.d.   Papers. Subject, Lodges: File 914, Dossiers 8, 10, 13, 14. Municipal Archive, Santiago, Cuba.
Luz Unida Numero 10,973 (United Light No. 10,973)
1925–61   Papers. Subject, Lodges: File 929, Dossier 2. Municipal Archive, Santiago, Cuba.
Sociedad De Antillanos Amantes de la Democracia (Antillean Lovers of Democratic Society).
N.d.   Papers. Subject, Caimanera: File 197, Dossier 1. Municipal Archive, Santiago, Cuba.
U.S. Department of Commerce, Bureau of the Census
1945 *Cuba: Summary of Biostatistics and Charts, Population, Natality and Mortality Statistics.* Washington, D.C., May.

Secondary Sources

Abraham, Sara
2001   "The Shifting Sources of Racial Definitions in Trinidad and Tobago, and Guyana: Research Agenda." *Ethnic and Racial Studies* 24(6):979–97.
Abu El-Haj, Nadia
2007   "The Genetic Reinscription of Race." *Annual Review of Anthropology* 36:283–300.
Aceto, Michael
2002   "Ethnic Personal Names and Multiple Identities in Anglophone Caribbean Speech Communities in Latin America." *Language in Society* 31(4):577–608.
Adams, Richard, Jr., J. B. Afoh-Manin, Roslyn Alic-Batson, Marva Allen, Molefi Kete, Peter Bailey, Gloria Batiste-Roberts, Lili Bernard, Marie Brown, Khepra Burns, et al.
2009   "Acting on Our Conscience: A Declaration of African American Support for the Civil Rights Struggle in Cuba, 11/03/09." http://www.afrocubaweb.com/actingonour-conscience.htm (accessed March 18, 2015).

AfroCubaWeb

N.d.   "El Doce—1912: The 1912 Massacre of AfroCubans." http://www.afrocubaweb.com/ history/eldoce.htm (accessed September 7, 2014).

Allen, Jafari S.

2007   "Means of Desire's Production: Male Sex Labor in Cuba." *Identities* 14(1–2):183–203.

2011   *¿Venceremos? The Erotics of Black Self-Making in Cuba*. Durham, N.C.: Duke University Press.

Alonso, José F., and Armando M. Lago

1995   "A First Approximation Model of Money, Prices, and Exchange Rates in Revolutionary Cuba." In *Cuba in Transition: Volume 5*, Papers and Proceedings of the 5th Annual Meeting of the Association for the Study of the Cuban Economy (ASCE), 102–43. Washington, D.C.: ASCE.

Alvarado Ramos, Juan Antonio

2006   *Relaciones Raciales en Cuba*. Cuba Transition Project. Institute for Cuban and Cuban-American Studies. University of Miami.

Álvarez Estévez, Rolando

1988   *Azúcar e Inmigración 1900–1940*. Havana: Editorial De Ciencias Sociales.

Álvarez Estévez, Rolando, and Marta Guzmán Pascual

2008   *Cuba en el Caribe y el Caribe en Cuba*. Havana: Fundación Fernando Ortiz.

Andrews, George Reid

1997   "Black Workers in the Export Years: Latin America, 1880–1930." *International Labor and Working-Class History* 51:1–23.

2004   *Afro-Latin America 1800–2000*. Oxford, UK: Oxford University Press.

Aranda Covarrubias, Gisela

2011   *Población Afrodescendiente Cubana Actual*. Havana: Instituto Cubano de Investigación Cultural.

Arguelles, Lourdes, and B. Ruby Rich

1984   "Homosexuality, Homophobia, and Revolution: Notes Toward an Understanding of the Cuban Lesbian and Gay Male Experience, Part I." *Signs* 9(4):683–99.

Argyriadis, Kali

2008   "Speculators and Santuristas: The Development of Afro-Cuban Cultural Tourism and the Accusation of Religious Commercialism." *Tourist Studies* 8(2):249–65.

Austin, Diane

1983   "Culture and Ideology in the English-speaking Caribbean: A View from Jamaica." *American Ethnologist* 10(2):223–40.

Austin Broos, Diane

1992   "Redefining the Moral Order: Interpretations of Christianity in Post-Emancipation Jamaica." In *The Meaning of Freedom: Economics, Politics and Culture after Slavery*, edited by Seymour Drescher and Frank McGlynn, 221–46. Pittsburgh: University of Pittsburgh Press.

Ayala, César J.

1999   *American Sugar Kingdom: The Plantation Economy of the Spanish Caribbean, 1898–1934*. Chapel Hill: University of North Carolina Press.

Azicri, Max

2000   *Cuba Today and Tomorrow: Reinventing Socialism*. Gainesville: University Press of Florida.

Azikiwe, Abayomi, S. E. Anderson, Kazembe Balagun, Amina and Amiri Baraka, Rev. Luis Barrios, Judy Bourne, Jean Damu, Lena Delgado de Torres, James Early, and Herman and Iyaluua Ferguson, et al.

2009   "We Stand With Cuba! African Americans Express Solidarity with the Cuban Revolution." *Pan African News Wire*, December 20. http://panafricannews.blogspot.com/2009/12/we-stand-with-cuba-african-americans.html (accessed March 18, 2015).

Baker, Lee

1998   *From Savage to Negro: Anthropology and the Construction of Race, 1896–1954*. Berkeley: University of California Press.

Baloyra, Enrique A.

1994   "Where Does Cuba Stand?" In *Cuba and the Future*, edited by Donald E. Schulz, 23–40. Westport, Conn.: Greenwood Press.

Banerjee, Sukanya

2010   *Becoming Imperial Citizens: Indians in the Late Victorian Empire*. Durham, N.C.: Duke University Press.

2012   "Introduction: Routing Diasporas." In *New Routes for Diaspora Studies*, edited by Sukanya Banerjee, Aims McGuinness, and Steven C. McKay, 1–22. Bloomington: Indiana University Press.

Barreiro, José

2003   "Survival Stories." In *The Cuba Reader: History, Culture, Politics*, edited by Aviva Chomsky, Barry Carr, and Pamela Smorkaloff, 28–38. Durham, N.C.: Duke University Press.

Barrow, Christine

1998   "Caribbean Masculinity and Family: Revisiting 'Marginality' and 'Reputation'." In *Caribbean Portraits: Essays on Gender Ideologies and Identities*, edited by Christine Barrow, 339–58. Kingston, Jamaica: Ian Randle.

Basch, Linda, Nina Glick Schiller, and Cristina Szanton Blanc

1994   *Nations Unbound: Transnational Projects, Postcolonial Predicaments, and Deterritorialized Nation-States*. 1st ed. London: Routledge.

Basdeo, Sahadeo

2005   "Cuba-CARICOM Relations since 1972: Challenge and Change in Regional Cooperation." In *Foreign Policy Toward Cuba: Isolation or Engagement?* edited by M. Zebich-Knos and Heather N. Nicol, 107–124. Lanham, Md.: Lexington Books.

BBC (British Broadcasting Company)

2010   "Cuba to Cut One Million Public Sector Jobs." Sept. 14. http://www.bbc.com/news/world-latin-america-11291267 (accessed September 7, 2014).

Beckles, Hilary

2003   *Great House Rules: Landless Emancipation and Workers' Protests in Barbados 1838–1938*. Kingston, Jamaica: Ian Randle.

Beckles, Hilary, and Verene Shepherd, eds.

1996   *Caribbean Freedom: Economy and Society from Emancipation to the Present*. Princeton, N.J.: Markus Weiner Publishers.

Behar, Ruth

1995   "Introduction" and "Queer Times in Cuba." In *Bridges to Cuba/Puentes a Cuba*, edited by Ruth Behar, 1–20 and 394–415. Ann Arbor: University of Michigan Press.

2002   *Adio Kerida (Good Bye Dear Love)*. Film. *Women Make Movies*. http://www.ruthbehar.com/AdioKerida.htm (accessed February 2012).

2007   *An Island Called Home: Returning to Jewish Cuba*. New Brunswick, N.J.: Rutgers University Press.

Belliard, Marianella

2001   "'Whiteout': Myth, Identity and Racial Erasure in Cuba and the Dominican Republic (1844–2000)." PhD diss., New York University.

Bengelsdorf, Carollee

1994   *The Problem of Democracy in Cuba: Between Vision and Reality*. New York: Oxford University Press.

Bennett, Dawne

2005   "CARICOM Signs Free Trade Agreement with Cuba." http://www.caribbeannewsnow.com/caribnet/2005/12/12/trade.shtml (accessed August 2006).

Benson, Devyn Spence

2012   "Owning the Revolution: Race, Revolution, and Politics from Havana to Miami, 1959–1963." *Journal of Transnational American Studies* 4(2). http://escholarship.org/uc/item/5sb9d392.

2013   "Cuba Calls: African American Tourism, Race, and the Cuban Revolution, 1959–1961." *Hispanic American Historical Review* 93(2):239–71.

2009   "Not Blacks, But Citizens: Race and Revolution in Cuba." PhD Diss., University of North Carolina–Chapel Hill.

Benzing, Cynthia

2005   "Cuba—Is the Special Period Really Over?" *International Advances in Economic Research* 11(1):69–82.

Berg, Mette Louise

2011   *Diasporic Generations: Memory, Politics, Generation among Cubans in Spain*. New York: Berghahn Books.

Besson, Jean

1992   "Freedom and Community: The British West Indies." In *The Meaning of Freedom: Economics, Politics and Culture after Slavery*, edited by Seymour Drescher and Frank McGlynn, 183–219. Pittsburgh: University of Pittsburgh Press.

1993   "Reputation and Respectability Reconsidered: A New Perspective on Afro-Caribbean Peasant Women." In *Women and Change in the Caribbean: A Pan-Caribbean Perspective*, edited by Jane Momsen, 15–37. Bloomington: Indiana University Press.

Betancourt, Juan R.

1955   *Doctrina Negra: La Única Teoría Certera Contra la Discriminación Racial en Cuba*. Havana: P. Fernández y Cie.

Biehl, João, Bryon Good, and Arthur Kleinman
2007   "Rethinking Subjectivity." Introduction to *Subjectivity: Ethnographic Investigations*, edited by João Biehl, Bryon Good, and Arthur Kleinman, 1–24. Berkeley: University of California Press.

Bloch, Alexia
2005   "Longing for the Kollectiv: Gender, Power, and Residential Schools in Central Siberia." *Cultural Anthropology* 20(4):534–69.

Blue, Sarah
2007   "The Erosion of Racial Equality in the Context of Cuba's Dual Economy." *Latin American Politics and Society* 49(3):35–68.

Blum, Denise
2008   "Socialist Consciousness Raising and Cuba's School to the Countryside Program." *Anthropology and Education Quarterly* 39(2):141–60.
2011   *Cuban Youth and Revolutionary Values: Educating the New Socialist Citizen*. Austin: University of Texas Press.

Bolland, O. Nigel
1981   "Systems of Domination after Slavery: The Control of Land and Labor in the British West Indies after 1838." *Comparative Studies in History and Society* 23(4): 591–619.
1992   "The Politics of Freedom in the British West Indies." In *The Meaning of Freedom: Economics, Politics and Culture after Slavery*, edited by Seymour Drescher and Frank McGlynn, 113–46. Pittsburgh: University of Pittsburgh Press.

Boudreault-Fournier, Alexandrine
2008   "Positioning the New Reggaetón Stars in Cuba: From Home-Based Recording Studios to Alternative Narratives." *Journal of Latin American and Caribbean Anthropology* 13(2):336–60.

Bourgois, Phillippe
1989   *Ethnicity At Work: Divided Labor on a Central American Banana Plantation*. Baltimore, Md.: John Hopkins University Press.

Bowles, Samuel
1971   "Cuban Education and the Revolutionary Ideology." *Harvard Educational Review* 41(4):472–500.

Brady, Anita, and Tony Shirato
2010   *Understanding Judith Butler*. London: Sage Publications.

Brah, Avtar
1996   *Cartographies of Diaspora: Contesting Identities*. London: Routledge.

Brenner, Philip, William M. Leogrande, Donna Rich, and Daniel Siegel, eds.
1989   *The Cuba Reader: The Making of a Revolutionary Society*. New York: Grove.

Brereton, Bridget
1989   "Society and Culture in the Caribbean: The British and French West Indies 1870–1980." In *The Modern Caribbean*, edited by Franklin Knight and Colin Palmer, 85–110. Chapel Hill: University of North Carolina Press.

Brock, Lisa, ed.
1998   *Between Race and Empire: African Americans and Cubans before the Cuban Revolution*. Philadelphia: Temple University Press.

Brodber, Erna

2004   *The Second Generation of Freeman in Jamaica, 1907–1944.* Gainesville: University Press of Florida.

Brodkin, Karen

2000   "Global Capitalism: What's Race Got to Do With It?" *American Ethnologist* 27(2): 237–56.

Bronfman, Alejandra

2004   *Measures of Equality: Social Science, Citizenship, and Race in Cuba, 1902–1940.* Chapel Hill: University of North Carolina Press.

Brotherton, Sean

2008   "'We Have to Think Like Capitalists But Continue Being Socialists': Medicalized Subjectivities, Emergent Capital, and Socialist Entrepreneurs in Post-Soviet Cuba." *American Ethnologist* 35(2):259–74.

2012   *Revolutionary Medicine: Health and the Body in Post-Soviet Cuba.* Durham, N.C.: Duke University Press.

Brundenius, Claes

2002   "Whither the Cuban Economy after Recovery?: The Reform Process, Upgrading Strategies and the Question of Transition." *Journal of Latin American Studies* 34:365–95.

Bryan, Patrick

1991   *The Jamaican People, 1880–1902: Race, Class and Social Control.* London: Macmillan Caribbean.

2001   "Jamaica and Cuba 1918–1939." In *Intra-Caribbean Migration: the Cuban Connection (1898–Present)*, edited by Annette Insanally. Mona, Jamaica: University of the West Indies, Latin American-Caribbean Centre.

Bryce-Laporte, Roy S.

1972   "Black Immigrants: The Experience of Invisibility and Inequality." *Journal of Black Studies* 3(1):29–56.

1998   "Crisis, Contraculture, and Religion Among West Indians in the Panama Canal Zone." In *Blacks and Blackness in Latin America and the Caribbean*, vol. 1, *Central America and the Northern South American Lowlands*, edited by Norman Whitten and Arlene Torres, 100–118. Bloomington: University of Indiana Press.

Buijtenhuijs, Robert

1973   *Mau Mau Twenty Years After: The Myth and the Survivors.* Vol. 4. The Hague: Mouton.

Bull, Andy

2007   "The Curious Revival of Cricket in Cuba." http://blogs.guardian. co.uk/sport/2007/01/07-week/ (accessed February 12, 2008).

Burchardt, Hans-Jürgen

2002   "Contours of the Future: The New Social Dynamics in Cuba." *Latin American Perspectives* 29(3):57–74.

Burroway, Michael, and Katherine Verdery, eds.

1999   *Uncertain Transition: Ethnographies of Change in the Postsocialist World.* Boulder, Colo.: Rowman and Littlefield.

Butler, Judith
1993   *Bodies that Matter: On the Discursive Limits of "Sex."* New York: Routledge.
Butterworth, Douglas
1980   *People of Buena Ventura: Relocation of Slum Dwellers in Post-revolutionary Cuba.* Urbana: University of Illinois Press.
Buyandelgeriyn, Manduhai
2008   "Post-Post-Transition Theories: Walking on Multiple Paths." *Annual Review of Anthropology* 37:235–50.
Cabezas, Amelia
2004   "Between Love and Money: Sex, Tourism, and Citizenship in Cuba and the Dominican Republic." *Signs* 29(4):987–1015.
2009   *Economies of Desire: Sex and Tourism in Cuba and the Dominican Republic.* Philadelphia: Temple University Press.
Campbell, Carl
2002   "British Aid and West Indian Education: 1835–45." In *In the Shadow of the Plantation: Caribbean History and Legacy*, edited by Alvin O. Thompson and Woodville K. Marshall, 283–96. Kingston, Jamaica: Ian Randle.
Cancio Isla, Wilfredo
2004   "El éxodo de los balseros: Una tragedia que difícilmente se repetirá." *El Nuevo Herald*, August 9. http://www.latinamericanstudies.org/exile/tragedia.htm (accessed September 7, 2014).
Cannon, Terrence
1981   *Revolutionary Cuba.* Havana: Editorial José Martí.
Cannon, Terry, and Johnetta Cole
1978   *Free and Equal: The End of Racial Discrimination in Cuba.* New York: Venceremos Brigade.
Capelli, Luciano, and Yazmín Ross, dirs.
2000   *El Barco Prometido/The Promised Ship.* Film. Río Nevado Producciones. Distributed by Latin American Video Archives, New York.
Carr, Barry
1998a   "'Omnipotent and omnipresent?' Labor shortages, Worker Mobility, and Employer Control in the Cuban Sugar Industry, 1910–1934." In *Identity and Struggle at the Margins of the Nation-State: The Laboring Peoples of Central America and the Hispanic Caribbean*, edited by Aviva Chomsky and Antonio Lauria-Santiago, 260–91. Durham, N.C.: Duke University Press.
1998b   "Identity, Class and Nation: Black Immigrant Workers, Cuban Communism, and the Sugar Insurgency, 1925–1934." *Hispanic American Historical Review* 78(1):83–116.
Carter, Henderson
2002   "The Bridgetown Riot of 1872." In *In the Shadow of the Plantation: Caribbean History and Legacy*, edited by Alvin O. Thompson and Woodville K. Marshall, 334–50. Kingston, Jamaica: Ian Randle.
Casal, Lourdes
1979   "Race Relations in Contemporary Cuba." In *The Position of Blacks in Brazil and*

Cuban Society, edited by Anani Dzidzienyo and Lourdes Casal, 11–27. London: Minority Rights Group.

Casey, Matthew

2012   "From Haiti to Cuba and Back: Haitians' Experience of Migration, Labor, and Return, 1900–1940." PhD diss., University of Pittsburgh.

Castillo Bueno, María de los Reyes

2000   *Reyita: The Life of a Black Cuban Woman in the Twentieth Century*. Durham, N.C.: Duke University Press.

Cervantes-Rodríguez, Margarita

2010   *International Migration in Cuba: Accumulation, Imperial Designs, and Transnational Social Fields*. University Park: Pennsylvania State University Press.

Chailloux Laffita, Graciela I..

2005   "Introducción" In *¿De Dónde Son los Cubanos?* edited by Graciela Chailloux Laffita, 1–4. Havana: Editorial de Ciencias Sociales.

Chailloux, Graciela, and Robert Whitney

2001   "I Am the Caribbean: A West Indian Melting Pot in Cuba." In *Intra-Caribbean Migration: The Cuban Connection (1898–Present)*, edited by Annette Insanally, 39–62. Mona, Jamaica: University of the West Indies.

2005   "British Subjects y Pichones en Cuba." In *¿De Dónde Son los Cubanos?* edited by Graciela Chailloux Laffita, 53–91. Havana: Editorial de Ciencias Sociales.

Chailloux, Graciela, Robert Whitney, and Roberto Claxton

2006   "Diasporic Voices: A Collection of Interviews with English-speaking Migrants to Cuba and Their Descendants" In *Regional Footprints: The Travels and Travails of Early Caribbean Migrants*, edited by Annette Insanally, Mark Clifford, and Sean Sheriff, 133–54. Mona, Jamaica: University of the West Indies, Latin American and Caribbean Centre.

Chari, Sharad, and Katherine Verdery

2009   "Thinking Between the Posts: Postcolonialism, Postsocialism, and Ethnography After the Cold War." *Comparative Studies in Society and History* 51(1):6–34.

Charlton, Audrey

2005   "'Cat Born in Oven Is Not Bread': Jamaican and Barbadian Immigrants in Cuba Between 1900 and 1959." PhD diss., Teacher's College, Columbia University.

Cheng, Yinghong

2009   *Creating the New Man: From Enlightenment Ideals to Socialist Realities*. Honolulu: University of Hawaii Press.

Chivallon, Christine

2002   "Beyond Gilroy's Black Atlantic: The Experience of the African Diaspora." *Diaspora* 11(3):359–82.

Chomsky, Aviva

1996   *West Indian Workers and the United Fruit Company in Costa Rica, 1870–1940*. Baton Rouge: Louisiana State University Press.

1998   "The Aftermath of Repression: Race and Nation in Cuba after 1912." *Journal of Iberian and Latin American Studies* 4(2):1–40.

2000   "'Barbados or Canada?' Race, Immigration, and Nation in Early-Twentieth-Century Cuba." *Hispanic American Historical Review* 80(3):415–62.

Clark, Juan

1975   "The Exodus from Revolutionary Cuba (1959–1974): A Sociological Analysis." PhD diss., University of Florida.

Clarke, Kamari

2010   "New Spheres of Transnational Formations: Mobilizations of Humanitarian Diasporas." *Transforming Anthropology* 18(1):48–65.

Clarke, Kamari, and Deborah Thomas

2006   *Globalization and Race: Transformations in the Cultural Production of Blackness.* Durham, N.C.: Duke University Press.

Clealand, Danielle Pilar

2012   "The Power of the Frame." Conference paper presented at Cuban Research Institute, Florida International University, May 23, 2013.

Clifford, James

1994   "Diasporas." *Cultural Anthropology* 9(3):302–38.

Cohen, Robin

2008   *Global Diasporas: An Introduction.* Seattle: University of Washington Press.

Conniff, Michael

1985   *Black Labor on a White Canal: Panama, 1904–1981.* Pittsburgh: University of Pittsburgh Press.

Cooper, Frederick, Thomas Holt, and Rebecca Scott

2000   *Beyond Slavery: Explorations of Race, Labor and Citizenship in Post-emancipation Societies.* Durham: University of North Carolina Press.

Copeland-Carson, Jacqueline

2004   *Creating Africa in America: Translocal Identity in an Emerging World City.* Philadelphia: University of Pennsylvania Press.

Cornebise, Michael

2003   "The Social Construction of Tourism Space in Cuba." PhD Diss. University of Tennessee–Knoxville.

Corrales, Javier

2004   "The Gatekeeper State: Limited Economic Reforms and Regime Survival in Cuba, 1989–2002." *Latin American Research Review* 39(2):35–65.

Cotman, John Walton

2006   "Caribbean Convergence: Contemporary Cuba-CARICOM Relations." In *Redefining Cuban Foreign Policy: The Impact of the "Special Period,"* edited by H. Michael Erisman and John Kirk, 121–49. Gainesville: University Press of Florida.

Craton, Michael

1988   "Continuity, Not Change: The Incidents of Unrest Among Ex-Slaves in the British West Indies, 1838–1876." *Slavery and Abolition* 9(8):144–70.

1997   *Empire, Enslavement, and Freedom in the Caribbean.* Kingston, Jamaica: Ian Randle.

Crawford, Sharika

2011   "A Transnational World Fractured But Not Forgotten: British West Indian Migration to the Colombian Islands of San Andrés and Providence." *New West Indian Guide* 85(1–2):31–52.

Daniel, Yvonne

1995   *Rumba: Dance and Social Change in Contemporary Cuba.* Bloomington: Indiana University Press.

Davidson, Julio O'Donnell

1996   "Sex Tourism in Cuba." *Race and Class* 38(1):39–49.

Davis, Annalee

2007   *On the Map: Intra-Caribbean Migration from Guyana to Barbados.* Film. Caribbean Tales Worldwide Distribution.

De Grandis, Rita, and Zilá Bernd, eds.

1999   *Unforseeable Americas: Questioning Cultural Hybridity in the Americas.* Amsterdam: Rodopi.

De la Cadena, Marisol

2001   "Reconstructing Race, Racism, Culture and Mestizaje in Latin America." *NACLA Report on the Americas* 34(6):16–28.

De la Fuente, Alejandro

1995   "Race and Inequality in Cuba, 1899–1981." *Journal of Contemporary History* 30(1): 131–67.

1997   "Two Dangers, One Solution: Immigration, Race, and Labor in Cuba 1900–1930." *International Labor and Working Class History* 51:30–49.

1998   "Race, National Discourse, and Politics in Cuba: an Overview." *Latin American Perspectives* 25(3):43–69.

1999   "Myths of Racial Democracy: Cuba, 1900–1912." *Latin American Research Review* 34(3):39–73.

2001a   "The Resurgence of Racism in Cuba." *NACLA Report on the Americas* 34(6):29–34.

2001b   *A Nation for All: Race, Inequality, and Politics in Twentieth-Century Cuba.* Chapel Hill: University of North Carolina Press.

2007   "Race, Culture, Politics." In *Looking Forward: Comparative Perspectives on Cuba's Transition,* edited by Marifeli Pérez-Stable, 138–62. Notre Dame, Ind.: University of Notre Dame Press.

2009   "The New Afro-Cuban Cultural Movement and the Debate on Race in Contemporary Cuba." *Journal of Latin American Studies* 40(4):697–720.

De la Fuente, Alejandro, and Laurence Glasco

1997   "Are Blacks 'Getting Out of Control'? Racial Attitudes, Revolution, and Political Transition in Cuba." In *Toward a New Cuba? Legacies of Revolution,* edited by Miguel A. Centeno and Mauricio Font, 53–71. Boulder, Colo.: Lynn Rienner Publishers.

De la Rey, Cheryl, Amina Mama, and Zine Magubane

1997   "Beyond the Masks." *Agenda* 32:17–23.

Delgado, Kevin M.

2009   "Spiritual Capital: Foreign Patronage and the Trafficking of Santería." In *Cuba in the Special Period: Culture and Ideology in the 1990s,* edited by Ariana Herdnadez-Reguant, 51–68. New York: Palgrave Macmillan.

Derrick, Jorge

2001   "Jamaica and Cuba 1918–1939." In *Intra-Caribbean Migration: The Cuban Connection (1898–Present)*, edited by Annette Insanally, 29–37. Mona, Jamaica: University of the West Indies.

Dickerson, Debra

2004   *The End of Blackness: Returning the Souls of Black Folk to Their Rightful Owners.* New York: Pantheon.

Dominguez, Jorge

1978   *Cuba: Order and Revolution.* Cambridge, Mass.: Harvard University Press.

Do Nascimento, Abdias

1977   *Racial Democracy in Brazil: Myth or Reality?: A Dossier of Brazilian Racism.* Ibadan, Nigeria: Sketch Publishing.

Dore, Elizabeth

2009   "Cubans' Memories of the 1960s: The Ecstasies and the Agonies." *ReVista* (Winter). http://www.drclas.harvard.edu/publications/revistaonline/winter-2009/cubans-memories-1960s.

Duany, Jorge

1994   "Beyond the Safety Valve: Recent Trends in Caribbean Migration." *Social and Economic Studies* 43(1):95–122.

1998   "Reconstructing Racial Identity: Ethnicity, Color, and Class among Dominicans in the United States and Puerto Rico." *Latin American Perspectives* 25(3):147–72.

2002   *Puerto Ricans on the Move: Identities on the Island and in the United States.* Durham: University of North Carolina Press.

2005   "Dominican Migration to Puerto Rico: A Transnational Perspective." *Centro* 17(1):242–69.

2012   *Blurred Borders: Transnational Migration between the Hispanic Caribbean and the United States.* Chapel Hill: University of North Carolina Press.

Duharte, Rafael, and Elsa Santos

1997   *El Fantasma de la Esclavitud: Prejucios Raciales en Cuba y America Latina.* Bonn, Germany: Pahl-Rugenstein.

Dye, Alan

1998   *Cuban Sugar in the Age of Mass Production: Technology and the Economics of the Sugar Central, 1899–1929.* Stanford, Calif.: Stanford University Press.

Echeverri-Gent, Elisvinda

1992   "Forgotten Workers: British West Indians and the Early Days of the Banana Industry in Costa Rica and Honduras." *Journal of Latin American Studies* 24:275–308.

Eckstein, Susan

1994   *Back From the Future: Cuba Under Castro.* Princeton, N.J.: Princeton University Press.

2004   "Dollarization and Its Discontents: Remittances and the Remaking of Cuba in the Post-Soviet Era." *Comparative Politics* 36(3):313–30.

Edwards, Brent Hayes

2001   "The Uses of Diaspora." *Social Text* 19(1):45–73.

2003   *The Practice of Diaspora: Literature, Translation, and the Rise of Black International-ism*. Cambridge, Mass.: Harvard University Press.

Ellis, Carolyn, and Michael Flaherty, eds.

1992   *Investigating Subjectivity: Research on Lived Experience*. Newbury Park, Calif.: Sage Publications.

Emmer, Pieter

2000   "'A Spirit of Independence' or Lack of Education for the Market? Freedmen and Asian Indentured Labor Force in the Post-Emancipation Caribbean, 1834–1917." *Slavery and Abolition* 21(2):150–68.

Espino Prieto, Rodrigo, and Pablo Rodriguez Ruiz

2006   "Raza y Desigualdad en la Cuba Actual." *Temas* 45(January–March):44–54.

Espronceda Amor, Maria Eugenia

1999   "La Formación de la Estructura Parental en Condiciones de Inmigración: Estudio Comparado." Master's thesis, University of Oriente.

Estévez Rivero, Sandra

2003   "El Movimiento Garveyista en Santiago de Cuba (1920–1935)." *Del Caribe* 41:71–75.

Facio, Elisa, Maura Toro-Morn, and Anne Roschelle

2004   "Tourism, Gender, and Globalization: Tourism in Cuba During the Special Period," *Transnational Law and Contemporary Problems* 14(1):119–42.

Fagen, Richard

1969   *The Transformation of Political Culture in Cuba*. Palo Alto, Calif.: Stanford University Press.

Faist, Thomas, and Ranier Bauböck, eds.

2010   *Diaspora and Transnationalism: Concepts, Theories and Methods*. Amsterdam, Neth-erlands: Amsterdam University Press.

Fanon, Frantz

2008   *Black Skin, White Masks*. New translation by Richard Philcox with foreword by Kwame Anthony Appiah, 2008. New York: Grove Press. Originally published 1952 as *Peau noire, masques blancs*. Paris: Éditions du Seuil.

Fernandes, Sujatha

2006   *Cuba Represent! Cuban Arts, State Power, and the Making of New Revolutionary Cul-tures*. Durham, N.C.: Duke University Press.

Fernández, Damian

1994   "Informal Politics and the Crisis of Cuban Socialism." In *Cuba and the Future*, edited by Donald E. Schulz, 69–82. Westport, Conn.: Greenwood Press.

Fernández, Nadine

1996   "The Color of Love: Young Interracial Couples in Cuba." *Latin American Perspectives* 23(1):99–117.

1999   "Back to the Future? Women, Race and Tourism in Cuba." In *Sun, Sex and Gold: Tourism and Sex Work in the Caribbean*, edited by Kemala Kempadoo. Lanham, Md.: Rowman & Littlefield.

2010   *Revolutionizing Romance: Interracial Couples in Contemporary Cuba*. New Bruns-wick, N.J.: Rutgers University Press.

Fernández Díaz, Ariel
2007   Author notes from "Cuba Represent! Rap Music and Racial Politics in Contemporary Cuba." Lecture and dialogue with Sujatha Fernandes, February 2, 2007, Graduate Center, CUNY.

Fernández Robaina, Tomás
1990   *El Negro en Cuba, 1902–1958. Apuntes para la Historia de la Lucha Contra la Discriminación Racial*. Havana: Editorial de Ciencias Sociales.

Ferrer, Ada
1999   *Insurgent Cuba: Race, Nation, and Revolution, 1868–1898*. Chapel Hill: University of North Carolina Press.

Fikes, Kesha, and Alaina Lemon
2002   "African Presence in Former Soviet Spaces." *Annual Review of Anthropology* 31:497–524.

Foner, Nancy
1998   "West Indian Identity in the Diaspora: Comparative and Historical Perspectives." *Latin American Perspectives* 25(3):173–88.
2001   "Introduction: West Indian Migration to New York City: An Overview." In *Islands in the City: West Indian Migration to New York*, edited by Nancy Foner, 1–22. Berkeley: University of California Press.
2006   *In a New Land: a Comparative View of Immigration*. New York: New York University Press.

Font, Mauricio Augusto, and Alfonso V. Quiroz, eds.
2005   *Cuban Counterpoints: The Legacy of Fernando Ortiz*. Lanham, Md.: Lexington Books.

Fox, Patricia
2006   *Being and Blackness in Latin America: Uprootedness and Improvisation*. Gainesville: University Press of Florida.

Frederick, Rhonda
2005   *"Colón Man a Come": Mythographies of the Panama Canal Migration*. Lanham, Md.: Lexington Books.

Frederik, Laurie
2005   "Cuba's National Characters: Setting the Stage for the Hombre Novísimo." *Journal of Latin American and Caribbean Anthropology* 10(2):401–36.
2012   *Trumpets in the Mountains: Theater and the Politics of National Culture in Cuba*. Durham, N.C.: Duke University Press.

Freeman, Carla
2000   *High Tech and High Heels in the Global Economy: Women, Work, and Pink Collar Identities in the Caribbean*. Durham, N.C.: Duke University Press.
2007   "The 'Reputation' of Neoliberalism." *American Ethnologist* 34(2):252–67.

Friedman, Jack R.
2007   "Shame and the Experience of Ambivalence on the Margins of the Global: Pathologizing Past and Present in Romania's Industrial Wastelands." *Ethos* 35(2):235–64.

Furé Davis, Samuel
2011   *La Cultura Rastafari en Cuba*. Santiago de Cuba: Editorial Oriente.

Garnes, Walterio Lord
2009   "Marcus Garvey and the UNIA in the Memory of West Indian Residents in Cuba."
        76 King Street Liberty Hall 1:130–44.
Garvey, Marcus
1973   "The Race Question in Jamaica (1916)." In *Consequences of Class and Color: West
        Indian Perspectives*, edited by David Lowenthal and Lambros Comitas, 4–12. Garden
        City, N.J.: Anchor Press.
2011   *The Marcus Garvey and Universal Negro Improvement Association Papers*. Vol. 11,
        The Caribbean Diaspora, 1910–1920, edited by Robert A. Hill. Durham, N.C.: Duke
        University Press.
Gilroy, Paul
1993   *The Black Atlantic: Modernity and Double-Consciousness*. Cambridge, Mass.: Har-
        vard University Press.
2000   *Against Race: Imagining Political Culture Beyond the Color Line*. Cambridge, Mass.:
        Harvard University Press.
2003   "The Black Atlantic as a Counterculture of Modernity." In *Theorizing Diaspora: A
        Reader*, edited by Jana Evans Braziel and Anita Mannur, 49–80. Malden, Mass.:
        Blackwell.
Giovannetti, Jorge L.
2001   "Black British Subjects in Cuba: Race, Ethnicity, Nation, and Identity in the Migra-
        tory Experience, 1898–1938." PhD diss., University of North London.
2002   "Historia Visual y Etnohistoria en Cuba: Inmigración antillana e identitdad en 'Los
        Hijos de Baraguá.'" *Caribbean Studies* 31(2):216–52.
2006a   "The Elusive Organization of 'Identity': Race, Religion, and Empire among Carib-
        bean Migrants in Cuba." *Small Axe* 10(1):1–27.
2006b   "Black British Caribbean Migrants in Cuba: Resistance, Opposition, and Strategic
        Identity in the Early Twentieth Century." In *Intra-Caribbean Migration: The Cuban
        Connection (1898–Present)*, edited by Annette Insanally, 103–20. Mona, Jamaica:
        University of the West Indies.
2006c   "Grounds of Race: Slavery, Racism, and the Plantation in the Caribbean." *Latin
        American and Caribbean Ethnic Studies* 1(1):5–36.
Gleijeses, Piero
2002   *Conflicting Missions: Havana, Washington, and Africa, 1959–1976*. Chapel Hill: Uni-
        versity of North Carolina Press.
Glick Schiller, Nina
2005   "Transnational Social Fields and Imperialism: Bringing a Theory of Power to Trans-
        national Studies." *Anthropological Theory* 5:439–61.
Glick Schiller, Nina and Georges Eugene Fouron
2001   *Georges Woke Up Laughing: Long Distance Nationalism and the Search for Home*.
        Durham, N.C.: Duke University Press.
Global Voices Online
2013   "Racism Greets Imported Cuban Doctors in Brazil." http://globalvoicesonline.
        org/2013/09/11/racism-greets-imported-cuban-doctors-in-brazil/ (accessed October
        4, 2013).

Godfried, Eugene

2000   "Reflections on Race and the Status of People of African Descent in Revolutionary Cuba." afrocubaweb.com/eugenegodfried/reflectionsonrace.htm (accessed April
2003).

Gómez Navia, Raimundo

2005   "Lo Haitiano en lo Cubano." In ¿De Dónde Son los Cubanos? edited by Raimundo
Gómez Navia and Graciela Chailloux, 5–51. Havana: Editorial de Ciencias Sociales.

Gonzalez, Edward, and Kevin F. McCarthy

2004   *Cuba After Castro: Legacies, Challenges, and Impediments.* Santa Monica, Calif.:
RAND Corporation.

González Suárez, Dominga

1987   "La Inmigración Antillana en Cuba." *Economia y Desarrollo* 100(Sept./Oct.):50–61.

Goodrich, Jonathan

1993   "Socialist Cuba: A Study of Health Tourism." *Journal of Travel Research* 32(1):36–41.

Gordon, Edmund

1998   *Disparate Diasporas: Identity and Politics in an African-Nicaraguan Community.*
Austin: University of Texas Press.

Gordon, Edmund, and Mark Anderson

1999   "The African Diaspora: Toward an Ethnography of Diasporic Identification." *Journal
of American Folklore* 112(445):282–97.

Gordon, Shirley C.

1963   *A Century of West Indian Education.* London: Longmans, Green.

Graham, Richard, ed.

1990   *The Idea of Race in Latin America, 1870–1940.* Austin: University of Texas Press.

Graham, Tracy

2013   "Jamaican Migration to Cuba, 1912–1940." PhD Diss., University of Chicago.

Grant, Cedric

2005   "Caribbean Community and Cuba Relations: Thirty Years Revisited." In *Foreign
Policy Toward Cuba: Isolation or Engagement?* edited by Michele Zebich-Knos and
Heather N. Nicol, 125–38. Lanham, Md.: Lexington Books.

Greenbaum, Susan

2002   *More Than Black: Afro-Cubans in Tampa.* Gainesville: University of Florida Press.

Gropas, Maria

2007   "The Repatriotization of Revolutionary Ideology and Mnemonic Landscape in Present-Day Havana." *Current Anthropology* 48(4):531–49.

Guarnizo, Luis Eduardo

2003   "The Economics of Transnational Living." *International Migration Review* 37(3):
666–99.

Guerra, Lillian

2009   "'To condemn the Revolution is to condemn Christ': Radicalization, Moral Redemption and the Sacrifice of Civil Society in Cuba, 1960." *Hispanic American Historical
Review* 89(1):73–110.

2010   "Beyond Paradox: Counter-Revolution and the Origins of Political Culture in the

Cuban Revolution: 1959–2009." In *A Century of Revolution: Insurgent and Counter-insurgent Violence During Latin America's Long Cold War*, edited by Greg Grandlin and Gilbert Joseph, 199–238. Durham: University of North Carolina Press.

2012   *Visions of Power in Cuba: Revolution, Redemption, and Resistance, 1959–1971*. Chapel Hill: University of North Carolina Press.

Guevara, Ernesto

1977   *El Socialismo y El Hombre Nuevo*. 1st ed. Mexico: Siglo Veintiuno.

Guevara, Ernesto, and Fidel Castro

2009 [1968]   *Socialism and Man in Cuba*. Atlanta: Pathfinder Press.

Guridy, Frank A.

2003   "'Enemies of the White Race': The Machadista State and the UNIA in Cuba." *Caribbean Studies* 31(1):107–37.

2010   *Forging Diaspora: Afro-Cubans and African Americans in a World of Empire and Jim Crow*. Chapel Hill: University of North Carolina Press.

Haddad, Angela

2003   "Critical Reflexivity, Contradictions and Modern Cuban Consciousness." *Acta Sociologica* 46(1):51–68.

Hagedorn, Katherine

2001   *Divine Utterances: The Performance of Afro-Cuban Santería*. Washington, D.C.: Smithsonian Institution.

Hahamovitch, Cindy

2011   *No Man's Land: Jamaican Guestworkers in America and the Global History of Deportable Labor*. Princeton, N.J.: Princeton University Press.

Hale, Charles

1996   "Mestizaje, Hybridity, and the Cultural Politics of Difference in Post-Revolutionary Central America." *Journal of Latin American Anthropology* 2(1):36–61.

Hall, Catherine, ed.

2000   *Cultures of Empire: Colonizers in Britain and the Empire in the Nineteenth and Twentieth Centuries*. Manchester, UK: Manchester University Press.

Hall, Douglas

1978   "The Flight from the Plantations Reconsidered: The British West Indies, 1838–42." *Journal of Caribbean History* 10(11):7–24.

Hall, Stuart

1981   "Notes on Deconstructing 'The Popular.'" In *People's History and Socialist Theory*, edited by Raphael Samuel, 227–40. London: Routledge.

1987   "Minimal Selves." In *Identity: The Real Me: Postmodernism and the Question of Identity*, edited by Homi K. Bhaba, 44–46. London: Institute of Contemporary Arts.

1990   "Cultural Identity and Diaspora." In *Identity, Community, Culture, Difference*, edited by Jonathan Rutherford, 222–37. London: Lawrence and Wishart.

2000   "Old and New Identities, Old and New Ethnicities." In *Theories of Race and Racism: A Reader*, edited by Les Back and John Solomos, 144–53. London: Routledge.

Hansen, Jonathan

2011   *Guantánamo: An American History*. New York: Hill and Wang.

Hansing, Katrin

2006   *Rasta, Race, and Revolution: The Emergence and Development of the Rastafari Movement in Socialist Cuba.* Berlin: LIT Verlag.

Harpelle, Ronald N.

1993   "The Social and Political Integration of West Indians in Costa Rica: 1930–1950." *Journal of Latin American Studies* 25(1):103–18.

2001   *The West Indians of Costa Rica: Race, Class, and the Integration of an Ethnic Minority.* Quebec: McGill–Queen's University Press.

Harrison, Faye V.

1995   "The Persistent Power of 'Race' in the Cultural and Political Economy of Racism." *Annual Review of Anthropology* 24:47–74.

1999   "Introduction: Expanding the Discourse on 'Race.'" *American Anthropologist* 100(3): 609–31.

Hartman, Sadiya

1997   *Scenes of Subjection: Terror, Slavery, and Self-Making in Nineteenth Century America.* New York: Oxford University Press.

Hasenbalg, Carlos

1996   "Racial Inequalities in Brazil and throughout Latin America: Timid Responses to Disguised Racism." In *Constructing Democracy: Human Rights, Citizenship, and Society in Latin America*, edited by Elizabeth Jelin and Eric Hershberg, 161–76. Boulder, Colo.: Westview Press.

Hay, Michelle

2009   *"I've Been Black in Two Countries": Black Cuban Views on Race in the U.S.* El Paso, Tex.: LFB Scholarly Publishing.

Helg, Aline

1995   *Our Rightful Share: the Afro-Cuban Struggle for Equality, 1886–1912.* Chapel Hill: University of North Carolina Press.

Henken, Ted A.

2002   "Condemned to Informality: Cuba Experiments with Self-Employment During the Special Period (The Case of the Bed and Breakfasts)." *Cuban Studies* 33:1–29.

2007   *Cuba: A Global Studies Handbook.* Santa Barbara, Calif.: ABC-CLIO Publishers.

Hernandez-Reguant, Ariana, ed.

2009   *Cuba in the Special Period: Culture and Ideology in the 1990s.* New York: Palgrave Macmillan.

Hill, Robert A., ed.

2011   *The Marcus Garvey and Universal Negro Improvement Association Papers.* Vol. 11, *The Caribbean Diaspora, 1910–1920.* Durham, N.C.: Duke University Press.

Hintzen, Percy

2001   *West Indian in the West.* New York: New York University Press.

2004   "Imagining Home: Race and the West Indian Diaspora in the San Francisco Bay Area." *Journal of Latin American Anthropology* 9(2):289–318.

2010   "Race and Diasporic Imaginings among West Indians in the San Francisco Bay Area." In *Global Circuits of Blackness: Interrogating the African Diaspora*, edited by

Jean Muteba Rahier, Percy Hintzen, and Felipe Smith, 49–73. Urbana-Champaign: University of Illinois Press.

Hintzen, Percy, and Jean Rahier, eds.

2003   *Problematizing Blackness: Self-Ethnographies by Black Immigrants to the United States*. New York: Routledge.

Hintzen, Percy, and Jean Rahier

2010   "Introduction: Theorizing the African Diaspora: Metaphor, Miscognition, and Self-Recognition." In *Global Circuits of Blackness: Interrogating the African Diaspora*, edited by Jean Muteba Rahier, Percy Hintzen, and Felipe Smith, x–xxvi. Urbana-Champaign: University of Illinois Press.

Hodge, G. Derrick

2001   "Colonization of the Cuban Body: Nationalism, Economy, and Masculinity of Male Sex Work in Havana." *NACLA Report on the Americas* 34(5):20–28.

Hoetnick, H.

1967   *Caribbean Race Relations: A Study of Two Variants*. London: Oxford University Press.

Hoffman, Bert

2001   "Transformation and Continuity in Cuba." *Review of Radical Political Economics* 33(1):1–20.

Holt, Thomas

1992   *The Problem of Freedom: Race, Labor, and Politics in Jamaica and Britain 1832–1938*. Baltimore, Md.: John Hopkins University Press.

Hörschelmann, Kathrin

2002   "History After the End: Post-Socialist Difference in a (Post)modern World." *Transactions of the Institute of British Geographers* 27(1):52–66.

Howard, Philip

1998   *Changing History: Afro-Cuban Cabildos and Societies of Color in the Nineteenth Century*. Baton Rouge: Louisiana State University Press.

Hutnyk, John

2005   "Hybridity." Racial and Ethnic Studies 28(1):79–102.

Itzigsohn, José

2000   "Immigration and the Boundaries of Citizenship: The Institutions of Immigrants' Political Transnationalism." *International Migration Review* 34(4):1126–54.

Jackson, Shona

2006   "Guyana, Cuba, Venezuela and the 'Routes' to Cultural Reconciliation between Latin America and the Caribbean." *Small Axe* 10(1):28–58.

Jamaica Information Service

2007   "Region Observes Cuba/CARICOM Day," December 8. http://jis.gov.jm/region-observes-caricomcuba-day/ (accessed March 2012).

James, C.L.R. (Cyril Lionel Robert)

1973   "The Middle Classes." In *Consequences of Class and Color: West Indian Perspectives*, edited by David Lowenthal and Lambros Comitas, 79–94. Garden City, N.J.: Anchor Press.

James, Winston

1998   *Holding Aloft the Banner of Ethiopia: Caribbean Radicalism in Early Twentieth-Century America*. London: Verso.

Jatar-Hausmann, Ana Julia

1999   *The Cuban Way: Capitalism, Communism and Confrontation*. West Hartford, Conn.: Kumarian Press.

Jones, Alberto

2001a   "Guantánamo Remembered." *AfroCubaWeb*. www.afrocubaweb.com/albertojones/albertojones3.htm (accessed May 2001).

2001b   "Joining the British West Indian Welfare Center." *AfroCubaWeb*. http://www.afrocubaweb.com/cacf.htm (accessed March 6, 2015).

2005   "The Caribbean American Children's Foundation Newsletter #10." *AfroCubaWeb*. http://www.afrocubaweb.com/cacf.htm##10 (accessed September 6, 2014).

Kapcia, Antoni

2008   *Cuba in Revolution: A History Since the Fifties*. London: Reaktion Books.

Kasinitz, Philip

1992   *Caribbean New York: Black Immigrants and the Politics of Race*. Ithaca, N.Y.: Cornell University Press.

Kaya, Ayhan

2007   "German-Turkish Transnational Space: A Separate Space of Their Own." *German Review* 30(2):483–502.

Kearney, Michael

1995   "The Local and the Global: The Anthropology of Globalization and Transnationalism." *Annual Review of Anthropology* 24:547–65.

Kempadoo, Kamala, ed.

1999   *Sun, Sex, Gold: Tourism and Sex Work in the Caribbean*. Lanham, Md.: Rowman and Littlefield.

2004   *Sexing the Caribbean: Gender, Race, and Sexual Labour*. New York: Routledge.

Kildegaard, Arnie C., and Roberto Orro Fernández

1999   "Dollarization in Cuba and Implications for the Future Transition." In *Cuba in Transition: Volume 9*, Papers and Proceedings of the 9th Annual Meeting of the Association for the Study of the Cuban Economy (ASCE), 25–30. Washington, D.C: ASCE.

Kleinman, Arthur, and Erin Fitz-Henry

2007   "The Experiential Basis of Subjectivity: How Individuals Change in the Context of Societal Transformation." In *Subjectivity: Ethnographic Investigations*, edited by João Biehl, Byron J. Good, and Arthur Kleinman, 52–65. Berkeley: University of California Press.

Knight, Franklin

1970   *Slave Society in Cuba During the Nineteenth Century*. Madison: University of Wisconsin Press.

1978   *The Caribbean: Genesis of a Fragmented Nationalism*. Oxford, UK: Oxford University Press.

1985   "Jamaican Migrants and the Cuban Sugar Industry." In *Between Slavery and Free*

Labor: The Spanish-Speaking Caribbean in the Nineteenth Century, edited by Manuel Moreno Fraginals, Frank Moya Pons, and Stanley Engerman, 84–114. Baltimore, Md.: Johns Hopkins University Press.

Knight, Franklin, and Colin Palmer, eds.

1989   *The Modern Caribbean.* Chapel Hill: University of North Carolina Press.

Kraidy, Marvin

2005   *Hybridity, Or the Cultural Logic of Globalization.* Philadelphia: Temple University Press.

Leiner, Marvin

1994   *Sexual Politics in Cuba: Machismo, Homosexuality, and AIDS.* Boulder, Colo.: Westview Press.

Levitt, Peggy

1998   "Social Remittances: Migration-Driven Local Level Forms of Cultural Diffusion." *International Migration Review* 32(4):926–48.

Levitt, Peggy, and Nina Glick Schiller

2004   "Conceptualizing Simultaneity: A Transnational Social Field Perspective on Society." *International Migration Review* 38:1002–39.

Lewis, David

1995   "The Latin Caribbean and Regional Cooperation: A Survey of Challenges and Opportunities." *Journal of Interamerican Studies and World Affairs* 37(4):25–55.

Lewis, Earl

1995   "To Turn as on a Pivot: Writing African Americans into a History of Overlapping Diasporas." *American Historical Review* 100(3):765–87.

Lewis, Oscar, Ruth Lewis, and Susan Rigdon

1977a   *Four Men: Living the Revolution. An Oral History of Contemporary Cuba.* Urbana: University of Illinois Press.

1977b   *Four Women: Living the Revolution. An Oral History of Contemporary Cuba.* Urbana: University of Illinois Press.

1978   *Neighbors: Living the Revolution. An Oral History of Contemporary Cuba.* Urbana: University of Illinois Press.

Lewis, Rupert

1988   *Marcus Garvey: Anti-Colonial Champion.* Trenton, N.J.: Africa World Press.

Lipman, Jana

2009   *Guantánamo: A Working Class History between Empire and Revolution.* Berkeley: University of California Press.

Look Lai, Walter

1993   *Indentured Labor, Caribbean Sugar: Chinese and Indian Migrants to the British West Indies, 1838–1919.* Baltimore, Md.: John Hopkins University Press.

Lopéz, Kathy

2009   "The Revitalization of Havana's Chinatown: Invoking Chinese Cuban History." *Journal of Chinese Overseas* 5(1):177–200.

2013   *Chinese Cubans: A Transnational History.* Chapel Hill: University of North Carolina Press.

Lovell, Anne M.

1997   "'The City Is My Mother': Narratives of Schizophrenia and Homelessness." *American Anthropologist* 99(2):355–68.

Lowenthal, David

1973   *West Indian Societies*. Oxford, UK: Oxford University Press.

Lowenthal, David, and Lambros Comitas, eds.

1973   *Consequences of Class and Color: West Indian Perspectives*. Garden City, N.J.: Anchor Press.

Mabardi, Sabine

2000   "Encounters of a Heterogeneous Kind: Hybridity in Cultural Theory." *Critical Studies* 13(1):1–20.

Maguire, Emily A.

2011   *Racial Experiments in Cuban Literature and Ethnography*. Gainesville: University Press of Florida.

Mahler, Sarah

2001   "Transnational Relationships: The Struggle to Communicate Across Borders." *Identities* 7(4):584–619.

Mahler, Sarah, and Patricia Pessar

2001   "Gendered Geographies of Power: Analyzing Gender Across Transnational Spaces." *Identities* (Special Issue: Gendering Transnational Spaces) 7(4):441–59.

Malkalani, Minkah

2009   "Introduction: Diaspora and the Localities of Race." *Social Text* 98 (Spring):1–9.

Malkin, Elisabeth

2010   "Cuba's Public Sector Layoffs Signal Major Shift." *New York Times*, September 13. http://www.nytimes.com/2010/09/14/world/americas/14cuba.html?_r=0 (accessed September 7, 2014).

Mama, Amina

1995   *Beyond the Masks: Race, Gender and Subjectivity*. London: Routledge.

Marshall, Dawn I.

1985   "The History of Caribbean Migrations." *Caribbean Review* 14(2):6–9, 52–53.

Marshall, Sharon

2006   "Nothing in My Hands: Some Personal Accounts of Migration from Barbados to Cuba." In *Regional Footprints: The Travels and Travails of Early Caribbean Migrants*, edited by Annette Insanally, Mark Clifford, and Sean Sheriff, 121–32. Mona, Jamaica: University of the West Indies, Latin American and Caribbean Centre.

Martí, José

1893   "My Race." *Patria*, April 16. http://www.historyofcuba.com/history/race/MyRace.htm (accessed September 6, 2014).

Martínez, Iván César

2007   *The Open Wound: The Scourge of Racism in Cuba from Colonialism to Communism*. Kingston, Jamaica: Arawak Publications.

Martinez-Alier, Verena

1989   *Marriage, Class and Colour in Nineteenth-Century Cuba: A Study of Racial Attitudes and Sexual Values in a Slave Society*. Ann Arbor: University of Michigan Press.

Martinez-Echazabal, Lourdes
1998   "Mestizaje and the Discourse of National/Cultural Identity in Latin America, 1845–
        1959." *Latin American Perspectives* 25(3):21–42.

McGarrity, Gayle
1992   "Race, Culture, and Social Change in Contemporary Cuba." In *Cuba in Transition:
        Crisis and Transformation*, edited by Sandor Helbsky, John Kirk, Carollee Bengels-
        dorf, Richard L. Harris, Jean Stubbs, and Andrew Zimbalist, 193–206. Boulder,
        Colo.: Westview Press.

1996   "Cubans in Jamaica: A Previously Neglected Segment of the Cuban Diaspora." *Ca-
        ribbean Quarterly* 42(1):55–83.

1997   "Los determinantes socio históricos de los diferentes patrones de adaptación de in-
        migrantes cubanos en Jamaica." *Revista de Ciencias Sociales* (Puerto Rico), no. 3,
        Nueva época (June 1997): 82–109.

McGillivray, Gillian
2009   *Blazing Cane: Sugar Communities, Class, and State Formation in Cuba, 1868–1959.*
        Durham, N.C.: Duke University Press.

McLeod, Marc C.
1998   "Undesirable Aliens: Race, Ethnicity, and Nationalism in the Comparison of Haitian
        and British West Indian Immigrant Workers in Cuba, 1912–1939." *Journal of Social
        History* 31(3): 599–623.

2000   "Undesirable Aliens: Haitian and British West Indian Immigrant Workers in Cuba,
        1898–1940." PhD diss., University of Texas–Austin.

2003   "'Sin dejar de ser cubanos': Cuban Blacks and the Challenges of the Garveyism in
        Cuba." *Caribbean Studies* 31(1):75–105.

2010   "'We Cubans Are Obligated Like Cats to Have a Clean Face': Malaria, Quarantine,
        and Race in Neocolonial Cuba, 1898–1940." *The Americas* 67(1):57–81.

McPherson, Marlene
2007   "Norma Ming Connects with Her Roots." *Jamaica Gleaner*, May 27. http://jamaica-
        gleaner.com/gleaner/20070527/out/out2.html (accessed August 13, 2014).

Mesa-Lago, Carmelo
2001   "The Cuban Economy in 1999–2001: Evaluation of Performance and Debate on the
        Future." In *Cuba in Transition*, vol. 11, Papers and Proceedings of the 11th Annual
        Meeting of the Association for the Study of the Cuban Economy (ASCE), 1–17.
        Washington, D.C.:ASCE.

Mesa-Lago, Carmelo, and Marianne Masferrer
1974   "The Gradual Integration of the Black in Cuba: Under the Colony, the Republic, and
        the Revolution." In *Slavery and Race Relations in Latin America*, edited by Robin
        Brent Toplin, 348–84. Westport, Conn.: Greenwood Press.

Michalowski, Raymond
1996   "Ethnography and Anxiety: Field Work in the Vortex of U.S.-Cuba Relations."
        Qualitative Sociology 19(1):59–82.

Minority Rights Group, ed.
1995   *No Longer Invisible: Afro-Latin Americans Today*. London: Minority Rights Group
        Publications.

Mintz, Sidney

1958   "Historical Sociology of the Jamaican Church-Founded Free Village System." *De West Indische Gids* 38(1–2):46–70.

1974   *Caribbean Transformations*. New York: Columbia University Press.

1997   "The Localization of Anthropological Practice—From Area Studies to Transnationalism." *Critique of Anthropology* 18(2):117–33.

Mintz, Sidney, and Sally Price, eds.

1985   *Caribbean Contours*. Baltimore, Md.: John Hopkins University Press.

Moberg, Mark

1996   "Myths that Divide: Immigrant Labor and Class Segmentation in the Belizean Banana Industry." *American Ethnologist* 23(2):311–30.

Mohanram, Radhika

2007   *Imperial White: Race, Diaspora, and the British Empire*. Minneapolis: University of Minnesota Press.

Moore, Brian L., and Michelle A. Johnson

2004   *Neither Led nor Driven: Contesting British Cultural Imperialism in Jamaica, 1865–1920*. Kingston, Jamaica: University of the West Indies Press.

Moore, Carlos

1988   *Castro, the Blacks, and Africa*. Los Angeles: University of California, Ralph J. Bunche Center for African American Studies.

2008   *Pichón: A Memoir: Race and Revolution in Castro's Cuba*. Chicago: Lawrence Hill Books.

Moore, Robin

1998   *Nationalizing Blackness: Afro-Cubanismo and Artistic Revolution in Havana, 1920–1940*. Pittsburgh: University of Pittsburgh Press.

Morales Domínguez, Esteban

2013   *Race in Cuba: Essays on the Revolution and Racial Inequality*. New York: Monthly Review Press.

Moreiras, Alberto

1999   "Hybridity and Double-Consciousness." *Cultural Studies* 13(3):377–407.

Morejón, Nancy, Miguel Barnet, Esteban Morales, Eduardo Roca (Choco), Heriberto Feraudy, Rogelio Martínez Furé, Pedro de la Hoz, Fernando Martínez Heredia, and Omara Portuondo, et al.

2009   "Mensaje Desde Cuba a los Intelectuales y Artistas Afroamericanos." December 2. http://www.afrocubaweb.com/mensajedesdecuba12-09.htm#Mensaje%20desde% 20Cuba (accessed March 18, 2015).

Moreno Fraginals, Manuel, Frank Moya Pons, and Stanley L. Engerman, eds.

1985   *Between Slave and Free Labor: The Spanish Caribbean in the Nineteenth Century*. Baltimore, Md.: John Hopkins University Press.

Mukhopadhyay, Carol C., and Yolanda T. Moses

1997   "Reestablishing 'Race' in Anthropological Discourse." *American Anthropologist* 99(3):517–33.

Mullings, Leith
2005   "Interrogating Racism: Toward an Antiracist Anthropology." *Annual Review of Anthropology* 34:667–93.

Muñiz, Humberto García, and Jorge Giovannetti
2003   "Garveyismo y racismo en el Caribe: El caso de la población cocola en la República Dominicana." *Caribbean Studies* 31(1):139–211.

Naranjo Orovio, Consuelo
1997   "Immigration, 'Race' and Nation in Cuba in the Second Half of the 19th Century." *Ibero-Amerikanisches Archive* 24 (3–4):303–26.

Nassy Brown, Jacqueline
1998   "Black Liverpool, Black America, and the Gendering of Diasporic Space." *Cultural Anthropology* 13(3):291–325.

2005   *Dropping Anchor, Setting Sail: Geographies of Race in Black Liverpool.* Princeton, N.J.: Princeton University Press.

Nelson, Lowry
1970   "Cuban Population Estimates, 1953–1970." *Journal of Interamerican Studies and World Affairs* 12(3):392–400.

Nettleford, Rex, Barry Chevannes, Rupert Lewis, and Maureen Warner-Lewis
2009   "Letter from Jamaica, 11/26/09." http://www.afrocubaweb.com/actingonourconscience.htm (accessed August 27, 2014).

Newman, Michael
2005   *Socialism: A Very Short Introduction.* New York: Oxford University Press.

Newton, Velma
1984   *The Silver Men: West Indian Labour Migration to Panama 1850–1914.* Kingston, Jamaica: Sir Authur Lewis Institute of Social and Economic Studies.

Noguera, Pedro
2003   "Anything but Black: Bringing Politics Back to the Study of Race." In *Problematizing Blackness: Self Ethnographies by Black Immigrants to the United States,* edited by Percy Hintzen and Jean Rahier, 193–200. New York: Routledge.

Núñez, Gerardo Gonzalez, and Ericka Kim Verba
1997   "International Relations between Cuba and the Caribbean in the 1990s: Challenges and Perspectives." *Latin American Perspectives* 24(5):81–95.

Núñez González, Niurka, Maria Magdalena Perez Alvarez, Pablo Rodriguez Ruiz, Hernan Tirado Toirac, Odalys Buscaron Ochoa, Lazara Y Carranza Fuentes, Rodrigo Espina Prieto, Ana Julia Garcia Dally, and Estrella Gonzalez Noriega
2011   *Relaciones Raciales en Cuba: Estudios Contemporáneos.* Havana: Fundación Fernando Ortíz.

Olwig, Karen Fog
1990   "'The Struggle for Respectability': Methodism and Afro-Caribbean Culture on 19th Century Nevis." *New West Indian Guide* 64(2–4):93–114.

2002   "A 'Respectable' Livelihood: Mobility and Identity a Caribbean Family." In *Work and Migration: Life and Livelihoods in a Globalizing World,* edited by Ninna Nyberg Sorensen and Karen Fog Olwig, 85–105. London: Routledge.

2009   "A Proper Funeral: Contextualizing Community among Caribbean Migrants." *Journal of the Royal Anthropological Institute* 15(3):520–37.

Ong, Aihwa

1996   "Cultural Citizenship as Subject-Making: Immigrants Negotiate Racial and Cultural Boundaries in the United States." *Current Anthropology* 37(5):737–62.

O'Reggio, Trevor

2006   *Between Citizenship and Alienation: The Evolution of Black West Indian Society in Panama, 1914–1964*. Lanham, Md.: University Press of America.

Ortiz, Fernando

1940   *Cuban Counterpoint: Tobacco and Sugar*. Durham, N.C.: Duke University Press.

Palmer, Colin

2000   "The African Diaspora." *Black Scholar* 30(3–4):56–60.

Pappademos, Melina

2011   *Black Activism and the Cuban Republic*. Chapel Hill: University of North Carolina Press.

Parla, Aysa

2009   "Remembering across the Border: Postsocialist Nostalgia among Turkish Immigrants in Bulgaria." *American Ethnologist* 36(4):750–67.

Patterson, Tiffany, and Robin D. G. Kelley

2000   "Unfinished Migrations: Reflections on the African Diaspora and the Making of the Modern World." *African Studies Review* 43(1):11–45.

Pérez, Louis A., Jr.

1995   *Cuba: Between Reform and Revolution*. New York: Oxford University Press.

1999   *On Becoming Cuban: Identity, Nationality, and Culture*. Chapel Hill: University of North Carolina Press.

Pérez de la Riva, Juan

1975   "La Inmigración antillana en Cuba durante el primer tercio del siglo XX." *Revista Biblioteca Nacional Jose Martí* 17(2):75–87.

Pérez López, Jorge

1995   *Cuba's Second Economy: From Behind the Scenes to Center Stage*. Piscataway, N.J.: Transaction Publishers.

2002   "The Cuban Economy in an Unending Special Period." In *Cuba in Transition: Volume 12*. Proceedings of the Twelfth Annual Meeting of the Association for the Study of the Cuban Economy (ASCE), 507–21. Washington, D.C.: ASCE.

2006   "The Cuban Economy in 2005–2006: The End of the Special Period?" In *Cuba in Transition: Volume 16*, Proceedings of the Sixteenth Annual Meeting of the Association for the Study of the Cuban Economy (ASCE), 1–13. Washington, D.C.: ASCE.

Pérez Sarduy, Pedro, and Jean Stubbs, eds.

2000   *Afro-Cuban Voices: On Race and Identity in Contemporary Cuba*. Gainesville: University of Florida Press.

Pérez-Stable, Marifeli

1999   *The Cuban Revolution: Origins, Course, and Legacy*. New York: Oxford University Press.

2011   *The United States and Cuba: Intimate Enemies*. New York: Routledge.

Perry, Mark D.
2008   "Global Black Self-Fashionings: Hip Hop as Diasporic Space." *Identities* 15(6):635–64.

Pertierra, Ana Cristina
2011   *Cuba: The Struggle for Consumption.* Coconut Creek, Fla.: Caribbean Press.

Pessar, Patricia, and Sarah Mahler
2003   "Transnational Migration: Bringing Gender In." *International Migration Review* 37(3):812–46.

Petras, E. M.
1988   *Jamaican Labor Migration: White Capital and Black Labor, 1850–1930.* Boulder, Colo.: Westview Press.

Piedra Rencurrel, José Francisco
2002   "Remarks." In *Intra-Caribbean Migration: The Cuban Connection (1898–Present),* 4–5. Mona, Jamaica: University of the West Indies.

Pierre, Jemima
2004   "Black Immigrants in the United States and the 'Cultural Narratives' of Ethnicity." *Identities* 11(2):141–70

Portes, Alejandro, Luis Guarnizo, and Patricia Landolt
1999   "The Study of Transnationalism: Pitfalls and Promise of an Emergent Research Field." *Racial and Ethnic Studies* 2(2):217–37.

Purcell, Trevor W.
1993   *Banana Fallout: Class, Color, and Culture Among West Indians in Costa Rica.* Afro-American Culture and Society series, no. 12. Los Angeles: University of California Press.

Puri, Shalini
2003   "Theorizing Diasporic Cultures: The Quiet Migration." In *Marginal Migrations: The Circulation of Cultures within the Caribbean,* edited by Shalini Puri, 1–16. New York: Palgrave Macmillan.
2004   *The Caribbean Post-Colonial: Social Equity, Post-Nationalism, Cultural Hybridity.* New York: Palgrave Macmillan.

Putnam, Lara
2002   *The Company They Kept: Migrants and the Politics of Gender in Caribbean Costa Rica, 1870–1960.* Chapel Hill: University of North Carolina Press.
2013   *Radical Moves: Caribbean Migrants and the Politics of Race in the Jazz Age.* Chapel Hill: University of North Carolina Press.
2014   "Citizenship from the Margins: Vernacular Theories of Rights and the State from the Interwar Caribbean." *Journal of British Studies* 53(January):162–91.

Queeley, Andrea
2009   "The Passing of a Black Yankee: Fieldnotes/Cliff Notes of a Wannabe Santiaguera." In *Fieldwork Identities in the Caribbean,* edited by Erin Brooke, 77–104. Coconut Creek, Fla.: Caribbean Studies Press.
2010   "*Somos Negros Finos*: Anglophone Caribbean Cultural Citizenship in Revolutionary Cuba." In *Global Circuits of Blackness: Race, Citizenship, and Modern Subjectivities,* edited by Jean Muteba Rahier, Percy C. Hintzen, and Felipe Smith, 201–22. Champaign: University of Illinois Press.

Rabinow, Paul, ed.

1994   *The Essential Works of Michel Foucault (1954–1984).* Vol. 1, *Ethics, Subjectivity, and Truth.* New York: New Press.

Radhakrishnan, R.

1993   "Postcoloniality and the Boundaries of Identity." *Callaloo* 16(4):750–71.

Ricardo, Roger Luis

1993   *Guantánamo, the Bay of Discord: The Story of the U.S. Military Base in Cuba.* Minneapolis: Ocean Press.

Richardson, Bonham C.

1989   "Caribbean Migrations, 1838–1985." In *The Modern Caribbean*, edited by Franklin Knight and Colin Palmer, 203–28. Durham: University of North Carolina Press.

Ritter, Archibald R. M.

2007   "Economic Illegalities and the Underground Economy in Cuba." In *A Contemporary Cuba Reader: The Revolution under Raúl Castro*, edited by Philip Brenner, Marguerite Rose Jiménez, John M. Kirk, and William M. Leogrande, 203–15. Lanham, Md.: Roman and Littlefield.

Rivkin-Fish, Michele

2009   "Tracing Landscapes of the Past in Class Subjectivity: Practices of Memory and Distinction in Marketizing Russia." *American Ethnologist* 36(1):79–95.

Robotham, Don

1998   "Transnationalism in the Caribbean: Formal and Informal." *American Ethnologist* 25(3):307–21

2000   "Blackening the Jamaican Nation: The Travails of a Black Bourgeoisie in a Globalized World." *Identities* 7(1):1–37.

2005   *Culture, Society and Economy: Bringing Production Back In.* London: Sage.

Rodriguez-Mangual, Edna M.

2004   *Lydia Cabrera and the Construction of an Afro-Cuban Cultural Identity.* Chapel Hill: University of North Carolina Press.

Rogers, Ruel

2001   "'Black like who?' Afro-Caribbean Immigrants, African Americans, and the Politics of Group Identity." In *Islands in the City: West Indian Migration to New York*, edited by Nancy Foner, 163–92. Berkeley: University of California Press.

2006   *Afro-Caribbean Immigrants and the Politics of Incorporation: Ethnicity, Exception, or Exit.* New York: Cambridge University Press.

Roland, L. Kaifa

2010   *Cuban Color in Tourism and La Lucha: An Ethnography of Racial Meaning.* New York: Oxford University Press.

Rolando, Gloria

1996   *Los Hijos de Baraguá—My Footsteps in Baraguá.* Film. Havana: Mundo Latino.

2001   *Raices de mi Corazón (Roots of My Heart).* Film. Havana: Mundo Latino.

Roque Cabello, Marta Beatriz, and Manuel Sánchez Herrero

1998   "Background: Cuba's Economic Reforms: An Overview." In *Perspectives on Cuban Economic Reforms*, edited by Jorge F. Pérez-López and Matías F. Travieso Díaz, 9–17.

Special Studies, no. 30. Phoenix: Arizona State University Center for Latin American Studies.

Rose, James L. G.

2002   "'Behold the Tax Man Cometh': Taxation as a Tool of Oppression in Early Post-Emancipation British Guiana, 1838–48." In *In the Shadow of the Plantation: Caribbean History and Legacy*, edited by Alvin O. Thompson and Woodville K. Marshall, 297–313. Kingston, Jamaica: Ian Randle.

Rosendahl, Mona

1997   *Inside the Revolution: Everyday Life in Socialist Cuba*. Ithaca, N.Y.: Cornell University Press.

Routon, Kenneth

2010   *Hidden Powers of the State in the Cuban Imagination*. Gainesville: University Press of Florida.

Rubiera Castillo, Daisy, and Inéz María Martiatu Terry

2011   *Afrocubanas: Historia, Pensamiento y Prácticas Culturales*. Havana: Editorial de Ciencias Sociales.

Rush, Anne Spry

2011   *Bonds of Empire: West Indians and Britishness from Victoria to Decolonization*. Oxford, UK: Oxford University Press.

Safran, William

1991   "Diasporas in Modern Societies: Myths of Homeland and Return." *Diaspora* 1(1) (Spring):83–99.

Sampson, Steve

1991   "Is There an Anthropology of Socialism?" *Anthropology Today* 7(5):16–19.

Sánchez, Dominga González

1988   "La Inmigración Negra y La Situación Socioeconomica de Negros y Mulatos en el Campo." *Economia y Desarrollo* 104(May/June):104–15.

Sánchez Guerra, José

2004   *Los anglo-caribeños en Guantánamo (1902–1950)*. Guantánamo, Cuba: Editorial El Mar y la Montaña.

Sanders, Ronald

2004   "CARICOM-Cuba Day: 8th December: A time for celebration." *Caribbean NetNews*. http://www.caribbeannewsnow.com/caribnet/2004/12/07/sanders.htm.

Saney, Isaac

2004   *Cuba: A Revolution in Motion*. Blackpoint, Nova Scotia: Blackpoint Publishing.

Sawyer, Mark

2005   *Racial Politics in Post-Revolutionary Cuba*. Cambridge, UK: Cambridge University Press.

Scarano, Francisco A.

1989   "Labor and Society in the Nineteenth Century." In *The Modern Caribbean*, edited by Franklin Knight and Colin Palmer, 51–84. Chapel Hill: University of North Carolina Press.

Scarpaci, Joseph L.

1995   "The Emerging Food and Paladar Market in Havana." In *Cuba in Transition: Volume 5*, Papers and Proceedings of the 5th Annual Meeting of the Association for the Study of the Cuban Economy (ASCE), 74–84. Washington, D.C.: ASCE.

Schwab, Stephen Irving Max

2009   *Guantánamo, USA: The Untold History of America's Cuban Outpost*. Lawrence: University Press of Kansas.

Scott, Rebecca

1985   *Slave Emancipation in Cuba: The Transition to Free Labor, 1860–1899*. Princeton, N.J.: Princeton University Press.

1997   "Raza, clase y acción colectiva en Cuba, 1895–1912: Formación de alianzas interraciales en el mundo de la caña." In *El Caribe entre Imperios*, edited by Arcadio Díaz Quiñones, special issue of *Op. Cit.: Revista del Centro de Investigaciones Históricas* 9:131–63.

2008   *Degrees of Freedom: Louisiana and Cuba After Emancipation*. Cambridge, Mass.: Harvard University Press.

Serbin, Andres

1991   "The CARICOM States and the Group of Three: A New Partnership Between Latin America and the Caribbean?" *Journal of Interamerican Studies and World Affairs* 33(2):53–80.

1994   "Transnational Relations and Regionalism in the Caribbean." *Annals of the American Academy of Political and Social Science* 533 (May):139–50.

Serviat, Pedro

1986   *El Problema Negro y Su Solución Definitiva*. Havana: Editora Politica.

Shannon, Jordan

2008   "*Lo que el ajiaco no lleva*: Haitianness, Race and Culture in the Construction of Cubanidad." Master's thesis, Stone Center for Latin American Studies, Tulane University.

Smith, Michael Peter, and Luis Eduardo Guarnizo, eds.

1998   *Transnationalism from Below*. New Brunswick, N.J.: Transaction Publishers.

Smith, Raymond T.

1982   "Race and Class in the Post-Emancipation Caribbean." In *Racism and Colonialism: Comparative Studies in Overseas History*, vol. 4, edited by H. L. Wesseling, 91–119. New York: Springer.

1996   *The Matrifocal Family: Power, Pluralism and Politics*. New York: Routledge.

Somers, Margaret R.

1994   "The Narrative Construction of Identity: A Relational and Network Approach." *Theory and Society* 23(5):605–49.

Spivak, Gayatri

1988   "Subaltern Studies: Deconstructing Historiography." In *Other Worlds: Essays in Cultural Politics*, edited by Ranajit Guha and Gayatri Spivak, 197–221. Oxford, UK: Oxford University Press.

Sporn, Pam, dir.

2000   *Cuban Roots/Bronx Stories*. Film. New York: Latino Public Broadcasting Third World Newsreel.

Stoler, Ann

1989   "Making Empire Respectable: The Politics of Race and Sexual Morality in Twenti-
        eth-Century Colonial Cultures." *American Ethnologist* 16(4):634–60.

Stone, Elizabeth, ed.

1981   *Women and the Cuban Revolution: Speeches and Documents by Fidel Castro, Vilma
        Espin, and Others.* New York: Pathfinder Press.

Stubbs, Jean

1989   *Cuba: The Test of Time.* London: Latin American Bureau.

Sutton, Constance

1974   "Cultural Duality in the Caribbean." *Caribbean Studies* 14(2):96–101.

Tanikella, Leela

2003   "The Politics of Hybridity: Race, Gender, and Nationalism in Trinidad." *Cultural
        Dynamics* 15(2):153–81.

Taylor, Edward J.

1999   "The New Economics of Labour Migration and the Role of Remittances in the Mi-
        gration Process." *International Migration* 37(1):63–88.

Taylor, Henry Louis

2009   *Inside El Barrio: A Bottom-Up View of Neighborhood Life in Castro's Cuba.* West
        Hartford, Conn.: Kumarian Press.

Thomas, Deborah

2004   *Modern Blackness: Nationalism, Globalization and the Politics of Culture in Jamaica.*
        Durham, N.C.: Duke University Press.

2006   "Public Bodies: Virginity Testing, Redemption Songs, and Racial Respect in Jamai-
        ca." *Journal of Latin American and Caribbean Anthropology* 11(1):1–31.

2007   "Blackness across Borders: Jamaican Diasporas and New Politics of Citizenship."
        Identities 14(1–2):111–33.

2008   "Walmart, 'Katrina,' and Other Ideological Tricks: Jamaican Hotel Workers in Mich-
        igan." *Gendering Diaspora* 90:68–86.

Thomas, Deborah, with Tina M. Campt

2006   "Diasporic Hegemonies: Slavery, Memory, and Genealogies of Diaspora." *Trans-
        forming Anthropology* 14(2):163–72.

Thomas, Deborah, and Kamari Clarke

2013   "Globalization and Race: Structures of Inequality, New Sovereignties, and Citizen-
        ship in a Neoliberal Era." *Annual Review of Anthropology* 42:305–25.

Thomas, Hugh

1998   *Cuba, or, The Pursuit of Freedom.* New York: Da Capo.

Tolen, Rachel

1991   "Colonizing and Transforming the Criminal Tribesman: The Salvation Army in Brit-
        ish India." *American Ethnologist* 18(1):106–25.

Trouillot, Michel-Rolph

1992   "The Caribbean Region: An Open Region in Anthropological Theory." *Annual Re-
        view of Anthropology* 21:19–42.

1997   *Silencing the Past: Power and the Production of History.* Boston: Beacon Press.

Truitt, Allison

2008   "On the Back of a Motorbike: Middle-Class Mobility in Ho Chi Minh City, Vietnam." *American Ethnologist* 35(1):3–19.

Tsang, Martin

2014   "Con la Mocha al Cuello: The Emergence and Negotiation of Afro-Chinese Religion in Cuba." PhD diss., Florida International University.

Twine, Francis Winddance

1998   *Racism in a Racial Democracy: The Maintenance of White Supremacy in Brazil.* New Brunswick, N.J.: Rutgers University Press.

Ulysse, Gina

2007   *Downtown Ladies: Informal Commercial Importers, A Haitian Anthropologist, and Self-Making in Jamaica.* Chicago: University of Chicago Press.

Vertovec, Steven

2009   *Transnationalism.* New York: Routledge.

Vickerman, Milton

1999   *Crosscurrents: West Indian Immigrants and Race.* New York: Oxford University Press.

Wade, Peter

1993   *Blackness and Race Mixture.* Baltimore, Md.: Johns Hopkins University Press.

Walderinger, R., and Fitzgerald, D.

2004   "Transnationalism in Question." *American Journal of Sociology* 109 (5):1177–95.

Waters, Mary C.

2001a   "Growing up West Indian and African American: Gender and Class Differences in the Second Generation." In *Islands in the City: West Indian Migration to New York*, edited by Nancy Foner, 193–215. Berkeley: University of California Press.

2001b   *Black Identities: West Indian Immigrant Dreams and American Realities.* Cambridge, Mass.: Harvard University Press.

Weedon, Chris

2004   *Identity and Culture: Narratives of Difference and Belonging.* Berkshire, UK: McGraw-Hill/Open University Press.

Welch, Pedro L. V.

2002   "Post-Emancipation Adjustments in the Urban Context: Views from Bridgetown, Barbados." In *In the Shadow of the Plantation: Caribbean History and Legacy*, edited by Alvin O. Thompson and Woodville K. Marshall, 266–82. Kingston, Jamaica: Ian Randle.

West-Durán, Alan.

2013   "Zurbano and *The New York Times*: Lost and Found in Translation." *AfroCubaWeb*, April 6. http://www.afrocubaweb.com/alan-west-zurbano-nyt.html (accessed September 6, 2014).

Whitney, Robert, and Graciela Chailloux Laffita

2013   *Subjects or Citizens: British Caribbean Workers in Cuba: 1900–1960.* Gainesville: University Press of Florida.

Williams, Brackette

1989   "A Class Act: Anthropology and the Race to Nation Across Ethnic Terrain." *Annual Review of Anthropology* 18:401–44.

Wilson, Peter
1973   *Crab Antics: The Social Anthropology of English-Speaking Negro Societies of the Carib-*
        bean. New Haven, Conn.: Yale University Press.
Wirtz, Kristina
2004   "Santeria in Cuban National Consciousness: A Religious Case of the Doble Moral."
        Journal of Latin American and Caribbean Anthropology 9(2):409–38.
2007   *Ritual, Discourse, and Community in Cuban Santeria: Speaking a Sacred World.*
        Gainesville: University Press of Florida.
Wodak, Ruth, and Martin Reisigl
1999   "Discourse and Racism: European Perspectives." *Annual Review of Anthropology*
        28:175–99.
Wolf, Eric
1994   "Perilous Ideas: Race, Culture, People." *Current Anthropology* 35(1):1–12.
Wright, Michelle
2004   *Becoming Black: Creating Identity in the African Diaspora.* Durham, N.C.: Duke Uni-
        versity Press.
Wynter, Cadence A.
2001   "Jamaican Labor Migration to Cuba, 1885–1930." PhD. diss., University of Illinois–
        Chicago.
Yelvington, Kevin
1995   *Producing Power: Ethnicity, Gender, and Class in a Caribbean Workplace.* Philadel-
        phia: Temple University Press.
Zeitlin, Maurice
1967   *Revolutionary Politics and the Cuban Working Class.* Princeton, N.J.: Princeton Uni-
        versity Press.
Zeleza, Paul Tiyambe
2005   "Rewriting the African Diaspora: Beyond the Black Atlantic." *African Affairs*
        104(414):35–68.
2010   "Reconceptualizing African Diasporas: Notes From a Historian." *Transforming An-*
        thropology 18(1):74–78.
Zimbalist, Andrew
1994a   "Reforming Cuba's Economic System from Within." In *Cuba at a Crossroads: Poli-*
        tics and Economics after the Fourth Party Congress, edited by Jorge F. Pérez-López,
        220–37. Gainesville: University Press of Florida.
1994b   "Treading Water: Cuba's Economic and Political Crisis." In *Cuba and the Future,*
        edited by Donald E. Schulz, 7–22. Westport, Conn.: Greenwood Press.
Zurbano, Roberto
2013   "For Blacks in Cuba, the Revolution Hasn't Begun." *New York Times Review,* March
        23. http://www.nytimes.com/2013/03/24/opinion/sunday/for-blacks-in-cuba-the-
        revolution-hasnt-begun.html?_r=0 (accessed March 18, 2015).

Index

Page numbers in *italics* indicate illustrations.

Born and raised in Berkeley, California, Andrea J. Queeley is a cultural anthropologist who seeks to expand and deepen critical understandings of the global Black experience with a geographic focus on the Americas. Her work contributes to a broader and interdisciplinary inquiry into how racialized subjects negotiate structural inequalities in contexts of political, economic, social, and environmental crisis. She currently lives in Miami, Florida.

Contemporary Cuba

EDITED BY JOHN M. KIRK

Afro-Cuban Voices: On Race and Identity in Contemporary Cuba, by Pedro Pérez-Sarduy and Jean Stubbs (2000)

Cuba, the United States, and the Helms-Burton Doctrine: International Reactions, by Joaquín Roy (2000)

Cuba Today and Tomorrow: Reinventing Socialism, by Max Azicri (2000)

Cuba's Foreign Relations in a Post-Soviet World, by H. Michael Erisman (2000)

Cuba's Sugar Industry, by José Alvarez and Lázaro Peña Castellanos (2001)

Culture and the Cuban Revolution: Conversations in Havana, by John M. Kirk and Leonardo Padura Fuentes (2001)

Looking at Cuba: Essays on Culture and Civil Society, by Rafael Hernández, translated by Dick Cluster (2003)

Santería Healing: A Journey into the Afro-Cuban World of Divinities, Spirits, and Sorcery, by Johan Wedel (2004)

Cuba's Agricultural Sector, by José Alvarez (2004)

Cuban Socialism in a New Century: Adversity, Survival, and Renewal, edited by Max Azicri and Elsie Deal (2004)

Cuba, the United States, and the Post-Cold War World: The International Dimensions of the Washington-Havana Relationship, edited by Morris Morley and Chris McGillion (2005)

Redefining Cuban Foreign Policy: The Impact of the "Special Period," edited by H. Michael Erisman and John M. Kirk (2006)

Gender and Democracy in Cuba, by Ilja A. Luciak (2007)

Ritual, Discourse, and Community in Cuban Santería: Speaking a Sacred World, by Kristina Wirtz (2007)

The "New Man" in Cuba: Culture and Identity in the Revolution, by Ana Serra (2007)

U.S.-Cuban Cooperation Past, Present, and Future, by Melanie M. Ziegler (2007)

Protestants, Revolution, and the Cuba-U.S. Bond, by Theron Corse (2007)

The Changing Dynamic of Cuban Civil Society, edited by Alexander I. Gray and Antoni Kapcia (2008)

Cuba in the Shadow of Change: Daily Life in the Twilight of the Revolution, by Amelia Rosenberg Weinreb (2009)

Failed Sanctions: Why the U.S. Embargo against Cuba Could Never Work, by Paolo Spadoni (2010)

Sustainable Urban Agriculture in Cuba, by Sinan Koont (2011)

Fifty Years of Revolution: Perspectives on Cuba, the United States, and the World, edited by Soraya M. Castro Mariño and Ronald W. Pruessen (2012)

Cuban Economists on the Cuban Economy, edited by Al Campbell (2013)

Cuban Revelations: Behind the Scenes in Havana, by Marc Frank (2013; first paperback printing, 2015)

Cuba in a Global Context: International Relations, Internationalism, and Transnationalism, edited by Catherine Krull (2014)

Healthcare without Borders: Understanding Cuban Medical Internationalism by John M. Kirk (2015)

Rescuing Our Roots: The African Anglo-Caribbean Diaspora in Contemporary Cuba by Andrea J. Queeley (2015)